# SAVING YOUR BUSINESS

# SAVING YOUR BUSINESS

How to Survive Chapter 11
Bankruptcy and Successfully
Reorganize Your Company

## SUZANNE CAPLAN

**PRENTICE HALL**
Englewood Cliffs, New Jersey 07632

Prentice-Hall International (UK) Limited, *London*
Prentice-Hall of Australia Pty. Limited, *Sydney*
Prentice-Hall Canada Inc., *Toronto*
Prentice-Hall Hispanoamericana, S.A., *Mexico*
Prentice-Hall of India Private Limited, *New Delhi*
Prentice-Hall of Japan, Inc., *Tokyo*
Simon & Schuster Asia Pte. Ltd., *Singapore*
Editora Prentice-Hall do Brasil, Ltda., *Rio de Janeiro*

10   9   8   7   6   5   4   3   2   1

**Library of Congress Cataloging-in-Publication Data**

Caplan, Suzanne.
  Saving your business : how to survive Chapter 11 bankruptcy and
successfully reorganize your company / Suzanne Caplan.
    p.    cm.
  Includes index.
  ISBN 0-13-832684-3
  1. Bankruptcy—United States.   2. Corporate reorganizations—
United States.   3. Corporate turnarounds—United States.   4. Small
business—United States—Management.   I. Title.
HG3766.C23     1992
658.4'063—dc20                                              92-11279
                                                                CIP


ISBN 0-13-832684-3

**PRENTICE HALL**
Business Information & Publishing Division
Englewood Cliffs, NJ 07632

Simon & Schuster, A Paramount Communications Company

Printed in the United States of America

To Janie Packee
1966–81

Your courage has been my inspiration.

# INTRODUCTION

When you are a small business owner, the decision to file bankruptcy is not an easy one. It usually follows a prolonged period of business difficulties, much soul searching, and many sleepless nights. I know: I made that decision in 1986.

After the devastating recession in the early 1980s, I managed to steer my small manufacturing company into a relatively stable position by 1985. A commercial dispute threatened to inflict the fatal blow. The gnawing realization that I would be unable to meet current obligations drove me to seek legal advice, and I made the decision to file for court protection. During the next $4^{1}/_{2}$ years, my business life proved to be a constant roller coaster.

I struggled through the maze of bankruptcy, learning all that I could, and developing a strategy along the way. I sat in court listening to other cases and read a number of court dockets, which, as public records, are available to anyone. I made mistakes and scored successes, and during this time, there was always a business to manage.

By the time the court approved my reorganization plan in December 1990, I felt almost comfortable with bankruptcy—and I had learned more about operating a business than I had in the 14 years before the filing. I used this "knowledge under fire" as a basis for writing this book. *Saving Your Business* is meant to shed light on the process of bankruptcy and the strategies for a successful conclusion.

This book describes a management strategy for business bankruptcy—a strategy that can turn the decision to file bankruptcy from a step in the embalming process into a reorganizational period that continues the life of your business. This strategy emphasizes the importance of planning: recognizing the signs of impending bankruptcy and acting quickly to survive the bankruptcy process and save your business.

All of your creditors have the right to enforce a money judgment against you if you fail to make payment. Through the courts in their jurisdiction, creditors can sell your real estate and personal property in order to satisfy debts. Creditors can repossess encumbered property without court intervention if the law and the creditors' contracts permits the creditors to do so. If you wait to file bankruptcy until your creditors actually begin the bidding at a sheriff's sale of your property, your bankruptcy will suffer from the lack of management planning that necessitates an emergency filing.

As soon as you file a bankruptcy petition, the court issues an order for automatic stay (which is applicable to all creditors) and immediately operates to stop any actions to collect money or property from your company. The automatic stay order requires creditors to obtain permission from Bankruptcy Court before they can enforce their right to liquidate your company's assets. With few exceptions, creditors must leave your company in peace if the debts were incurred prior to the time when you filed bankruptcy.

My company continued to operate while taking advantage of the automatic stay offered by a Chapter 11 bankruptcy (reorganization). For purposes of this discussion, Chapters 11 and 7 of the Bankruptcy Code apply to business bankruptcy debtors. Chapter 7 bankruptcy will liquidate your company if you do not wish to continue to operate the business. The court will appoint a Trustee who will take charge of your company's assets. The Trustee may continue to operate the business, but the Trustee will ultimately sell the assets and disburse the net proceeds to creditors, in order of their priority. With few exceptions, Chapter 7 bankruptcy discharges your company from any liability for debts incurred prior to the bankruptcy filing, although you personally may remain liable for payment of the debts.

Chapter 11 allowed me to continue to operate the business without a Trustee, but it adds a burden that would not have existed in Chapter 7 bankruptcy. In addition to operating and generating cash flow, the business must also present to the court and creditors proof that the company can reorganize.

If you file a Chapter 11 bankruptcy and want to reorganize your company successfully, it is crucial that your management first recognizes the facts that brought about the bankruptcy and then formulates a strategy to correct the problems that led to bankruptcy. Your company must present a plan to the court and creditors that pays creditors more than they would have received if you had filed a Chapter 7 bankruptcy requiring a Trustee to liquidate your company's assets. This plan must be accompanied by a financial disclosure statement showing the business actually has the financial ability to carry out the plan. The plan must receive approval from your creditors and be confirmed by the court.

After any company files bankruptcy, creditors can ask the court to relieve them from the automatic stay order so that they can resume their pursuit of property. The court may grant relief from the automatic stay to creditors if the company's assets are no longer sufficient to act as a cushion to protect the interest of the creditors.

This book analyzes strategies used by business debtors—including my own company—in Chapter 11 bankruptcy cases that have resulted in the successful reorganization of an ongoing business and survived the bankruptcy proceeding. This book also reviews failed reorganization strategies to discover the planning flaws that led to failure.

There are three features that are common to a successful business reorganization. The first is the prebankruptcy planning and timing of the actual filing of the bankruptcy petition. Planning and strategy during the period just before you file for bankruptcy will determine whether your creditors will try to put your company out of business. Therefore, during this planning period, it is crucial that you communicate frequently and honestly with your creditors. If you file for bankruptcy without prior planning or as a last resort to stop creditors from liquidating your company's assets, your creditors' impatience and hostility will hamper your ability to manage the bankruptcy while you await court approval of your reorganization plan. If you file for bankruptcy as a last-minute decision, you may have already lost assets that are vital to the successful reorganization of your business.

The second feature of a successful Chapter 11 business reorganization is how you manage your business after you've filed for bankruptcy. There are several management strategies that will discourage the court from granting creditors relief from the automatic stay. These strategies therefore allow time for your business to get back on its feet and become profitable enough to create and fund a plan for reorganization.

The third feature of a successful reorganization is the design of the actual reorganization plan. The plan must be as generous as possible to all classes of creditors and must still be realistic for your company to accomplish. Creating an atmosphere that motivates creditors and the court to accept the plan is an important feature of prebankruptcy planning and business bankruptcy management. The time and effort it takes to design, sell, and complete the reorganization can be extensive, and it requires constant management effort. Entwined with the management strategy of a successful business reorganization are the Bankruptcy Code and a myriad of laws and statutes that apply to your operation. Solid legal advice is important to your success, as is finding the right attorney to advise you and give you the needed guidelines to design your reorganization plan. These guidelines pertain to both style and substance.

This book is not a how-to manual, because self-help can prove to be disastrous in a bankruptcy case. Rather, *Saving Your Business* is intended to fill in some of the management blanks to increase the chances that you will reorganize your bankrupt business successfully. Time is the primary ally of a company in Chapter 11 bankruptcy, and this book describes the strategy that can provide you with that time.

In December 1990, my company's reorganization plan was accepted by creditors and approved by the court. This was a result of intense planning and tough negotiation. Our payment schedule was structured so that even during an economic downturn, we could meet our debt service—which we have done successfully! Our first year out of bankruptcy was 1991, and although it was a tough year, we managed to turn a profit. We have recently moved into a new location which will allow us to manufacture more efficiently as well as being safer and more pleasant. I believe the worst is all behind us, and I look forward to future challenges.

# ACKNOWLEDGMENTS

No business makes it through the mine field of a reorganization without the help of good and loyal business friends. Above all others, there is Keith Novak, who worked long after others would have left. To those who continued to have faith: the Shermans, Joe Kenney and Joe Lear, Tom Nunnally, Tom Packee, Dave Meister, and Alex Kress, I will be eternally grateful. To those who continued to give advice: Norm Belt, Mark Bibro, Rod Townsend, Jr., Sam Mullin, and Jane Rectenwald, I will long carry your words of wisdom.

No individual makes it through the trauma of bankruptcy without the support of great family and friends—to Harriet and Betty to whom I am inextricably connected. To my friends: Jean Hunter, Paul Mason, Sarah Hargrave, Kathy Murray, and Barbara Davis, your support held me up during the darkest times, and I will never forget your kindness.

And lest it be said that I subscribe to Shakespeare's theory that we should "kill all lawyers," I wish to single out some very special practitioners: Mary Bower whose intellect and compassion are above the crowd. Rich Finberg, Barry Lipson, and Mike Malakoff who ride white horses for a contingency fee. Don Phillips whose humor and humanity are notable for a bankruptcy specialist. Dottie Servis whose clear-eyed honesty is a challenge to others. Dick Lerach, who is a tough adversary and an ethical man to be admired.

Finally, a book does not become a book without the expertise of others and I am grateful to Sherry Truesdell for turning my scribble into words; Patti Tihey for her editorial advice; Ruth Mills for her editorial focus; and Mike Snell, agent extraordinaire who has the courage to work with rookies.

# CONTENTS

# 2

## A Fool for a Client

### The Right Attorney Is the First Step to Success 15

# 3

## To File or not to File

### Reorganizing Without Filing for Bankruptcy 37

# 4

## Be Prepared

### What to Do before You File for Bankruptcy 51

*Part II*
*After You File: Fixing What Went Wrong 65*

# 5

## Let the Games Begin

### What to Expect Once You File Your Bankruptcy Petition 67

# 6

## Can We Talk?

### Opening Constructive Lines of Communication 84

# 7

## Greater than the Sum

### Analyzing Your Business to Cut Costs, Increase Profits, and Raise Cash 105

# 8

## Keep Your Eye on the Ball

### Running Your Company as a Viable Concern 122

*Part III*
*The Reorganization: A Chance to Start Over 131*

# 9

## Case Study

### One Company's Progress from Bankruptcy Petition to Reorganization Plan 133

# 10

## Let's Make a Deal

### Negotiating Payment Terms with Your Creditors 177

# 11

## The First Step Out of Bankruptcy

### Filing a Disclosure Statement 191

# 12

## Your Best Offer

### Filing Your Plan of Reorganization 203

# 13

## Making the Reorganization Work

### And What to Do If It Doesn't 218

# 14

## What's the Worst that Could Happen?

### Conversion to Chapter 7 Liquidation 227

# 15

## And Life Goes On 233

# I

# A BUSINESS IN TROUBLE

## IS CHAPTER 11 BANKRUPTCY THE ANSWER?

Even as his safety equipment company was growing in revenue from $600,000 to $3.2 million over three years, Roy Wooly (CEO) had a sense of foreboding. He brushed these feelings aside with the quick explanation that this level of success was an extraordinary accomplishment for someone of his humble beginnings. Roy had earned his degree with the aid of a combination of scholarships and part-time jobs, one of which was a shipper/receiver for a mid-size safety supply company. After graduation, he went to work in sales for that company, and within 6 years, was its second highest-paid salesman.

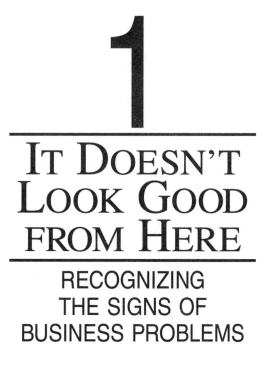

# IT DOESN'T LOOK GOOD FROM HERE

## RECOGNIZING THE SIGNS OF BUSINESS PROBLEMS

Shortly before his 30th birthday, Wooly established Ozark Safety Supply using several of his former customers as a base. In 1983, his second year in business, sales in the company approached $500,000, and two other salesmen from his former employer joined him. The growth explosion began.

The sudden growth and success of this company did not necessarily guarantee continued success. Raising capital, and managing and increasing equity are keys to long-term business success and existence. Wooly knew from day 1 that he was undercapitalized, but he was so caught up in the euphoria of building a successful business that he dismissed the risky implications of leveraging his growth with bank loans and vendor credit. Wooly always intended to increase the equity by retaining earnings. First, however, he found it necessary to establish an adequate warehouse. While he was doing that, it seemed reasonable to build plush offices. Then, the company needed a truck to replace the station wagons and vans the owner and his sales staff drove as delivery vehicles. When Roy decided he and his top salesman needed top-of-the-line cars, both leased Lincolns, and the rest of the sales staff leased Sables. And so the years passed, with the profits of the company committed to the trappings of success, which were seen as necessary, instead of building the cash cushion, as Wooly had once intended.

This business owner is fairly typical of many entrepreneurs. The lean years involve hard work and sacrifice. When some success is achieved, the perks are viewed as necessary, tangible evidence of that achievement. For many, little thought is given to providing a substantial cash cushion. The optimism necessary to build a business leaves little room for dwelling on the risks that can wreak havoc on the financial welfare of a company. Although there is a strong amount of faith and perseverance required to initiate and nurture a venture toward success, a strong dose of reality is needed on a regular basis. It is easy to become acclimated to the rhythm of your company and instinctively know when it is beginning to change course. The volume of customer traffic, mail or calls can give clear signals. The critical issue is to face the problem squarely and take corrective action. Avoidance won't make it go away.

## PROTECT YOUR COMPANY AGAINST TOUGH TIMES BY BUILDING A FINANCIAL CUSHION

Every sector of our economy goes through cycles and from time to time faces downturns of varying degrees. Most entrepreneurs start new businesses to meet a growing market, not a diminishing one. Once your new business is up and running, it is in a growth cycle, and it is difficult to imagine how it can turn in the opposite direction. You feel creative, energetic, resourceful, and confident that the direction you're going is up.

Even if you were well financed to begin with, it is critical that you retain cash so it is available when it is needed. Retain enough working capital to see you through any short-term financial crisis. If you began on the proverbial shoestring, then it is of absolute necessity that you continue to operate on that shoestring even after your business becomes profitable. You will need cash to fund expansion without getting heavily into debt. It is easy to fall into the trap of operating on the edge so that you are just one bad debt or one business interruption away from your own demise. If you don't learn this lesson in time for the first round, I can personally attest that you will learn it after a reorganization of your business. Every aspect of how I conduct my business now is far more conservative than it was before my bankruptcy.

## ACKNOWLEDGE THE SERIOUSNESS OF YOUR FINANCIAL PROBLEMS

To "run your own shop" is to face problems almost every day of the week. Employees who don't show up when they are desperately needed, shipments that are delayed or not shipped when promised, mechanical glitches, adverse weather conditions, and every other nightmare conceived challenge our ingenuity. We learn to be resourceful, and we learn not to be undermined by most problems that confront us. But when it comes to money, many of us are guilty of deluding ourselves that a "big deal" is just around the corner that will solve all of our problems. If you don't acknowledge them, temporary cash-flow problems or below-average profits will go untreated, and become threats to the survival of the business.

## DETERMINE THE NATURE AND EXTENT OF YOUR FINANCIAL PROBLEMS

The first step is to look at the reason your company is having financial distress. Where are the problems in your operation—in the marketplace you serve or in the general economic activity? If the market conditions for your product or service are in reasonably normal condition and your specific company is losing money, you should start your analysis with your last 3 years' operating statements. Are your costs under control? Or have they been slowly escalating, taking with them all of your profit? Analyze these numbers line by line to get a handle on the trouble area.

Sometimes entire industries are affected. In the winter of 1990–91, the airline industry was suddenly hit with the threat of war with Iraq and a dramatic rise in fuel costs. A major decline in passenger travel ensued; Eastern Airlines blamed its final failure (conversion from a Chapter 11 reorganization to a Chapter 7 liquidation) on the Persian Gulf situation, but the real seeds were planted by years of losses and acrimonious labor relations. In late March 1991, Midway Airlines filed for Chapter 11 protection, and its CEO claimed that Midway employees all deserved purple hearts because they had been casualties of the war. Most industry analysts, however, pointed to Midway's overambitious expansion, particularly to a second hub in Philadelphia, as the real core of its problems, not the Gulf War. The airline had little direct competition to its "second airport" concept in Chicago but found itself going head to head with a very aggressive USAir in Philadelphia.

The deep discounting that followed resulted in major losses for both airlines, and it was this prolonged period of losses that threatened Midway Airlines' financial viability.

The general economic conditions of the country have an impact on all business—but some businesses suffer more than others. Recessions end, but entire industries may be changed by the process; you have to determine whether your business will recover sufficiently to return to financial health.

Your company can suffer from one specific problem or a combination of several problems. That's where I found my company in the mid-1980s as manufactures of specialty industrial safety clothing. Our main market has traditionally been the metals industry, primarily steel. I took over the operation in 1972 and faced my first general recession only 2 years afterward. After a couple of rather tough years, the economy rebounded along with the steel industry and my own company as well.

The severe recession of the early 1980s did not end with any significant rebound in basic industries, however, and many companies, mine included, came out of that period very fragile.

*You must face the facts that brought you to your current condition, and determine when and if your company's recovery will begin.* What will it take to return your company to financial stability? Will it require a restructuring of your operation? Is it time to look at new and healthier markets? Or will your existing operation rebound? Whatever the circumstances, you will need action—and action begins with awareness. Face the facts!

## RECOGNIZE THE DIFFERENCE BETWEEN LONG-TERM AND SHORT-TERM PROBLEMS

It is critical for any company to separate its long-term structural problems from any short-term or cyclical difficulties. Many companies limp around for years with weak underpinnings—such as undercapitalization, or losses based on poor pricing and high costs—yet they continue to mask the damage to their cash flow. Often the CEO or managers won't confront these more serious issues, and when an unexpected crisis occurs, the entire organization erupts in chaos.

For Roy, the salesman-turned-CEO, mentioned at the beginning of this chapter, chaos began with the failure of one of his big customers. In 1985, the CEO had aggressively pursued asbestos removal contractors because they required protective clothing and respiratory protection. After 3 years of great business, the asbestos removal industry began to slow down, profit margins dwindled, and contractors began to go under. One contractor who closed had been one of the CEO's longtime customers and left him with a $60,000 debt. This was a major blow to the CEO's company, and left him with very little working capital. A loss this large may severely impact many small companies, but it becomes a genuine crisis to a business without much working capital.

When he established his company, this CEO knew that capital was a problem for him, yet he did very little while enjoying his short-term success to address this long-term problem. These problems that businesses confront can be separated into "chronic," or structural problems, and "acute," or short-term anomalies. To develop a strategy for a successful solution, the chronic problem must be faced and steps must be taken to correct them. A bankruptcy filing can address both chronic

**TABLE 1–1**

**Recognizing Chronic versus Acute Business Problems**

| CHRONIC PROBLEMS | | ACUTE PROBLEMS |
|---|---|---|
| Develop slowly<br>Continue over a<br>prolonged period | Onset and<br>duration | Develop within 60 days<br>May continue for a period<br>of 6 months or less |
| Are pervasive<br>throughout entire<br>operation<br>Affect costs across<br>the board | Scope | May only involve a single<br>customer or product line<br>Could be a single, large<br>charge-off |
| Conduct an<br>operational audit:<br>reduce overhead or<br>gradually increase<br>pricing | Strategy | Effect corrective action<br>immediately<br>Communicate candidly<br>with suppliers, lenders,<br>and creditors |
| May force financial<br>restructuring on<br>creditors<br>Loans may be<br>reduced by<br>diminished value<br>of assets<br>Supplier debt may be<br>reduced by 50% or<br>more | Bankruptcy<br>impact | Automatic stay will allow<br>at least 120, possibly<br>180, days to take action<br>to stem crisis situation<br>Overall debt may be<br>paid out over several<br>years |

and acute business problems, but the plans for each will differ substantially from beginning to end.

Table 1–1 provides some analytical guidelines for recognizing which of your business problems are chronic and which are acute. If your company's problems are *chronic*—that is, long-term, structural problems—they need attention *now*.

## LEARN THAT MANAGING CHRONIC FINANCIAL PROBLEMS DOESN'T CURE THEM

A company's chronic problems may fester for years. For example, consider the very long-term and bitter relations between Eastern Airlines and its unions. After years of give-backs, the machinists were ready for all-out war, even if the chief casualty would be the airline itself. While this animosity grew, passenger loads dropped. Caught in the crossfire of disgruntled employees, many frequent flyers began to avoid Eastern. Eastern tried all sorts of promotional fares to woo them back, and the losses that followed killed the airline. In the end, the fight was so bitter that on January 15, 1991, the day Eastern ceased flying, union machinists still picketing posted signs at vacant gates declaring, "We won."

Eastern had a long window of opportunity in which it could have forged a workable peace to end this chronic and debilitating problem. At one point, it became a personal grudge match between then-CEO Frank Borman and Charles Burns, head of the machinists. Then Eastern sold out to Continental Holdings, and this baggage went with the sale. Frank Lorenzo, CEO of Continental, did little to change these dynamics; in fact, he became a lightning rod to exacerbate the situation. In 1989, machinists went on strike, followed by all other employees including the relatively well-paid pilots. A year and a half later, the end of the airline was blamed on war in the Persian Gulf. But the war was only the *acute* problem; other airlines survived the same war.

Another structural or chronic problem is operating losses that continue over a long period. These have many causes, such as high fixed overhead, high labor costs, and poor pricing. Recent leveraged buyouts have created high carrying costs, which have become a structural impediment to many companies.

Many companies continue to operate for years with chronic problems eroding their finances, but they learn to make adjustments to compensate. These usually manifest in slow payables. In some cases, payments are made in a cycle of 45 to 60 days. But too many companies take a far riskier approach: They make payments only in response to a direct request for money, usually by telephone. This approach does not mask the issue and puts most suppliers on notice that they should watch that company's account. It also questions the credibility of the company and its managers.

## UNDERSTAND HOW UNTREATED PROBLEMS CREATE FINANCIAL VULNERABILITY

Unacknowledged or untreated problems will, if they do not destroy a company, become the chronic problems that slowly debilitate a company's resources. This was the case for XYZ Industrial Supply, an automotive supplier whose main business was items such as nuts, bolts, and abrasives, as well as general tools. For years, this Michigan-based company made regular profits from business with 4 major automotive plants located within 12 miles of its warehouse. Its location and well-managed inventory system made it a desirable supplier, and the greatest pressure the company experienced over the years was maintaining a demanding delivery schedule. When the automotive industry began its retrenchment, this supplier saw a major drop in its revenue. Over a 3-year period, 1 plant completely closed, and the remaining 3 scaled back operations by nearly 40%. The company's management was concerned, but like many who had come to believe that the plants would always be there, they took no steps to make real changes in their own operations. It took months for the company to initiate their first layoff, and it was only one entry clerk and one warehouseman—not much of a savings.

During the first year of the downturn, XYZ Industrial used cash flow and cash reserve to continue operations as usual. Inventory was allowed to deplete by 25%, but no serious changes were made in operations or marketing. There were other smaller industrial accounts to develop, but the company's salesmen were not used to this type of selling. It was of little interest to them because the return looked too small to bother. By the time year 2 began, cash reserves had dwindled, and lines of credit were being drawn. Some deeper cuts were made in overhead expenses, but none sufficient to stem the mounting losses. Now suppliers were receiving payments more slowly, and it was evident to most employees that their company was in real trouble. It was not until the year's end and a major occurrence, however, that the company's final crisis began.

Most major auto companies process payments like clockwork on certain dates. For XYZ, these dates were crucial times because they often issued checks in advance of monies received with no cash backup. In September 1989, a check for $47,000 did not arrive on the day it was expected. Panic did not set in until the second day, when a call was made to the accounting department, and it was determined that no check had been cut due to a keypunch error. The previous month's contract releases had to be reconstructed, and the process would take weeks to correct.

Only by scrambling was the company's controller able to cover the outstanding checks but was not able to meet the upcoming payroll. With a delay of a few days, the net pay was available, but a withholding deposit was not remitted. In October, when the quarterly return was due, the funds were so short that this was also not filed. Once this barrier had been crossed, it seemed easier to repeat it, and that was done twice the following year.

By year 3, the problems facing this company were both chronic and acute. Loan payments were not being made, suppliers were cutting off credit and now the Internal Revenue Service (IRS) was closing in on the unpaid taxes. Penalties and interest had been added, and the debt was too much to pay at one time. For the first time and only out of desperation, the CEO and top manager of the company consulted an attorney. Could anything be done to hold off the Feds who, by this time, had made a levy on their company bank account? As it happened, on the day the available funds were frozen, the balance was so low that little cash was turned over to the IRS. As receivables were collected, the crisis passed. After 2 weeks of unsuccessful negotiations with the IRS, the attorney recommended and the company agreed to file for Chapter 11 bankruptcy protection. This move froze all actions, including the IRS levy, but it also left a very weakened company resulting from 3 long years of unaddressed problems. It was extremely doubtful that the leadership that could not face the growing threat could acknowledge the real issues and create a plan to correct them, as well as pay off the existing debt.

*This is the type of chronic/acute double shot that my company experienced.* Our chronic problem had been a prolonged period of low profits. This was a result of the severe economic downturn in the steel and other primary industry that we traditionally served. Business fell by more than 40%—and what remained became brutally competitive. I took major steps to restructure the operation to account for these changes, and by 1984—2 years after the free-fall began—we were, at least, on balance. As in the case with most chronic problems, these difficult times had seriously eroded the financial stability of my business. Many projects had been deferred, and we had no cash cushion to rely on in case of any emergency. And the crisis did arrive.

In 1986, my company became embroiled in a commercial dispute regarding our largest customer. Realizing litigation would be necessary, and with no margin for error, I was forced to file for bankruptcy protection to keep the company operating while the outstanding issues were settled.

## OVERCOME A SUDDEN ECONOMIC CRISIS

Even when business circumstance deteriorates quickly, an early and realistic assessment and action will minimize the damage, and increase the chances for a successful restructuring. Jeffrey Collen was in the process of creating a chain of shoe stores when he faced a disaster in the making and turned it into a successful restart.

Jeff had expanded his small, neighborhood shoe store into a 3-store chain with plans for further expansion. His second store was in a suburban shopping mall, and the volume it generated allowed Collen to carry better lines and to buy for better prices. The third store was in a smaller mall, and it did not do great volume, but it did not have much overhead. In fall 1989, the highway department informed the tenants of the larger suburban mall about road construction that would begin in spring 1990. They brought charts and graphs to show how they planned the traffic to flow, and painted a rosy picture of how well they expected it to work.

Jeff Collen left the meeting with a rock in the pit of his stomach. His store was less than a year old and was barely covering its own overhead. With athletic shoes accounting for 40% of all sales, any spring disruption could be disastrous. At that moment, however, there was little he could do but adopt a "wait-and-see" attitude and go ahead with buying stock for his expected levels of business.

Business activity during Christmas 1989 was less than Collen had expected, and he started 1990 with more inventory than normal that only deep discounting moved. His cash position was not strong, and his small line of credit was almost fully used. Then, on Monday, April 17, the barriers went up along the highway leading to the mall. The first few days, merchants could have shot a cannon down the hallway of the shopping mall with little chance of hitting anyone. Most business owners were concerned but all hoped that the weekend would see their customers finding the traffic flow as easy as the highway department had promised. By late Saturday afternoon, the truth was apparent—it would be worse than anyone had anticipated.

During the next 3 weeks, sales were off more than 30%, and the store was losing money at a rate the owner couldn't afford. New fall merchandise had to be purchased, and it was clear that if the owner did not pay his outstanding bills, his suppliers would not ship. The bank was unwilling even to listen to a proposal to increase the line of credit, and the branch manager started making noises that it should be paid down instead. The owner was becoming distraught and wondered why he had ever gone into business for himself in the first place.

Fortunately for this merchant, numbered among his group of close friends was an attorney specializing in commercial law including bankruptcy. After listening to his story, particularly the fact that conditions could rebound in less than 4 months, the attorney suggested filing for Chapter 11 protection. This was done *before* lease payments were missed, *before* the bank had called in its loan, and *before* suppliers had taken any collection actions. All this store owner needed was some breathing room during the time of the highway construction, and the court action secured that for him. He also assured all creditors from the beginning that their payback would be 100% of what was owed, even if it would be over an extended period. Collen's shoe store spent less than 6 months in bankruptcy before a plan was approved. The owner learned a lot about inventory control and retail promotion in the process. And his lawyer friend kept the legal fees reasonable.

## IF YOUR COMPANY IS FINANCIALLY VULNERABLE, A SUDDEN EVENT CAN SPELL DISASTER

The crisis usually escalates when a sudden event adds additional pressure. There are an infinite variety of catastrophes that can confront a business. These include, but certainly are not limited to, the closing or failure of a customer, a general economic downturn, a strike, the loss of key managers, and fire and other natural disasters.

All of these problems create financial stress on any business, but they can be life threatening to a company that has a weakened foundation. This was the case for Roy Wooly, the salesman-turned-CEO. His early lack of capital and his inattention to correcting the situation was a stress on his business. Even though he was slow to pay, Roy's personal charm and vision for the growth of his own company and his suppliers made everyone more patient than they might have been. But when the CEO lost $60,000 on a defunct contractor, his cash-flow problems quickly grew to crisis proportions. Promises that had been made couldn't be kept and calls from creditors went unanswered. He described the right-hand bottom drawer of his desk as becoming a "nightmare of unopened mail."

Even at this point, there were many steps Wooly could have taken that would have stopped his downward spiral. His overhead expenses should have been cut quickly and deeply, but Roy couldn't see it. He felt that his business growth and success would continue and that there was little reason to make cuts in his life-style. Cutting costs would have allowed more money to flow to suppliers and would have relieved some of that pressure. Support staff could have been cut—unnecessary equipment sold and cheaper quarters found. Pounding the pavement for new business might have increased profits and given this company a chance to atone for its past excesses.

Even an infusion of outside capital would have created the time needed to effect a turnaround. He might have considered taking on a partner and using the investment money as working capital. The benefits are beyond just the money. A partner can provide an additional perspective to use when making decisions.

Many entrepreneurs reject the idea of bringing in a partner (as our safety equipment CEO did) because they want to control their own business. *But wouldn't it be preferable to share control of a company with renewed potential than to have full control over a sinking ship?*

## LOOK FOR SOLUTIONS BESIDES FILING FOR BANKRUPTCY

Bankruptcy reorganization should never be viewed as the only answer for a business in trouble, however. The CEO of the safety equipment company had several opportunities to put his own business on the right track, but he missed all the signs. He had made enough money in the early years to provide a real cash cushion sufficient to absorb a $60,000 loss. Even after that loss, reserves could have been created so that his enormous need for cash would not have taken precedence over his understanding of the critical importance of operating profit for the survival of a business.

At best, bankruptcy is one tool in the arsenal of business strategies that can be used to gain breathing room from threatened or attempted creditors' actions, or to force negotiated debt restructure and payments on creditors who are unwilling to negotiate outside of the court's jurisdiction. The cost of these two primary features of time and restructure can be high, in terms of legal fees and management effort necessary to prepare a bankruptcy filing, attend all required hearings, and complete all paperwork.

The single factor that contributes to the success of a business, whether it is in the start-up phase or in the period of reorganization, is the planning. A plan must be realistic to the conditions of the business itself, as well as the markets it serves, and creative in finding ways to solve problems and sell those solutions. For a company in reorganization, whether under bankruptcy protection or on its own, the first step is to take an analytical audit of its entire operation. It is critical to identify the strengths as well as the weaknesses.

If the problems have become long term and pervasive or structural, there is no quick fix. Every area that is creating financial pressure for the company must be dealt with. Overhead costs should be reviewed and slashed, when possible, with serious consideration to the need to maintain quality and customer service. If pricing is the issue, for example, a gradual implementation of increases can be instituted, along with a review of changes in product lines or service delivery. Enhancing the value can support an increased price.

The safety equipment company could have benefited from both a cut in costs and increased prices. Concentration in either area may have saved his company. Money spent on offices, automobiles, and entertaining could have provided his cash cushion. When his pricing was forced so low that profits were impossible, it was critical to develop new business that produced the needed profits. A cash surplus will provide time for this transition.

But even a substantial amount of cash cannot protect a company indefinitely if management remains unwilling to acknowledge the problems and institute the necessary changes. Our automotive supplier watched his company slowly die, taking no steps to reverse the downward spiral. It was death by attrition, and a bankruptcy filing could only prolong the agony, not stop it. A new business strategy was required.

## SUMMING UP

Recognizing the problem is the first step to making changes. The shoe store owner knew in advance that trouble was coming. The fact is that most of us do sense it before it happens. The key to success is facing the circumstance squarely and taking the necessary actions, which may include filing for protection under the Bankruptcy Code.

Bankruptcy is a unique legal problem. In many legal cases, the client is almost extraneous: The lawyer manages the case, negotiates the settlement, and consults with the client for approval—in other words, the lawyer is the expert and must direct the case. Bankruptcy, however, is more than a legal matter—it is also a business matter. Hence, the client must be much more closely involved in the entire process.

Obviously, businesses should not represent their own interests in most legal situations—and bankruptcy is one of the most complex circumstances a business can experience, with very high stakes. You must take the time and make the effort to find competent and creative counsel. You must not settle for a lawyer who does not work well with you and does not inspire confidence. To do so is to invite disaster. Knowing the local practitioners in advance of any emergency is sound business advice.

But how soon is soon enough? In his book, *Feast for Lawyers—Inside Chapter 11: An Exposé,* Sol Stein of Stein & Day Publishers describes having first dis-

# 2

# A FOOL FOR A CLIENT

## THE RIGHT ATTORNEY IS THE FIRST STEP TO SUCCESS

cussed a Chapter 11 bankruptcy filing 2 years before he actually sought bankruptcy protection. That may appear unusual, but it isn't really extraordinary at all. Many companies sense impending trouble well in advance of the time that their financial problems begin closing in on them, and you would be wise to begin to seek counsel and advice as early as possible. Waiting until a filing becomes inevitable will prove to be very costly to your company because there will be no time for advance planning.

## KNOW WHAT TO LOOK FOR IN A BANKRUPTCY LAWYER

The practice of bankruptcy law has been growing steadily during the past 5 years, and virtually all types of lawyers can be found in this specialty. Somewhere between the high-priced "too busy to take time" variety and the slightly sleazy bankruptcy-mill type is a growing cadre of bright, professional, and responsive lawyers joining the field. Your best bet will be an attorney with bankruptcy experience from a small or midsize firm. Because there may be occasions when arguments must be made to the court to convince the judge that your company needs some indulgence to be able to successfully reorganize, you will want an attorney with good verbal skills. And you will want to find one with whom you feel compatible. Compatibility is an intangible that is both difficult to explain and critically important. During financial restructuring, the attorney-client relationship will experience moments of great stress. You will experience many low periods and face substantial frustration. If the underlying relationship with your attorney is not a personally cordial one coupled with mutual respect, the strain can become debilitating. A list of specific areas of discussion with potential attorneys is discussed later in this chapter.

## BEGIN YOUR SEARCH BY DEVELOPING A LIST OF POTENTIAL CANDIDATES

You will want to make a complete search in your area of all attorneys who may be candidates to handle your case. Begin with as extensive a list as you can put together; look for referrals from several different sources. It's understandable that you would not want to broadcast the fact that you are considering a bankruptcy filing, but it's important enough to find the right match that you will want to know about the credentials of many attorneys.

If you have a regular company lawyer, that's one place to start. He or she may want to handle this matter because many general business attorneys are branching out into bankruptcy practice as this area has enjoyed substantial growth. But if this is a small practice without much experience in this specialty, it is a risk to choose this firm. There are several bankruptcy strategies that are the result of experience. You want to get the benefit of that experience.

The best referral may be from other business associates. If you know someone who has been through the bankruptcy process, they will be able to either recommend an attorney or perhaps warn you away from one. The information is valuable, and you should solicit this input.

If you can ask your banker without raising any great concern, do so. Local collection agencies regularly use attorneys to pursue lawsuits, and most lawyers who work in this area also practice bankruptcy. Their experience in creditors' rights is valuable to debtors also.

If you can't get any personal recommendations, try your local bar association. They will provide a group of names of individuals whose practice includes bankruptcy. Depending on how you feel about it, there are ads in the Yellow Pages that you should at least review.

## Observe Lawyers in Court for Other Bankruptcy Cases

The best place to learn about the practice of bankruptcy and the lawyers in the field is in an actual court. You can go to the clerk's office and read any docket (the case record), and you can sit in any court room and observe the proceedings. In one day of hearings, a judge may deal with 20 cases with a new case scheduled every 15 minutes. Most of what goes on is a presentation of a motion, and any objections and questioning of the attorneys by the judge.

There are several things to look for if you observe in the court. Is the attorney well prepared to argue his motion, and does he articulate his case in a convincing manner? Does the judge appear to hold the lawyer in high regard? Attorneys in bankruptcy practice appear in court frequently, and because most districts have only a handful of bankruptcy judges, the experienced practitioner is probably well known by each judge. I have watched judges deal with lawyers they do not seem to hold in high regard, and the change in judicial demeanor is evident. The questions will be more intense and appear skeptical, and the attorney in question will have a tougher time convincing the judge to decide in his client's favor.

Your company's attorney will be going to court to persuade the judge to give your company protection from all of your creditors until such time as you can reorganize your business and restructure your debt. Although the law was written to allow a company to "rehabilitate" itself, it isn't always easy to convince the court that your company is capable of completing the process. You will need an attorney who is knowledgeable and has credibility with the court. You can see these qualities best if you observe them in person.

There is one other quality that can be uncovered more accurately by observation than by any other fashion—the respect your candidate receives from his peers and his interaction with them. This is important because the best way to keep your legal expense at a reasonable level is to negotiate with your creditors through their attorneys and settle most issues before they come in front of the judge. A motion that has been agreed to by both sides will almost always be approved by the court. A lawyer who is respected by his colleagues is better able to succeed in these negotiations. This form of compromise works in your favor but not necessarily in the favor of the income of the lawyer. In a court setting, you can observe which lawyers work expeditiously and which appear to milk a case. The ones who seem to create extra work should be avoided completely—you'll be paying the tab!

## MEET SEVERAL CANDIDATES BEFORE YOU CHOOSE YOUR LAWYER

Before I made my choice of attorneys to handle my company's bankruptcy, I met with four potential candidates, each recommended by someone I knew. Most attorneys are willing to give a potential client at least some time in a face-to-face meeting to discuss a pending case. Any lawyer unwilling to do this should be scratched off your list. Your time will be limited, but I would suggest four areas of inquiry in this initial phase.

### Ask about the Lawyer's Legal Background

Find out how long your candidate has been in practice and how extensively the law firm's practice has included financial restructuring and bankruptcy law. How many other members of the firm are also involved in an active bankruptcy practice (two heads are better than one). You will want to know how many cases the firm and the individual has handled. What percentage has ended in successful reorganization? Most attorneys who have handled bankruptcies for many years will have a substantial number of earlier cases that ended in liquidation, but you should expect that the more recent and current cases are in the process of successful reorganization.

### Ask about the Attorney's Prior Business Experience

Legal talent and business acumen are neither mutually exclusive nor necessary companion skills. Most lawyers have basic business knowledge but varying degrees of genuine expertise in areas such as marketing, accounting, or production and distribution methods. You will want to explore both the types of business your candidate has represented and other areas of his or her expertise, such as real estate transactions or supply contracts if these are issues that may come up in the course of your case.

Your attorney will not operate your business, and you should not expect him to take on that role. This is the critical aspect of a reorganization, and you should be willing and able to continue this responsibility. But an attorney who can add to your body of knowledge or contribute resources is a real asset. Discuss this aspect.

## Ask about the Attorney's Bankruptcy Strategy

Most companies, including my own, have a general business strategy. It will manifest in how aggressively we price our product or the type of distribution we choose. If we are successful, that will reinforce our continued method of operation. Attorneys will also develop a strategy in how they handle their cases. The more success they have, the greater their belief in how a case should be handled. You should discuss this with your candidate.

Does he believe that you should aggressively pursue a reduction in all claims? Is he inclined to end the case as soon as possible, or does he recommend that you try to get additional time to complete your plan?

For example, my attorney believed that it was best to keep a low profile and negotiate as the occasion arose. Key to our success was our ability to extend my case long enough to settle a civil suit over a commercial dispute. Had we been more aggressive in our pursuit to dismiss some claims, I am convinced that one of my creditors would have forced us to file a bankruptcy plan before we were able to do so.

The wise business principal matches the problem with the problem solver. If you have any idea of what the game plan should be, the time to match the attorney capable of achieving it is during the search for legal counsel. For example, if the ultimate failure of the company is all but a foregone conclusion, then protecting your personal assets and limiting your exposure is the strategy, and you should seek the appropriate expertise to execute this strategy. But if your trouble spot is the discharge of a questionable debt, lease agreement, or partnership arrangement, then you need an attorney whose strategy is one of aggressive pursuit of disputes. Have these discussions in general terms in your preliminary meetings.

## Ask Your Candidates about Fees and Retainers

You will need to have a frank discussion about money with your potential lawyers. You need to know if you can afford the one you choose. You don't want to take the time to find a perfect attorney and learn that he costs more than you can afford.

The fee question has two parts. Attorneys charge an hourly rate that can range from slightly under $100 to $300. In most court districts, the bankruptcy judge sets the upward limit. Exhibit 2–1 shows a sample motion for court permission to pay fees to the debtor's attorney (see page 24). It is accompanied by sample time sheets and other documentation. The hourly fee has been approved by the court. You should review any fee application that is submitted because you will be paying the bill.

Once the retainer has been exhausted, your attorney will file a motion for the court to approve additional payments. You will make these payments.

The second aspect of the fee question is the initial retainer, which virtually all attorneys require. This is the money paid up front that is held by the law firm to cover their fees. Because many cases do fail, leaving few assets remaining to pay legal fees, many attorneys require retainers of $10,000 or more. One Pittsburgh attorney reported that many potential clients tell him, "If I had $10,000, I wouldn't be bankrupt."

It would be virtually impossible to estimate the cost of any case, particularly because much of the cost is in the time that can be spent filing motions and answers, and appearing at hearings in response to actions initiated by creditors. But it is a question worthy of discussion that should include ways to control costs.

## Consider the Intangibles as You Narrow Your Search

Now that you have met each person, you will have a general impression of the lawyers that you interviewed. Did one stand out because you seemed to hit it off—to understand each other? Did he ask questions about the business operation that indicated an interest in the possibility that the company could be reorganized? If this is the attorney that you chose, the two of you will be working closely together, and your goal should be the same. If I had the impression that my attorney didn't believe or didn't care whether my company could be turned around, I wouldn't be comfortable working with that lawyer. This may have varying importance to you, but it should at least be considered.

## CONDUCT THE FINAL INTERVIEW WITH YOUR POTENTIAL LAWYER

Once you have narrowed the choice of attorneys, more specific questions are in order. At this stage, you should be willing to pay for the time of the lawyers under consideration. This establishes attorney-client privileges and its accompanying confidentiality. There is still one other precaution to take to make sure that any information discussed does not come back to haunt you. If the law firm has not yet done so, make sure that they conduct a "conflict search." This means that the firm is not representing anyone with an action pending against your company, and you will want to mention other large creditors to be considered in that review. Do not assume that this is automatically done—ask about it. I recently heard about a fairly good-size firm that accepted a retainer, filed a bankruptcy petition, and then found that they represented one of the creditors.

During this final interview process, there is also the good news to be considered. You may find out while discussing the creditors in your case that one of the lawyers has a particularly good working relationship with the legal representative of one of your more difficult creditors. This could make future negotiations a bit smoother as the two lawyers work amicably to everyone's benefit.

Now is the time to begin to discuss the specific strategy that might be employed in your case. For the purposes of such a discussion, you will need the past few years' operating statements and a current balance sheet. If there are legal actions pending against your company, bring all the pertinent documentation. A key issue of strategy is a critical look at assets beyond how they are listed at book value. Are they worth more than their listed value and could be liquidated to satisfy debts? Are they worth less and should the secured lender be forced to reduce the amount of your loan? These are just two of the issues of strategy that might be included in these final interviews.

At the conclusion of this process you will have learned more about the bankruptcy law, heard more than one suggestion of a strategy, and found the best legal counsel for your company. This gives you a real head start on the success potential for your case than you would have if you had grabbed the first law firm you could find when the sheriff was at the door.

## Take a Realistic Approach to How Attorneys Normally Work

You should understand that most attorneys juggle cases by operating in a reactive way rather than a proactive one. If the court has given a 30-day deadline to file a motion or the response to one filed by the other side, there will be silence for the first 28 days followed by a flurry of activity on day 29 to meet the deadline. This can create serious hurdles for you because hastily crafted agreements usually require deep concessions that you will have little time to consider. I once had a new agreement with rather serious implications waved under my nose in the hall outside of the courtroom. I refused to agree to any issue I didn't have sufficient time to consider—and you should too.

You will not get any serious commitment from your attorney to change his method of operation. But what you should demand is to be given copies of all pertinent communications sent to your counsel about your case as soon as they are received—not when your lawyer is just getting around to dealing with them. This will give you time to consider the issue before decisions must be made.

*You must be willing to make complete disclosure to your attorney so that he or she is prepared to handle what might be coming in your case.* If you have unopened mail that you have been avoiding, now is the time to open it and take it to your attorney. If you have underpaid or not paid your taxes, face up to it and decide how you will correct the situation. If you have been avoiding paying a bill claiming that the merchandise was not received or that it came in damaged, let your counsel know that this is, in fact, a valid debt, not one that is in dispute. If your attorney finds out later that you have been less than candid with him, it will be very costly in terms of paid legal time to correct inaccuracies and costly in terms of your working relationship.

If you have chosen the right attorney, you will feel as if you have entered into a partnership with your attorney with a goal that you will decide together and both work to make a reality. There are several outcomes to a financial restructuring, and you should consider these early on in the case:

- You could reorganize and continue operating the business.
- You could sell it as an operating business.
- You could liquidate the assets to reduce the debt and as much of your exposure as possible.

If you believe the company can and should be saved and your attorney does not share this belief, you won't be working in the same direction. This is one of the issues to settle *before* you pay your attorney a retainer to handle your case and *before* you file for Chapter 11 bankruptcy.

You can work with an attorney for some time before you make the actual decision to file; during this time, you can pay an hourly fee for time spent in the planning. If you have any questions as to whether or not this is the lawyer you want for the long haul, it may be best to go the route of a trial marriage.

After you have filed a bankruptcy petition, it is rather difficult to change attorneys. The court will formalize the appointment of the lawyer you have chosen to represent your company. Any attorney representing a debtor (whether in a Chapter 11 Reorganization or a Chapter 7 Liquidation) must be confirmed by the court to be paid. A Chapter 11 debtor files a motion to employ counsel to represent his interests in the reorganization process; Exhibit 2–2 shows a sample motion for permission to employ counsel (see page 32). The debtor in the sample motion converted a Chapter 7 to a Chapter 11 and is proceeding through the process of reviewing claims and creating a plan of reorganization.

Your creditors will be notified who your attorney is, so a great deal of contact they might have been making with you will now go directly to your counsel. Creditors are no longer permitted by the Bankruptcy Code to contact you. Changing this whole process would be difficult so it is easy to understand why the court frowns on allowing you to change lawyers easily. You must file a motion and give good reason why you want to fire your existing lawyer. Creditors won't want you to take another hunk of what they now consider "their money" and pay a retainer to a new firm. There's a good chance they would object.

The benefit of this system is that your lawyer can't walk away from your case without asking for permission from the court also. Even if you are no longer able to pay his legal bills, he must continue adequate representation until he files a motion with the court, and the judge hears the reasons and makes the court's determination. So you are protected if the going gets particularly rough.

## SUMMING UP

The choice of a lawyer is a critical decision that requires time and effort to make effectively. Do your homework, use your instincts, and take as much time as you need to make a wise choice.

**Exhibit 2–1    Sample Application for Attorney's Fees**

## IN THE UNITED STATES BANKRUPTCY COURT
## FOR THE WESTERN DISTRICT OF PENNSYLVANIA

IN RE:   PITTSBURGH GLOVE                    Case No. _____
         MANUFACTURING COMPANY,
                                             Chapter 11
              Debtor

### Summary Cover Sheet/Fees and
### Expenses Application

1. Your applicant was appointed on August 21, 1986.

2. Your applicant represents the debtor in possession, Pittsburgh Glove Manufacturing Company.

3. The total amount of the compensation requested is $_____.

4. This compensation is interim compensation.

5. The total amount of expenses for which reimbursement is sought is none and is for the period from January 10, 1989 to October 4, 1990.

6. The dates and the amounts of previous compensation paid are: retainer paid August 14, 1986—$_____; March 16, 1989—$_____ and $_____ for expenses per court order.

7. The date and amount of any retainer are the sum of $_____ paid on August 1, 1986 for the filing of this case (duplicate of item set forth in paragraph 6 above).

Date: _____          _____

Exhibit 2–1    Sample Application for Attorney's Fees    **25**

**Exhibit 2–1**  *(continued)*

---

## In the United States Bankruptcy Court
## for the Western District of Pennsylvania

---

IN RE:    PITTSBURGH GLOVE                    Case No. _____
         MANUFACTURING COMPANY,
                                               Chapter 11
         Debtor

### Application for Fees and Expenses

AND NOW, comes _____, attorney for the debtor in possession, and sets forth the following in support of her application for fees and expenses:

1. On or about August 21, 1986, this Honorable Court appointed _____ and _____ to represent the debtor in possession, Pittsburgh Glove Manufacturing Company, in this proceeding. A true and correct copy of the order for appointment of attorneys is attached hereto, marked Exhibit "A" and made a part hereof.

2. This application is for interim compensation and expenses for the period beginning January 10, 1989 and continuing until October 3, 1990. The total amount of compensation for services rendered to the debtor in possession and the estate is the sum of $_____. The total amount of expenses is the sum of none.

3. A previous order of compensation was made by this Honorable Court on March 16, 1989 pursuant to an application for fees and expenses for the period beginning August 14, 1986 and continuing until January 10, 1989. At that time, the court approved the debtor's initial retainer paid to its attorneys in the sum of $_____ and approved an additional $_____ in expenses, plus additional fees of $_____, for a total of $_____ in fees for the period between August 14, 1986 through January 10, 1989, which amount includes the initial retainer paid. A true and correct copy of the order of court approving the aforesaid prior agreement, is attached hereto, marked Exhibit "B" and made a part hereof.

4. The only attorney contributing services for this case is Mary E. Bower, whose billing rate is $_____ per hour; and whose total hours are 58 hours for total fees incurred from the period January 10, 1989 through October 4, 1990 in the sum of $_____.

5. A chronological listing of time and services performed is attached hereto, marked Exhibit "C" and made a part hereof.

**Exhibit 2–1**  *(continued)*

6. An itemization of the expenses for which reimbursement is requested is as follows: none.

7. _____, the professional above named, was and is a disinterested person and has not represented or held an interest adverse to the interest of the estate on the matter in which she was employed in compliance with Bankruptcy Code Section 327(a).

### History of the Case

8. Pittsburgh Glove Manufacturing Company is a small manufacturing company incorporated in 1907 and operated by Suzanne Caplan, the current president, since 1972. The debtor was forced into bankruptcy due to certain economic conditions and certain unlawful commercial practices which gave rise to litigation which was commenced during the bankruptcy proceeding and resulted in a settlement approved by this court under seal which created the fund from which the plan of reorganization has been funded. The debtor has filed its plan of reorganization and disclosure statement as amended, and believes that the plan is a consentual plan which will most likely be approved by all creditors.

WHEREFORE, the applicant respectfully requests this Honorable Court to authorize the debtor in possession to pay the sum of $_____ to _____ for counsel fees and _____ for expenses.

Respectfully submitted,

_____

Exhibit 2–1    Sample Application for Attorney's Fees    **27**

**Exhibit 2–1**    *(continued)*

## IN THE UNITED STATES BANKRUPTCY COURT
## FOR THE WESTERN DISTRICT OF PENNSYLVANIA

IN RE:  PITTSBURGH GLOVE                    Case No. _____
       MANUFACTURING COMPANY,
                                 Chapter 11
        Debtor

### Exhibit "C"
### Chronological Summary of Time and
### Services Rendered on Behalf of
### Debtor during Period from January
### 10, 1989 through October 4, 1990

| DATE | ATTORNEY | DESCRIPTION OF SERVICES | HOURS | CODE PER EXHIBIT "D" |
|---|---|---|---|---|
| 1/16/89 | MEB | Prepare statement of operations for filing (covering period 10-1-88 to 12-31-88) | .25 | 4 |
| 1/17/89 | MEB | Prepare motion to disburse funds for working capital | 2.0 | 4 |
| 1/31/89 | MEB | Telephone call with _____, attorney for _____ regarding unpaid Nov. & Dec. payments | .25 | 2 |
| 2/8/89 | MEB | Telephone call with _____, attorney for _____ regarding leases on machinery; telephone call with Suzanne Caplan regarding compromise with _____ | .50 | 2 |
| 2/20/89 | MEB | Telephone call with _____ regarding _____ reinstatement of leases | .25 | 2 |

**Exhibit 2–1**   *(continued)*

| DATE | ATTORNEY | DESCRIPTION OF SERVICES | HOURS | CODE PER EXHIBIT "D" |
|------|----------|-------------------------|-------|----------------------|
| 2/10/89 | MEB | Telephone call with Suzanne Caplan regarding problems with _____ leases and with Office of Administration | .25 | 2 |
| 2/10/89 | MEB | Telephone call with _____ regarding settlement with _____ | .25 | 1 |
| 2/14/89 | MEB | Telephone call with _____ regarding the _____ dispute | .25 | 2 |
| 2/14/89 | MEB | Telephone call with _____ of _____ (unsecured creditor) re administrative debt for material in the amount of $550.00. | .25 | 4 |
| 2/15/89 | MEB | Telephone call with _____ re meeting with _____; telephone call with _____ re _____; call with Suzanne Caplan re the above | 1.0 | 1 |
| 2/15/89 | MEB | Letter to _____ re _____ leases | .25 | 2 |
| 2/20/89 | MEB | Telephone call with Suzanne Caplan re _____ and plan; finish preparing plan and disclosure statement | 3.25 | 1 |

Exhibit 2–1    Sample Application for Attorney's Fees    **29**

**Exhibit 2–1**  *(continued)*

| DATE | ATTORNEY | DESCRIPTION OF SERVICES | HOURS | CODE PER EXHIBIT "D" |
|------|----------|-------------------------|-------|----------------------|
| 2/23/89 | MEB | Telephone call with _____ re meeting with _____ and settlement with _____; telephone call re _____, _____ and _____ | .50 | 1 |
| 2/27/89 | MEB | Telephone call with _____ re _____ administrative claim | .25 | 4 |
| 2/27/89 | MEB | Letter to _____ re _____ administrative claim | .25 | 4 |
| 3/2/89 | MEB | Meeting with _____ & _____; meeting with _____ re global settlement | 3.25 | 1 |
| 3/3/89 | MEB | Research regarding _____ claims that it is secured in the settlement funds; letter to _____ | 2.50 | 1 |
| 3/8/89 | MEB | Telephone call with Suzanne Caplan & with _____ re working capital motion | .25 | 4 |
| 6/13/90 | MEB | Prepare notice postponing hearing date for disclosure | .25 | 1 |
| 6/25/90 | MEB | Telephone call with Suzanne Caplan re agreement with _____ | .25 | 1 |
| 7/19/90 | MEB | Attend disclosure statement hearing; discussion with _____ re agreement of 7/5 | 1.0 | 1 |

**Exhibit 2–1**    *(continued)*

| DATE | ATTORNEY | DESCRIPTION OF SERVICES | HOURS | CODE PER EXHIBIT "D" |
|------|----------|-------------------------|-------|----------------------|
| 7/30/90 | MEB | Letter to _____, telephone call with _____ re _____ adversary proceeding | .50 | 1 |
| 8/7/90 | MEB | Letter and answer to adversary no. _____ (_____ priority) | .75 | 1 |
| 9/4/90 | MEB | Telephone call with _____ re hearing date on disclosure statement | .25 | 1 |
| 9/6/90 | MEB | Telephone calls with _____ and client re: disclosure statement | .25 | 1 |
| 9/6/90 | MEB | Telephone call with _____ of _____ regarding plan | .25 | 1 |
| 9/6/90 | MEB | Telephone call with Suzanne Caplan re changes in plan | .25 | 1 |
| 9/10/90 | MEB | Telephone call with _____ re plan and abandonment | .25 | 1 |
| 10/1/90 | MEB | Meeting with Suzanne Caplan re revisions to plan | .75 | 1 |
| 10/1/90 | MEB | Telephone call with _____ re revisions to plan | .25 | 1 |

Exhibit 2–1    Sample Application for Attorney's Fees    31

**Exhibit 2–1**    *(continued)*

---

### Exhibit "D"

Category listing of time and services on behalf of Pittsburgh Glove Manufacturing Company, Debtor, during the time period from January 10, 1989 to October 4, 1990.

I. Category 1—Preparation of plan and disclosure statement and negotiations related to plan and disclosure

HOURS:   34.5

II. Category 2—Negotiations with creditors involved with executory contracts

HOURS:    1.75

III. Category 3—Negotiation and hearing regarding confidentiality order

HOURS:   11.00

IV. Category 4—Miscellaneous activities such as preparing monthly statements of operations and miscellaneous motions discussions with creditors

HOURS:   10.75

TOTAL HOURS:   58.00

Billing Summary:

58 hours @ $      /hr. 5   $

Total amount due:          $

---

**Exhibit 2–2   Sample Motion for Leave to Employ Counsel to the Debtor**

---

IN THE UNITED STATES BANKRUPTCY COURT
FOR THE WESTERN DISTRICT OF PENNSYLVANIA

---

IN RE:

                                 Bankruptcy No. 91
                                 Chapter
     Debtor.                Motion No. 91–

---

    Movant.

### Application for Leave to Employ
### Counsel to the Debtor

AND NOW COMES the Debtor, _____, by and through his counsel, _____, Esquire and the law firm of _____ and files the following Application for Leave to Employ Counsel:

1. These proceedings were commenced by the filing of a Voluntary Petition under Chapter \_\_\_\_\_ of the United States Bankruptcy Code on _____ \_\_\_\_\_, 19\_\_\_\_.

2. On _____ \_\_\_\_\_, 19\_\_\_\_, upon consideration of the debtor's Motion, the Court entered an Order converting this case to a proceeding under Chapter \_\_\_\_\_.

3. The debtor continues to be in need of services of legal counsel to assist in the administration of these proceedings, to represent him on matters involving legal issues that are present or are likely to arise in the case and to prepare any and all legal documentation on behalf of the debtor. In addition, counsel may be necessary to perform the following functions: (a) examine proofs of claim for legal sufficiency and validity, (b) furnish information on legal matters in view of possible legal action or consequences, (c) recover assets of the estate through legal proceedings whereby negotiation in the context of possible legal action, (d) prepare a Disclosure Statement and Plan of Reorganization and negotiate treatment of claims with creditors, and (e) review reports for legal sufficiency.

4. The debtor, subject to the approval of this Honorable Court, wishes to retain _____, Esquire and the law firm of _____ as legal counsel in these proceedings on an hourly basis, as may be adjusted from time to time, plus expenses. The compensation and reimbursement will be requested at the appropriate time by proper application in accordance with the Bankruptcy Code and Rules.

Exhibit 2–2   Sample Motion for Leave to Employ Counsel to the Debtor      33

**Exhibit 2–2**   *(continued)*

5. The debtor believes that _____, Esquire and the law firm of _____ are well qualified to perform all of the legal services required.

6. Neither _____, Esquire nor the law firm of _____ represent any interest adverse to the debtor's estate, the debtor or creditors of the debtor's estate and are disinterested persons within the meaning of 11 U.S.C. Section 101. (See attached Verified Statements Pursuant to Bankruptcy Rule 2014.)

WHEREFORE, the debtor respectfully requests this Honorable Court to enter an Order authorizing the retention of counsel.

**Exhibit 2–2**   *(continued)*

---

## Verified Statement Pursuant to
## Bankruptcy Rule 2014

I, _____, individually and on behalf the firm of _____ declare under penalty of perjury that I have read the foregoing Application for Leave to Employ Counsel to the Debtor and that the averments set forth therein are true and correct to the best of my knowledge, information, and belief. Neither _____, Esquire, nor the firm of _____ have any connection with the debtor, creditors, or other parties-in-interest, or their respective attorneys or accountants except the following:

None.

_____

---

Exhibit 2–2   Sample Motion for Leave to Employ Counsel to the Debtor     35

**Exhibit 2–2**   *(continued)*

## Certificate of Service

I hereby certify that a true and correct copy of the fore-going Application for Leave to Employ Counsel to the Debtor was served upon the following individuals this _____ day of _____, 1991, United States mail, first-class, postage prepaid, addressed as follows:

_____

**Exhibit 2–2**    *(continued)*

## IN THE UNITED STATES BANKRUPTCY COURT
## FOR THE WESTERN DISTRICT OF PENNSYLVANIA

IN RE:

                                        Bankruptcy No. 91
                                        Chapter
    Debtor.                     Motion No. 91–

    Movant.

### Order of Court

AND NOW, this _____ day of _____, 1991, upon consideration of the within Application, the debtor's retention of counsel is hereby confirmed and the debtor is hereby granted leave to employ the services of _____ and the law firm of _____ as counsel in these proceedings as of the date of the filing of this application.

                                        _____

Virtually all businesses face cash-flow problems from time to time. For the most part, these are temporary situations, albeit uncomfortable ones. Many entrepreneurs have experienced the stress of making a payroll when cash is very short. One story, which has reached folklore proportions, involves Fred Smith, CEO of Federal Express, who flew to Las Vegas to try to win a big enough jackpot to enable him to make payroll and continue his early venture. Fortunately for him, he did, and the rest is history.

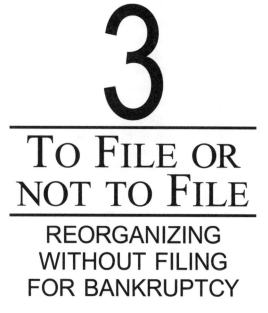

# TO FILE OR NOT TO FILE

## REORGANIZING WITHOUT FILING FOR BANKRUPTCY

Most companies cannot recover financially by betting on the toss of the dice, however. We are forced to face our difficulties and find solutions. And it isn't always easy to find effective guidance. The best scenario would have a management team in place, aided by the company accountant, who has previously worked closely with management. The decisions to be made will be based on solid business acumen, combined with good instincts.

For many smaller companies, including my own, this in-house group of advisers does not exist. Forming one to discuss the financial survival of the company would itself be a virtually impossible task. Because the most obvious solution to a cash shortage is cutting expenses—including wages and benefits, this could turn into a group where everyone is jockeying for position rather than finding creative solutions.

## Don't Let Your Attorney Make the Decision to File for Bankruptcy

A key reason why many people develop an animosity toward lawyers is based on a misunderstanding of the profession itself. Lawyers are not members of clergy, nor are they social workers. They are well-schooled professionals who are paid to do legal work—not to listen and sympathize.

Most of us would not go to a car dealer to seek advice as to whether or not we needed a new car. Any salesperson worth his or her salt should be able to convince us that we do, even if the only reason is a different color. I would be stunned to leave a dealer's showroom convinced that the old car I am driving meets my current needs best.

A similar analogy is an appointment with a surgeon to determine whether surgery is indicated or a more conservative approach is advisable. Much unnecessary surgery has been documented over the years, but when consulting with someone whose training, orientation, and income is based on a surgical approach, it is to be expected that a surgical solution will be offered.

Using this logic, it is only fair and reasonable to expect an attorney to recommend legal answers and a bankruptcy specialist to recommend filing a bankruptcy petition. Even one who proposes extensive preplanning will still focus your time and energy in this direction. While filing may not only be premature, it also may be completely unnecessary.

## Get the Information that Will Give You the Edge in Negotiating with Your Creditors

There is a very good reason to spend the time and money on an attorney at these early stages. First, locating the best bankruptcy specialist is time-consuming and a tough accomplishment in the intense stress after a crisis is well under way.

Information empowers you as you develop the strategy for solving financial problems without going as far as filing for bankruptcy. For example, it is important to learn what would most likely happen to creditors if a case were filed: How they would be repaid and what they would be repaid under a plan forms good parameters for negotiated settlements.

Although you do not want to burden discussions by the constant threat of a bankruptcy filing, it is reasonable to let creditors know that if amicable discussion fails, a filing is possible, and that you understand what their rights would and would not be under that circumstance. Bankruptcy should not be used as a threat but as a reality that will have to be faced. In today's business world, most creditors have some awareness of what might happen to their claims.

There are three main objectives normally sought when filing for a Chapter 11 reorganization:

- Cutting costs
- Extending payback time
- Reducing debt

It is important to realize, however, all of these objectives are also achievable through negotiation. The next section of this chapter describes in detail how to meet these objectives by negotiating.

## LEARN HOW TO CUT COSTS BY NEGOTIATING WITH YOUR CREDITORS

Virtually all contracts—including those with landlords, suppliers, and labor unions—can be voided by action of the bankruptcy court. This fact is now widely known, so reopening these written agreements is now far easier. If these overhead costs are the cause of financial distress, try reducing them through negotiation.

## Reduce Your Real Estate Expenses

With commercial real estate vacancies at an all-time high in most of the nation, most landlords will be realistic enough to talk to a tenant in distress. It may include permitting a company to move before the end of its lease or allowing the business to stay at a reduced rent.

Any landlord that has had experience evicting a tenant knows it can take several months to secure a judgment and even more time to execute it. A bankruptcy can add even more time if the tenant decides to fight eviction. All this time passes with no money coming in from the rental property.

Of course, it is better to find an amicable solution. One solution is an out-and-out release. Many of the major retail companies, such as Bloomingdales and Neiman-Marcus, gave up some store space that proved unprofitable business operations. No landlord is happy to have space vacant, but given that the end result of an expensive and time-consuming fight will result in just that, the sooner the space is available to rent, the better. Offering to help restore the space and, perhaps, to find a replacement tenant may ease the way, too. It is always good to leave any business encounter on amicable terms.

The need for temporary or even permanently reduced rent can also be addressed. If the space is in demand, you are less likely to negotiate successfully, but even then it is still possible. It may be accomplished by re-adding the rent reduction during the current period to the end of the lease. This will make the total value the same, yet give you the help you need during some tough times.

In less desirable space, a permanent reduction is easier. I know at least one highly priced mall in Pittsburgh that has negotiated lower rents with some tenants with the proviso that if a full-price tenant comes along, the space would be vacated.

The building that my own manufacturing company was housed in during our difficult years was an old structure in a deteriorating neighborhood. I always felt that my landlord had the choice of me or no one, at least not without making substantial improvements. I did not verbalize my beliefs. Rather, I tried to secure some understanding and tolerance based on my current situation. I tried to make up for the shortage by paying for some repairs that probably were not my responsibility. Why create animosity? If you do file bankruptcy, that creates adversaries, and adversaries can create trouble and cost money. This is a recurring theme.

## Cut the Cost of High-Priced Supply Contracts

During the years of high inflation, it seemed desirable to lock in current prices with long-term contracts. But this practice began to change in the late 1980s. With a more global economy and growing worldwide recession, some prices stabilized, and some actually fell. If your company were contractually locked into the higher prices, this could be a real problem.

Suppliers may not realize that these contracts can be revoked in a bankruptcy proceeding, and they may be reluctant to reopen negotiations. But renegotiation is still possible.

Big customers, such as the auto companies, have, for many years, demanded and received concessions from virtually all suppliers when the industry enters a downturn. It would be foolhardy for a supplier's future business with these giants not to accommodate these requests.

For other companies, however, this can prove to be more difficult. For example, Columbia Gas, one of the Northeast's largest natural gas suppliers, attempted to renegotiate high-priced natural gas contracts that forced it into a serious loss position. They even publicly suggested that a bankruptcy filing might be necessary, all to no avail. Finally, Columbia went into bankruptcy court to seek protection, and one of their first acts was to invalidate these contracts. The court obliged them in one hearing, making it difficult to explain how the suppliers would not have benefited by the earlier negotiations.

*It is crucial to determine the benefit that might be achieved by forcing lower prices compared with the cost of this action on supplier goodwill.* Are you a big customer? Does your supplier have a profit margin large enough that it can absorb a price cut? Do you have other alternative suppliers if negotiations fail?

If high-cost material or product threatens the survival of your company, then it is really in the best interest of your suppliers to accommodate your company in some way. If you file bankruptcy, your suppliers become unsecured creditors, and, most likely, they will end up with pennies on the dollars they are owed.

## Cut the Cost of High Wages

Wages for non-union workers can be renegotiated at any time, and a company can open this issue at times of a cash crunch. What can be at issue here is the morale of your employees during tough times. If renegotiations are done arbitrarily, the resulting internal animosity can cost more than the money saved.

My small manufacturing company was in the hands of my production manager for several years while I handled the bankruptcy and the civil litigation. It is only in retrospect that I realize how much pressure he absorbed and how much we owe to him. My recommendation: *if your managers are sufficiently skilled to be kept on during tough times, they should be rewarded, not penalized.*

The issue of union contracts is far more emotionally charged. They can be reopened voluntarily if both sides agree, but there are risks in forcing the issue, particularly when there has been acrimonious relationships in the past. You may risk a strike and any accompanying bad publicity. If yours is a consumer business, that can be very costly. If animosity grows, products or customer service could suffer, and that could result in a severe customer loss.

The airline industry has experienced difficult concession negotiations, several of which have ended in strikes and, ultimately, formal bankruptcy proceedings. Eastern Airlines was the most notorious example. After several give-backs were accepted over the years, lines were drawn in 1989. The company held fast to its demands, and a strike ensued that forced a bankruptcy filing. Several airlines, including TWA and Pan Am, achieved cost savings without being driven into bankruptcy court, although Pan Am eventually filed for bankruptcy for a series of other reasons.

When management and union have had a long history of adversarial negotiations, it can be almost impossible to conduct voluntary negotiations, although most union leaders realize that labor contracts can be voided by action of the bankruptcy court. Even after the action of a court order, strikes can ensue, so it is a worthwhile effort to forge a new pact with the mutual interest of the company's survival as the tie that binds.

## FIND ADDITIONAL TIME TO PAY EXISTING DEBTS

If the financial crisis facing your company is of a temporary nature, it may be possible to negotiate reductions and extensions without getting anywhere near a bankruptcy court. Fixed debt is normally the major burden for a small company and is usually owed to its major bank. The current business climate is very conducive to renegotiation with most banks.

Many banks are experiencing some degree of problems with their loan portfolios. An active loan can be carried as a full asset to the bank. But a loan that is "nonperforming" (i.e., not paying interest) will eventually be written off either in whole or in part. Therefore, it is in the bank's enlightened self-interest to make payment adjustments that assure the solvency of and eventual payback from the customer. In addition, no bank ever really likes to repossess assets that have secured a loan.

Bankers do not like to serve as real estate brokers or used machinery dealers. It is a time-consuming and costly venture for them. In addition, the liquidation value of most assets is usually far less than the value carried, so any sell-off will result in a write down. All of these factors serve as incentives for a bank to renegotiate terms when a customer gets into difficulty.

The important point to remember is to contact your banker *before* you have missed payments and not on the day before a payment is due. As soon as you realize that the funds won't be available, share that information. Bankers hate surprises.

In addition, put together as complete a package for your meeting as you might have done when applying for the original loan. Substantiate the current reason for your difficulties, what is being done to correct them, and when you project a turnaround. Documentation can include copies of open orders, contracts, or your own cash-flow projections. If you have not already discovered it, the insight here is that bankers like paper. A complete file looks good and makes them more secure.

## Learn What to Do about Vendor Credit that Can't Be Repaid

Vendor credit is the riskiest kind of credit to extend, although many companies do not realize how vulnerable they are. The debts incurred are unsecured, and collection efforts are more threat than substance. Even if an unpaid vendor decides to go to court to sue for payment and wins a judgment, that judgment does not force a debtor to pay. Once the judgment is filed, the creditor then has to execute, which is a costly procedure. They must seize some property and sell it to raise cash to satisfy the debt.

Even after a seizure, the actions can be reversed by a bankruptcy filing, which could force the creditor to return the money. Plus, the costs will be the burden of the creditor, meaning that the debt might grow big—up to 50%—and still be unpaid.

There is no harm in attempting to educate your vendors to the cruel world of credit, but it is not a wise idea to use this knowledge as a threat. The best policy is to be candid about your financial difficulties and attempt to work out a solution.

If you are overstocked with their product, perhaps you can return items for a credit to offset your balance. Most vendors, even those with rigid return policies, would rather have goods back than not get paid for them.

There are more creative ways to make peace with your vendors. What if you turn past-due balances into a loan of sorts, which you will pay over the next 6 months or a year with a small amount of interest? You can then agree to pay all future supply bills in a timely matter. This means that your vendor will get every dollar due and save a customer in the process.

**Understand why you shouldn't play hardball with vendors.** Ignoring unpaid bills and leaving phone calls unanswered is not prudent business practice. Although irate creditors may find it difficult to collect from you, they can make your life miserable.

Individual vendors may know that they can join forces with each other and force you into involuntary bankruptcy. All it takes are three creditors that are owed a total of $5,000. In some instances, attorneys who frequent these courts may see the same name on several judgments and contact the creditors to "inform them of their rights." This is a form of ambulance chasing, but if you are the debtor, you're the one who is likely to be hit by this wagon.

Having angry creditors in the wings can also make a bankruptcy a miserable, expensive, and losing proposition. These are the creditors who will jump at the chance to serve on the creditors' committee, and they will object to most of what you may attempt as a part of a reorganization plan.

The advice here: *If you owe someone money, don't hide; apologize.* And then attempt to make good on your obligations.

## REDUCE YOUR EXISTING DEBT LOAD

Technically, any company having greater debts than assets is insolvent. Because there are many ways to value assets, it is all in the interpretation.

There are many reasons why what had once been a perfectly reasonable debt load becomes a burden that a company must get out from under to survive. One that I am familiar with involves a manufacturer who took on a large government contract. It appeared that his business would increase by 40% and he needed space and machinery to support this increased volume.

With government contract in hand, his bank was happy to lend money, and even suggested a more ambitious expansion. When the contract ended prematurely, and no new ones followed, the company was swamped with debt and debt service. A year earlier, most business advisers would have recommended the move forward even considering that everything was at risk. Before the situation deteriorated too far, the entire new venture was disbanded: Machines were sold, inventory liquidated, and space vacated. All proceeds were used to pay down debts, and the balance was rescheduled with generous terms.

But what if the debt has been growing for years, and there are no longer assets to sell? These negotiations can be some of the toughest a business owner can face, and to achieve success, you had better go into them armed and prepared to the teeth. First, you should analyze how a bankruptcy could impact any of your company's secured debt. If a loan were made years ago and the value of the security has eroded over that time, it is possible that only a portion of the debt is currently secured. The balance would be treated under the bankruptcy code as an unsecured debt and may end up being paid off at pennies on the dollar.

For example, a $100,000 loan made in 1986 and secured by assets now worth $60,000 would now have a $40,000 unsecured component. A reasonable plan of reorganization that paid 30% to unsecured debt would make that loan worth $72,000. It may be possible to negotiate this sort of reduction without filing for bankruptcy.

Develop the documentation of current asset values and a model of how a court-imposed settlement might restructure the loan. Sweeten the pot with a higher offer as an incentive to a private deal without the court. Most bankers know that any bankruptcy is risky, with additional assets being used up to pay legal fees. A very astute bank officer would be willing to talk but this will not be easy. Even if it isn't successful, you will have learned skills and opened lines of communication that could be used to encourage cooperation at a later date.

## How You Can Benefit from a Chapter 11 Filing

There are many factors to consider in determining whether or not to file a bankruptcy petition. If your problems are caught early enough or if they are temporary in nature, it may be possible to get the benefits without going through the bankruptcy process.

There are drawbacks and benefits to a formal filing and when making that decision, you should consider each carefully. First, consider the benefits:

- You can stop, and in some cases, reverse collection actions.
- You can legally establish debt load, interest rate, and payback terms.
- You can force any uncooperative creditor to accept the deal.

## Advantage #1:
## A Filing Stops All Credit Actions

A bankruptcy filing can stop a sheriff's sale even if it is in progress. No company wants it to get that far, because much damage has occurred, but, occasionally there is an aggressive creditor who rushes through the whole process without listening to reason. It can feel like the legal equivalent of breaking both legs. A Chapter 11 bankruptcy filing is your way to fight back, because it can stop the actions at any stage.

One such creditor is the IRS, whose collection action exceeds all others. They have the right to levy your bank account and seize other assets, and once their wheels are in motion, the train is tough to stop. A Chapter 11 filing may be the only method.

Banks also may go forward on foreclosure actions particularly on real estate they think can be easily liquidated. A major unsecured creditor may also take collection actions to the seizure level, and leasing companies may proceed with repossession.

In virtually all cases, a bankruptcy filing prevents these seizures, and in many cases it can reverse actions that have recently occurred. The time frame of 90 days before a bankruptcy is the "preferential" period, and actions taken during this time are put under scrutiny and can be nullified.

This means that if your company has recently lost real estate or equipment, you can force its return by filing Chapter 11. In addition, if your company was forced by legal action, or even the threat of legal action, to make a larger payment on a loan or vendor debt, it is possible to have this reversed by the courts. You may get the money back.

# Advantage #2:
# The Reorganization Plan Establishes Your Debt and Payback Agreements

If you were to cease paying debts for a period, interest will continue to accrue, and the amount owed will become impossible to pay. For many debts, the additional interest ceases on filing, and even when that is not the case by statute, many creditors are willing, at the time of the plan, to receive the principal amount alone. After the case has gone on for some time, creditors begin to believe that they will not be paid at all. A fair plan that pays most of the debt will usually be well received.

In addition, disputes over debts can be settled by the bankruptcy court, even those involving taxes. Most companies that file have at least some unpaid taxes, and it is frequently the case that the amount is in dispute. Most bankruptcy court judges will be willing to decide all but the most complicated issues. By the time the case has come to its conclusion, the total company debt will be absolutely fixed.

The reorganization plan sets forth any payback amounts agreed on by consent as well as those that have been offered by the debtor. Once a plan has been voted on and confirmed by the court, your company can go forward knowing exactly how much it will cost to retire all of the remaining outstanding debts. Any claims not made to the court in the proper manner by the final date set by the court will no longer be in effect and will not be collectible. If you agree to a reasonable payback, you can emerge intact.

## Advantage #3:
## All Creditors, Even Dissenters, Will Accept Amount in Approved Plan

Once a bankruptcy is filed, each debt becomes classified in a class or type. Generally, these are:

- Priority, which are primarily taxes
- Secured, normally bank and other loans
- Unsecured, which is vendor credit

In a plan, all members of a class must be treated equally, and the majority must vote in favor. A plan can be approved over the objections of some creditors, and they are bound by the terms of the plan whether they like it or not.

This can be important if you have one or two creditors who have developed some animosity and seem to enjoy appearing in your worst nightmares. If enough of the other creditors vote in your favor, they can be neutralized.

## RECOGNIZE THE PROBLEMS INVOLVED IN A CHAPTER 11 FILING

The decision to file is a tough one because there are many drawbacks that have to be considered. The one that immediately comes to mind is the cost. The last thing most companies in financial distress need is another expense. In addition, the entire process can be very time-consuming—from preparing the original petition to court appearances and the various reports that are required. Also, consider the change in attitude that you might have to endure from customers, vendors, and competitors. The equal treatment of each class means any sweetener you offer as incentive to one will have to be given to all. If you're a tough negotiator, you may be able to get a better deal one on one.

## Problem #1: The Cost Does Not Have to Be Exorbitant, but You Will Incur Costs

The overriding theme of this entire book is to encourage you to participate and even to control bankruptcy proceedings to your own benefit. By that effort, you can cut your legal costs in half. Paying an attorney $150 or more an hour to make calls or prepare documents is both costly and can be damaging if they are not completely reflective of your position. Some of this work is best done by you.

But there will be costs. For example, the filing fee is $500, plus the hourly fee for your attorney. There is also a quarterly fee paid to the U.S. Trustee (the minimum is $150). And should your creditors get active and form a committee and hire an attorney, *you* will be paying these expenses. An acrimonious Chapter 11 filing can quickly drain most of your cash resources and make operating your business virtually impossible. Convincing everyone that this is not in anyone's best interest is your greatest challenge.

# Problem #2: Time in Court Is Time Away from Business

My own attorney required that I attend every hearing even when there were no issues of disagreement. While waiting for my own case to be called, I observed that many owners did not appear. In one respect, this is how I received my education and how I eventually became almost comfortable with the process. Conversely, there were times when it was incredibly inconvenient to take hours out of my schedule to sit in a courtroom.

There were monthly reports to file and other documents to produce in support of some motions. At one point, when asking for release of funds for working capital, I prepared an entire pro-forma package as if I were applying for a loan. And then the judge gave his approval without asking for any additional testimony!

The advice here would be to determine how this kind of intrusion might affect you and use this as one criterion for your decision as to whether to file for bankruptcy.

# Problem #3: How Others View a Bankrupt Company

By the time I filed for bankruptcy in 1986, attitudes were already beginning to change. At one time, vendors and customers would run as far away as possible from a company filing for bankruptcy. That is generally not the case now. In certain industries, such as retailing and the airlines, it is easier to name who is not in bankruptcy than who has filed.

Each business sector has its own experiences, and you are the best judge of how important this is in your industry. Will it affect your ability to secure the merchandise you need? Will it concern your customers to the point that you will substantially lose business? These are some of the questions you should be asking yourself. But also consider that at this point, many people accept this tough fact of business with little extra attention.

Once your schedule of debts has been recorded, each class of creditor is established, and members of each class must be treated uniformly. Room for individual negotiation becomes limited. This is usually not a problem because most offers to unsecured vendors are less than 50 cents on the dollar. But there could be some extraordinary debt that may be reduced or even canceled, or perhaps exchanged for an interest in the company. If this is the case, the scrutiny of the court may put a damper on this sort of free-form dealing.

## How to Decide If You Should File for Bankruptcy

The decision to file is a difficult one to make, and either choice—to file or not to file—will bring on its own set of difficulties. The decision is part analysis and part instinct, and in the end can only be made by the business owner.

Early on in this chapter, I suggested that the decision should not be made by an attorney. There are several reasons why:

1.  You, as the business owner, are in a better position (if given enough information) to know what effects this decision will have on your company and your life.
2.  Few attorneys have the time or business background to see both the pros and the cons of this decision.
3.  It is understandable that an attorney's views are skewed toward filing for bankruptcy.

Good accountants or controllers may be one of your most valuable assets. If they have followed your company through its ups and downs, they may be able to draw projections that will give you ideas regarding how to restructure current debt. They may also be able to help you to identify areas ripe for cost cutting or price adjustments that could change the financial health of your company.

Other business associates are a good source of advice as well as support. They can help to find new customers, vendors, and possibly even investors who might bring in needed capital and energy for a turnaround.

Finally, if it is possible, find someone who has been through the experience. This individual can give you keen insight and encouragement.

## SUMMING UP

The first decision that must be made in times of financial distress is how serious the situation is and how long it is likely to go on. Then you can determine how strong a medicine is going to be required to effect a cure. Perhaps it may be a small dose administered carefully—that is, not filing for bankruptcy—just honest and tough negotiation.

If you are reading this book out of idle curiosity, now is the time to consider some of the implications of bankruptcy. It may be the furthest thought in your mind, but it is not out of the question for any company. You don't plan on a fire, but you do carry insurance to protect your assets. Few of us dwell on our own death, but it is prudent to do at least some estate planning.

Most businesses have some tough times, and some circumstances are out of our control, such as physical disasters (fires and flood, etc.); the demise of a large customer; unpaid debts; and even criminal activity. Many of the management techniques for a successful reorganization are also good business practice.

It is always better to make friends than adversaries. We all strive to have cordial relationships with our customers, but how many of us treat our vendors as if our success depended on their cooperation? *Keep in mind that your suppliers can exert enough extra effort to have a direct impact on your bottom line.* On-time delivery, special deals, and back-

# 4

# BE PREPARED

## WHAT TO DO BEFORE YOU FILE FOR BANKRUPTCY

up support are a few ways vendors can make a difference. In return, suppliers need reasonable requests, appreciation for their work, and fair payment terms. And above all, they need loyalty and honesty. When times are good, treat your suppliers well; when times get tough, they will try to cooperate with you. Most companies will work with you on payment if you communicate with them. But silence is scary. Unanswered and unreturned phone calls increase the tension and the possibility of collection actions.

Having a trail of unpaid bills, uncollected judgments, and angry suppliers can be one of the most dangerous obstacles to a successful restructuring. An active and acrimonious creditor's committee can create substantial legal bills; take enormous amounts of time in court proceedings; and in the end, vote against any plan.

Conversely, if your vendors (the unsecured creditors) are supportive of your attempts to begin again, you are halfway home. Remember that when you deal with them.

Bankruptcy used to have such stigma attached that polite people didn't discuss it. No one would talk about the possibility with associates let alone creditors. This circumstance has changed, and it is now possible (in some cases desirable) to begin negotiations before any filing occurs.

First of all, you may be able to strike an agreement that will make bankruptcy unnecessary. Even if that isn't possible you have a chance to convince them of your serious intent to meet your obligations, however long and difficult it becomes. And you also have the opportunity to measure what you might be up against after your filing. How reasonable will your creditors be? Are they interested only in recovering their money, or are they also interested in a continuing business relationship and future profits?

*A word of caution and advice: Do not make any promises before or after a filing.* They could have contractual implications that could complicate your situation.

## Protect Your Funds by Maintaining a Bank Account and Bank Relationship with More than One Institution

Many companies can trace their success to a banking relationship that supplied capital when needed. This is developed over years and requires a personal knowledge by the banker of you and your business. Why then would you want to deal with a second bank?

If you file Chapter 11 and have an unpaid bank loan, there's a good chance that your account will be confiscated as an offset. Most security agreements list cash as one form of collateral so this is an easy and legal way to get repaid.

Therefore, *before* any filing, you will want to remove your funds and put them in another bank into what will eventually become your "debtor in possession" (DIP) account. Claims may be made on these funds, but for the time being they will be available. Although you can open a new account anytime, developing a new relationship with a banker will be far more difficult if you try to begin after you have filed for bankruptcy.

Most attorneys will recommend that you open new accounts and transfer all of your funds. But I was surprised to read the docket of a fair-sized chain of carpet stores in Pittsburgh and find out that they had left all their funds in the bank that was their primary lender. Immediately after their filing, all the funds were confiscated to offset loans. Imagine trying to run your company with all the cash gone! They tried, but it didn't work.

## GET FINANCING AFTER FILING FOR BANKRUPTCY

One of the main reasons to keep a bank in reserve is to use them for DIP financing. As strange as it may seem, it is very possible to get a loan after you file. In fact, several money center banks now have separate divisions handling just this type of financing. You'll often read about a major case being filed, and it will carry a notice about which bank or group of banks will provide financing.

Several large companies arrange these new lines of credit in advance of a filing, and there is no reason why you can't sit down with your "second" banker, explain your circumstance, and determine the bank's willingness to offer post-bankruptcy financing. Even if the bank is willing, you will need the approval of the court.

This court action may be the first of your case. Your attorney will file a motion to release security to the "new bank" to back up your loan. That means that your current secured lender will be required to release a portion of their claim against what may be limited assets.

For example, if you have a $100,000 bank loan that is secured by inventory and receivables valued at $150,000, your original loan may be oversecured. If you get approval for a DIP loan of $25,000, the new bank gets a "super priority" claim on $25,000 of your assets. If the company were eventually converted to a liquidation and the assets were converted to $110,000 of cash, the second bank gets the first $25,000 and the original lender only the balance of $85,000.

The easiest and most expeditious way to get this second financing is to file the motion with the approval of creditors. If you have a cooperative first lender and group of unsecured creditors, this is possible. Early in a case, it is important to convince all classes of creditors that this is still a viable business and their best chance for return will be from the reorganized company.

Every case has its own nuances so it is impossible to predict how any specific creditors or group of creditors will react. But be aware of the players and their motivations.

The creditors themselves want to get the highest return in the quickest possible time with the least wear and tear. The representing attorneys are looking to perform legal tasks for which they get paid. So it isn't unusual for them to create more work and delay than is required. They are working at giving their clients the greatest legal protection possible even if, at times, their obstreperous action thwarts any possible reorganization and eventually lessens the payback to all.

Even if creditors form opposition to this new secured lending, it is still possible to convince the judge to grant your motion over the objection of any or all creditors. The key factor here will be a well-drafted and well-supported motion as well as a convincing oral argument. Don't leave this task to your counsel—help create a good case for approval.

If you have a second banking relationship in place before you file, you can devote your time to establishing the loan proposal. It would be far more difficult to conduct the search for financing as well as document the case for its approval at the same time.

## ASSESS HOW MUCH TIME YOU HAVE BEFORE YOUR FINANCIAL DIFFICULTIES LEAD TO A BANKRUPTCY FILING

In most cases, there is some time between the onset of threatening problems and the moment the bankruptcy petition needs to be filed. It is possible to file very late and to stop or even reverse a sheriff's sale of assets. That is not recommended, however, because the battle lines that are drawn by that time will be difficult to reform into the cooperation needed to succeed.

There is, however, a wide margin between any premature action and the crisis scenario. It could be months or even years. Sol Stein, in his book, *A Feast for Lawyers,* reports seeing an attorney 2 years before he finally filed because a friend of his "smelled trouble." Stein doesn't make clear what kind of trouble he meant, but many entrepreneurs walk around with an underlying sense of impending disaster. The situation that forced my company to seek court protection began almost 2 years before we filed. During the days I busied myself with trying to create some solutions to our problems, which ultimately ended in litigation. At nights, I lost sleep worrying about the future. Bankruptcy was a word said in whispers, and there was a great stigma attached to it. Much has changed in the past few years.

The period between when trouble is felt and a disaster may happen is the time to learn all you can about the process. It is prudent self-defense. You wouldn't launch a product without a great deal of thought and planning. So why would you take on a critical phase such as a reorganization without the same effort?

You can estimate the time of crisis by the amount of cash reserve you currently hold, the point at which you will not be able to make necessary payments, or the likelihood that legal action will be undertaken against you. If these financial crises roam in front of you, now is the time to face the difficulty.

Of longer-term concern is the end of a large order or contract that is not likely to be renewed. A loss of as little as 10% of your cash flow may be enough to make it impossible to retire your obligations. Although the worst may not happen, having contingency plans won't hurt.

## Don't Wait Too Long to File

Although it is desirable to use as much time as possible to negotiate and to educate yourself about how to create a plan, waiting too long has serious ramifications. Creditors of all types will have run out of patience, and some may commence legal action. Not only does this begin a case with an adversarial tone, but it almost assures that you will be burdened by a gaggle of lawyers, all looking to do work for a fee. And you'll end up paying most of them!

Worst of all, at some point you may anger a creditor enough that his mission in life becomes putting you on the street. He no longer cares about collecting his debt, only about revenge. These are very dangerous adversaries; their willingness to spend time, money, and energy is monumental, and they may encourage others to follow. If your financial situation becomes precarious, don't play hardball. You may end up with an enemy more costly than a debt.

## UNDERSTAND THE PREFERENTIAL TRANSACTIONS THAT CAN BE REVERSED

The two main periods you have to consider are 90 days for all transactions and up to 1 year for those involving insiders. An insider is a member of the family, a partner, or an employee who exercises control on a director of the debtor.

## Transactions Made 80 Days before Filing Are Reversible

From the perspective of the legal system, a company that files for bankruptcy would be considered insolvent for the 90-day period before the filing. Any payments made to a lender or vendor that were not made equally to others in the same class could be reversed by the action of the court. This type of action most likely would be initiated by another member of the same class of creditor.

For example, if you had large outstanding debts to several creditors just before filing Chapter 11, you pay one and not the others. You may feel compelled to make payment to a supplier whose goodwill is central to any hope you have of reorganizing. And that may be true. However, if after filing, a creditor's committee forms that includes the unpaid vendors, they may demand and would probably be granted the right to reverse this transaction. The funds would be returned to the debtor ostensibly for equal distribution to other creditors.

Conversely, you also have the right to request a reversal—if, for example, a large creditor of yours files suit for an unpaid bill and wins a judgment. Perhaps you pay the amount and then discover that this depletes your cash reserve enough that it jeopardizes your ability to continue to do business. If you file bankruptcy within 90 days of that payment, you may initiate action to secure the return of that money.

The other entity most likely to seek reversal would be a trustee. In a normally progressing Chapter 11 case, a trustee would not be appointed. If any case drags on, and the court becomes convinced that management is not doing enough to bring the case to conclusion, the judge may appoint a trustee. Such was the case at Eastern Airlines when the company was taken away from the management of Continental Airlines and put under the control of Martin Shugrue, a court-appointed trustee. Some of the funds Eastern had paid to its parent Continental were returned after having been deemed preferential.

It is possible to avoid action of this type if no one raises the issues. In advance of your own filing, you should consider this possibility and how it could impact your plans.

**Use the 90-day period to your advantage.** Many troubled businesses get delinquent with the IRS on withholding tax. A portion of these taxes are the personal liability of the company owner. If it is at all possible, these taxes should be remitted before the filing so that this contingent liability to you is removed. It will substantially reduce the stress of the whole process.

The same goes for any loans in which you have a guarantee. It will probably be impossible to clear all of these, but a reduction would help.

And finally, paying off the critical vendors is also desirable. That may be accomplished by returning goods as well as cash payments. They may not extend credit after the filing, but they should appreciate not being a part of what can be a drawn-out legal process waiting for their money. Be as candid as you can to win their cooperation.

Always keep track of the dates all of the preceding transactions were completed so that the 90-day rule doesn't overturn them.

## Insider Transactions Made One Year before Filing Are Also Reversible

Those who have control of the company and its funds may find themselves under serious scrutiny by the creditors. There are many transactions that could be questioned but the main ones would be:

- Transferring assets such as a car
- Repaying loans
- Selling assets, perhaps property for less than its fair market value

This could present a serious problem for some business owners. It is not unusual for the principal of a company experiencing financial problems to forgo some of their own income as well as to add personal funds to the company to satisfy financial demands. If a bankruptcy occurs within the same year of these investments, it is possible that the principal will lose most of his lost wages as well as the additional money he invested. This is something you should think over carefully if this is your current situation.

It is also not advisable to attempt to extract as much as possible from any company contemplating filing a bankruptcy petition. If you have driven a company car, it is doubtful that you could transfer title to yourself for minimal value and have this fact not at least questioned by creditors. In some cases, it can get personally involved, and legal action may be initiated against you.

**Case example.**    A chain of discount jewelry and general merchandise stores in Pittsburgh has gone through just such a series of charges and countercharges. David Weis Wholesale Jewelers, Inc., attempted to liquidate on its own and was eventually forced into bankruptcy by its creditors. They also convinced the judge to appoint a trustee to oversee the court-supervised sell-off of the merchandise from the 28 former David Weis stores. Six months after this was complete, the trustee filed a civil suit demanding return of alleged improperly transferred assets such as paid-up insurance policies and luxury cars. There is also the issue of improper payments. The former owners are currently fighting this in court, but in addition to the possibility of losing, they now have mounting personal legal fees. This is hardly where you would want to be when you are trying to get on with your life.

## Protect Your Personal Assets If Time Is on Your Side

If a bankruptcy filing is a possibility somewhere in the distant future, now is the time to complete all the transactions that might be questioned if that day finally arrives. Any items that might be owned by your company for mostly your own use (i.e., a car, boat, real estate, even a plane) may be best preserved if they are bought by you for book value that is usually fully depreciated. Perhaps there are paid-up cash-value life insurance policies that may be transferred for some consideration. Keep careful records of each transaction, the justification for the value set, and the date the transaction was completed. Then keep in mind the target time of 1 year to avoid any charge of insider preference.

There are even longer statutes on transactions that might be considered fraudulent, and these limits usually coincide with the criminal laws in your state. This book is not meant to serve as a legal adviser, and I am unable to explain the nuances of these changes.

### REVIEW THE BANKRUPTCY PETITION BEFORE YOU FILE

You are making a serious error if the first time you see this document is the day that you sign it. This will be a time of high stress, and that isn't the right circumstance in which to answer the questions asked on the document. If in a calmer moment you may discover errors, it will require additional filings to correct them. You will find a sample petition in Chapter 9.

Sol Stein complained in his book, *A Feast for Lawyers,* about the fact that some assets were not listed on his petition so that his publishing company appeared to be insolvent when it was not. He claims to have mentioned this to his attorney several times, but it was never corrected. That may surprise you, but it doesn't surprise me. Few attorneys will revisit last week's work when they haven't begun this week's. They may be justified, but few of us will ever know for sure because we won't have the luxury (or trauma) of a replay.

The solvency of many companies is more subjective than most of us will admit. Do you value your inventory at cost or at liquidation value, considering that a distress sale may bring 10 cents on the dollar?

Is your machinery valued at book, at replacement, or at liquidation? That $1.00 could be set at $1.50 or 10 cents or anything in between.

*The basis for a winning strategy is to convince your creditors and the court that everyone will be better served by a going concern than one that is closed and dismantled.* Creditors who believe that your assets are substantial and can be easily converted to cash may push for that quick solution, so it is not always prudent to put a high value on those assets.

This aspect of how to manage a bankruptcy is by far the trickiest, and it clearly calls for good business instincts, not legal skills. A knowledge of the players and how they normally react is valuable as is the ability to convince them that their best interest is served by your concern.

The petition is the first piece of the puzzle—study it carefully, and review it *before* you take any action.

## PLAN FOR YOUR REORGANIZATION BEFORE YOU FILE FOR BANKRUPTCY

A good general goes into battle with a game plan and takes the time to implement it completely. Your reorganization plan is your battle plan. Whether or not the plan you file is the work of your accountant and attorney along with you, it's important to learn the rules of engagement as early as possible. Discuss with your attorney the various classes of creditors in your particular cases, and list the amount of debt you will have in each group. They are primarily the following:

- Administrative debt
     Unpaid wages after filing
     Legal and accounting fees for services after filing
     Any vendor credit (postfiling)
     All debts (including taxes) acquired postfiling
- Priority claims—any claims of taxing bodies (federal, state, or local) that must be paid in full
- Secured claims
- Unsecured claims—all other claims that have no security

Once you have filled out the original bankruptcy petition, you can transfer the numbers to a work sheet for the purpose of thinking about what you might reasonably be able to offer to creditors as part of a plan. The final numbers will most likely change for several reasons. One reason is that all of your unsecured creditors will not file a proof of claim either because they won't bother to find out how to do it, or they don't believe that they'll ever get anything back. This will reduce that class of creditor.

You may find the other main reason for change at the end of the case; this change deals with your secured lenders. If you no longer have assets that fully secured their loans, you may move to "cram down" the amount of the secured amount of their loan. For example, a loan for $100,000 granted years ago and secured by real estate valued at $125,000 at the time may now only be worth $90,000. It is possible to reduce the secured portion to 90,000 and drop the 10,000 to the unsecured column. If the plan offers 25 cents on the dollar to the unsecured, then the loan will be reduced from $100,000 to $92,500. For a company whose distress has reduced its asset values dramatically, the debt reduction can be substantial.

You need to think about your plan as soon as possible because a bankruptcy filing gives you only 120 days to file a plan, although that time is normally extended and can drag out for years. The early months are the most stressful—it is not the best time to *begin* to think about your plan. Start this process before you file.

## FILE A REORGANIZATION PLAN ALONG WITH THE BANKRUPTCY PETITION

As the numbers of Chapter 11 filings have increased and the cases have become more complicated, the costs have become astronomical. In some cases, the numbers of attorneys representing different groups of creditors and security holders, and employees and retirees number 10, 20, or more. Seeing a market develop, some lawyers have become specialists at locating and offering representation to obscure subgroups.

The judge handling my case also had charge of two major steel companies. I often observed their hearings, and it wasn't unusual to see 12 to 15 lawyers around the table. At $225 per hour per attorney, their cost could exceed $25,000 per day plus any support staff that was involved.

When Allegheny International, the parent company of Sunbeam appliance, emerged after 2 years in Chapter 11, the fees for their own representation exceeded $7 million. These costs are the primary reasons that most cases don't succeed. Additionally, the time that is involved creates even more reason for failure.

In response to this, a relatively new phenomenon is beginning to take hold. It is the idea of conducting all the negotiations with creditors *before* any filing and then including the plan along with the original petition. A smooth case can proceed from beginning to end in 60 to 90 days. This is a far cry from the 6 years Wheeling-Pittsburgh Steel and LTV spent under court protection and my own $4^1/_2$ years.

## Recognize the Benefit to the Debtor

The savings to the debtor are also beneficial to the creditors because there will be more to disburse as part of the plan. It is one of the main selling points to all parties involved.

The reason you want to confirm these agreements by a formal bankruptcy filing is that all creditors are formally signed off on the agreed plan. This prevents anyone from deciding at a later date that they are owed more, or that they require a faster payout.

## Discover that Creditors Also Benefit from Court Confirmation of a Reorganization Plan

If all creditors agree to the plan you work out, it is also in their best interest to have this agreement confirmed by the court. It assures them that other creditors have agreed to the same terms, and there will be no undisclosed surprises popping up out of the blue. It also provides the supervision of the court instead of individual creditors paying their own lawyer. This type of arrangement should give the greatest return with the lowest cost.

## Learn the Mechanics of Submitting a Reorganization Plan

The original bankruptcy petition is filed, listing the original debt to each class of creditor. For example, if you have a secured loan of 100,000, that amount is listed on the original petition even if your lender has agreed to accept 90,000 in full settlement. In addition, all unsecured vendor credit should be listed at its full claim regardless if you have offered 25 cents on the dollar, and that amount will satisfy these creditors.

It will be in the disclosure statement that you will restate the debt at its lower agreed to amount. You will record on this document that these various classes of creditors are impaired by the value of their claims being lower than the original claims.

Finally, when you file your plan, you will state the agreement that has been reached by the amount as well as the payout terms. This plan will be circulated to all creditors for their confirmation vote, and if all the deals are set, you should get 100% approval.

## Avoid Problems with the Prepackaged Bankruptcy-Reorganization Plan

Until the time that the plan is approved, no creditor is legally bound to accept the result of the negotiations. It is always possible that, once it is committed to writing in the plan, one or more creditors will change their minds. It may be that once they see what other classes of creditors are recovering, they will decide that they deserve more. Or it may be that once they review the total picture, they believe that it is possible for everyone to get more if they hold out longer. And then there is usually at least one disgruntled creditor that votes against the plan on general principles. You hope that there is only one.

The other problem with this quick process is that during the entire time, there may not have been enough attention given to the problems of the business itself and correction of the circumstance that brought you to bankruptcy. Even the best deal won't be good enough if you can't meet the obligations.

But this format is worth a try. If your early negotiations prove very amicable, you may want to suggest this type of prepackaged plan to creditors. The financial savings alone will make it attractive particularly if you are able to share money saved with creditors and the time saved can be used to revitalize the business. It's a great idea if you can sell it.

## WORK WITH YOUR ATTORNEY ON THE BANKRUPTCY FILING

My greatest criticism of lawyers may be the way in which most of them work. Earlier I wrote that few of them are willing to go back and do last week's work over. In addition, they almost never do next week's work in advance. If your case shows up next week, and you have some work to contribute or even critical decisions to make, you will probably find out only a few days at most before the due date. It creates a constant panic and stressful situation for the client, and I don't think most lawyers even think about it.

I assume that the reason for this particular behavior is that the issues of each case are so complex that they commit themselves to one case at a time and that time is when the action is going on. Too bad they can't use auxiliary personnel to prepare the next case and work with the client. Be ready for this, and if *you* know that something is pending, take charge of finding out in advance what is needed and what is likely to happen. Your lack of diligence on this issue will be rewarded by the kind of panic work that suffers from lack of time and a high level of stress.

## CONSIDER HIRING A TURNAROUND CONSULTANT TO HELP YOU REORGANIZE YOUR BUSINESS

The period during which a business is having problems is a tough time to go through for any owner. Speaking with a contractor who reorganized successfully 10 years ago, I asked him how long he knew he was getting in trouble. When I described my own circumstance and the "little man" hiding inside me who knew there was trouble coming even if I ignored him, I saw a smile of recognition. This 6th sense of foreboding wakes us up at night, ruins a vacation, or sometimes takes over for a few days of panic.

Now that you have come clean with the problems that may be threatening the very existence of your business, it is time to get all the help you need. It is impossible to make a diagnosis if some of the symptoms are being hidden. Now, at least, you can begin a course of treatment to recover.

It may be the time to consider a turnaround consultant as well as other sources of help. The "business doctors" can be very expensive, but the good ones are worth more than you will be required to pay. You need available cash to hire one, and you should make this contact *before* any filing. Once you have filed, you will need approval of the court to take this step, and because of the fees that may be involved, there may be objection from the creditors. So the time to begin this process is while you are still in complete control of every aspect of your business.

The answer may be to sell or close a portion or division of your business. You are relatively free to do this quickly if you are not operating under court supervision. The time lags of court approval have been known to undo what might have been a good deal.

If you are considering a consultant, interview more than one. Check out their credentials completely—calling every name they provide to you. It will be their successes that they will list, and you should try to find more objective views. One way to do this is while talking to a reference, casually ask if the company personnel know of anyone else in the area or industry who has used this consultant. You may get a new name in the process. Check with your banker or attorney as well as your associates. And in the end, follow your best instincts.

When negotiating with a consultant, try to be specific about cost and time. An open-ended monthly retainer may be an invitation to disaster. If you have creditors that are being patient, the clock will run out so time is critical.

The Small Business Administration (SBA) has a program of retired executives called SCORE, Service Corporation of Retired Executives, which may provide some help. Also, many universities have Small Business Development Centers where professors as well as students can provide comprehensive and free assistance to help make changes that will improve your business and turn it around.

If you are near a university with a master's of business administration program, find out if you qualify as a case study for their graduate students. I had one done years ago; the advice was excellent, and I am still kicking myself that I didn't take it.

The bankruptcy court can give you the time and the relief that you need, but the change is up to you.

## Summing Up

Advance planning can avert disaster. The most successful cases are the ones in which the business is proactive, seizing the initiative from the beginning. This is easier to achieve if you take the time and plan actions in advance.

# II

## AFTER YOU FILE

### FIXING WHAT WENT WRONG

The act of filing in itself is almost anticlimactic. The real stress is making the decision to file. A contractor from Pittsburgh reported that after almost a year of negotiating with creditors, he woke up in the middle of the night and realized something had to be done, or his difficulties could go on forever. One last meeting with his bankers was unsuccessful, and finally the petition was filed. At least now some conclusion would be achieved.

There is a feeling of relief once you've been to court. Now you know for sure that, for the time being, no credit actions can be taken against you. But that won't stop some relatively distressing phone calls. Many of your vendors/creditors may also be friends, and few will understand beyond the fact that they won't be getting paid anytime soon. This may create a financial problem for them. You will probably also receive some personal support, however, which will be appreciated.

And then there are the petty, stupid calls that can be funny or infuriating, or both. Mine came from an office supply company whose owner asked me if there was some way I could buy merchandise and pay extra so that he wouldn't have to take the "big hit." All this over an $81 bill!

# 5

## LET THE GAMES BEGIN

### WHAT TO EXPECT ONCE YOU FILE YOUR BANKRUPTCY PETITION

67

## KNOW THE SEQUENCE OF EVENTS IN THE BANKRUPTCY PROCESS

There is nothing that is very mysterious about the bankruptcy process, from the first filing to the confirmation of a plan. But for someone who doesn't know what to expect, it is confusing and distressing. And I have never known anyone who went through a bankruptcy whose attorney sat down in the beginning and laid out the whole schedule of events, and created a plan for a successful conclusion. You should be planning two steps ahead of the phase that you are currently passing through. Therefore, you should know that the following are the major events of a bankruptcy:

1. The case is filed and automatic stay is issued.
2. A complete bankruptcy petition is filed.
3. A motion is made by your attorney for use of cash collateral.
4. Creditors will be notified.
5. DIP financing may be secured.
6. A 341 Meeting will be scheduled (this is explained later in this chapter).
7. A creditors' committee may form.
8. Regular reports will be filed with the court.
9. You have a 120-day exclusive right to file a reorganization plan.
10. A bar date for claims will be set.
11. Contracts and leases will be assumed or rejected.
12. Assets may be sold.
13. A disclosure statement and plan will be filed.
14. A hearing will be held on disclosure statement.
15. Voting will be done on the plan.
16. Your reorganization plan will be confirmed.

You needn't go charging into your attorney's office with this list and demand that he tell you how he expects to handle each one of these events. First of all, it is impossible to predict exactly how your creditors or their attorneys will react, and you shouldn't make plans in a vacuum. You may not know who your judge is and that may make a difference. The reality is that no attorney has the time or inclination to plan a whole case before it begins. And finally, you must participate in the planning. And you can expect to have a growing familiarity with the process as time goes on. The rest of this chapter describes each of these events in detail.

## FILE A COMPLETE BANKRUPTCY PETITION

If your case is filed in an emergency situation, it is possible to file a short petition for a court order that will stop any collection actions such as a sheriff's sale. This court order is known as an automatic stay, and it takes effect as soon as your documents are logged into the court.

If you did not do so at the initial filing, you will have to complete the entire bankruptcy petition. Some attorneys now have computer software to accomplish this, but you will have to supply the numbers.

*Take your time and review all the questions completely. If you did not study your bankruptcy petition before, do it now.* Consider how the numbers plugged into this document will eventually become a factor in your reorganization plan.

Be sure and list all creditors to whom you owe any money—even those whose bills may be questioned. These accounts should be listed as "in dispute," and they will be settled later by action of the court. If the creditor does not file a proper proof of claim by the date set by the court, their debt will not be honored.

If any errors or omissions are made in the initial filing, a simple motion is filed to correct the original petition. The example in Exhibit 5–1 is very typical. It asks the court to allow your company to amend the schedules that are incomplete.

## MAKE SURE YOU HAVE PERMISSION TO USE YOUR FUNDS

If you haven't removed your funds from the bank that holds your secured loan, it will probably be confiscated by the bank as an offset. But even if your funds are in another bank, they may not be yours to use. And the funds that you may be collecting on your receivables are also in that category.

The company that operates after a bankruptcy filing is a new legal entity, the "debtor in possession." It is not entitled to the cash collateral (including receivables) that had been pledged by the prepetition company to secure a loan. To use this money, you must file a motion with the court for "use of cash collateral." This should be done promptly, and you may face opposition from the bank. In fact, your bank may file its own motion to prevent you from using this money.

**Exhibit 5–1    Sample Motion for Permission to Amend Schedules of Payment to Creditors**

---

## IN THE UNITED STATES BANKRUPTCY COURT
## FOR THE WESTERN DISTRICT OF PENNSYLVANIA

IN RE:

PITTSBURGH GLOVE
MANUFACTURING COMPANY

Case No. 86-_____
Chapter 11

### Motion for Leave to
### Amend Schedules

AND NOW, comes the debtor in possession, Pittsburgh Glove Manufacturing Company, by its attorney, Mary Bower, and sets forth the following in support of this motion to amend its schedules:

1. Through mistake or inadvertence, the debtor failed to list on its schedule A3, unsecured creditors without priority, the claim of _____. The claim of _____ is in the sum of _____, which the debtor in possession disputes.

2. Also through mistake or inadvertence, the debtor in possession failed to list on its schedule A1, creditors having priority, the claim of the _____, account number _____, in the sum of _____ as of August 1, 19___.

3. In addition, the debtor through mistake failed to list one of its leases on its statement of executory contracts.

4. Attached hereto, and marked Exhibits A, B and C are the debtor's proposed amended statement and schedules, which the debtor intends to file in the event that the court grants approval of this Motion to Amend.

WHEREFORE, debtor in possession respectfully requests this Honorable Court to grant leave to the debtor in possession to file the amended schedules and statement attached to this Motion as Exhibits A, B and C.

Respectfully submitted,

_____

Wolf and Bower
By Mary E. Bower
Attorney for debtor in
possession

Without any cash, most companies cannot go on, and the court is aware of this fact. Therefore, most judges will listen carefully to a well-crafted argument of the possibilities of the success of the reorganization and release at least a portion of the funds. And most banks, conscious that they will be shutting down the company trying to reorganize, will be willing to negotiate to take some payment in return for a release. A bank that does not cooperate runs the risk of legal action if their response is completely arbitrary, and they are aware of this. Your attempt at negotiating a compromise will also be persuasive to the judge if the bank is opposed, and the judge may very likely rule in your favor.

The filing of this motion is critical. It should include as much documentation as possible about your company and its chance for success. Discuss this early and completely with your attorney. This may also be the first time your case comes before the judge, whose impressions may well last for the duration of the case.

I was fortunate that from the inception of my case, we formed a cooperative and favorable attitude before our judge, and he assisted in bringing my case to a successful conclusion. In 4½ years, he never ruled against us.

## OBTAIN "DEBTOR-IN-POSSESSION" FINANCING FROM YOUR SECOND BANK

If you have found a second bank, the time to see them about a loan is as soon as you file for bankruptcy. If at all possible, prepare documentation for the second bank with any business information you have as well as your projections for the new postpetition company. Handle the loan negotiations just as you would have done for your company before you began any bankruptcy filing.

The real difference begins once the bank has agreed to give you funds. You then must seek permission of the court to "incur secured debt." The security that is released to your new bank is supersecurity—that is, their lien supersedes other liens that may be recorded. Any liquidation of assets would bring the first dollars to the "super" lien holder.

As in the use of cash collateral, the ultimate decision to approve will be made by the court. It is easier if you have approval of your existing secured lenders but not impossible if you don't.

In these early days following your bankruptcy filing, you must set the tone of your bankruptcy proceeding. One way to do this is to demonstrate your resolve and ability to see through the reorganization of your business to its successful conclusion. You will prove that by being prepared to take action to preserve the viability of your business. Do this in a proactive way. Another way is to show your conviction that you will be successful and your ability to convince all parties of your ultimate success.

This isn't easy. For most of us, this is one of the most stressful times of our business career. The financial pressures are enormous, and sap both energy and optimism. Try to think of the debtor-in-possession company as your second chance, and you have an opportunity to make it successful. Work with your attorney to make sure your presentations to the judge give that impression.

## MEET WITH YOUR CREDITORS

The first meeting of the debtor with his creditors is called a 341 meeting (because it is authorized under Section 341 of the Bankruptcy Code). The company owner or officers are required by law to attend and be questioned by the creditors and stockholders. The primary purpose of this meeting is to explain detailed information about the total financial picture of the company and its chance for a successful reorganization. Individual creditors may be primarily interested in their debt and how it might be paid.

Secured lenders may focus on the assets that secure their loans. Their questions will be directed at the location and condition of those assets. The purpose of these questions is to determine whether the value of these assets fully secure their outstanding loan balances. They also may want to determine whether or not these assets could easily be liquidated to satisfy the debt.

It will be your job to answer all questions honestly. But keep in mind that you also want to persuade everyone in the room that their best interest will be served by continuing the operations of your company. If you can convince most creditors that they have a real stake in the reorganized company, their cooperation will be forthcoming in the months ahead.

## Be Prepared for the 341 Meeting and Be Proactive

This may be the most challenging selling job of your entire career, and you should put on a real show. You are selling belief in your new company, so all the preparation and documentation you can add will be valuable. Although the meeting will be conducted by a member of the U.S. Trustee's office, and you will primarily be answering questions, there is absolutely no reason why you can't make a presentation.

*Tell your creditors what changes, cost reductions, streamlining, or new sales efforts you expect to institute and how long you expect it to be before results are achieved.* Don't be overly optimistic, but reassure all present that you are in charge of your company, and that you know what it takes to correct problems and bring a stronger and more profitable company out of bankruptcy. Also assure them that this "new" company has every intention of meeting its obligations.

## Expect Informal Negotiations to Go On before and after the Formal Meeting

In my 4½ years under court protection, I spent many hours in court and saw numerous "hall negotiations" go on—and I participated in many of them. These are the informal negotiations that go on in the hall before and after the hearings. They will start at your 341 meeting and continue throughout your case. Expect them, and even instigate the ones you want and feel comfortable about.

Before your 341 meeting, seek out your supportive creditors, and meet with them face to face. Do not make any promises, but you and your attorney should be prepared to make some compromises to gain some concessions. It may be initially about the issue of agreement for DIP financing. Remember that although there are legal strategies, the human strategies to motivate cooperation will also be effective.

## Avoid Acrimonious Meetings with Creditors

Many creditors attend the 341 meeting to ask questions of the debtor. Some, however, will be just as observant of the actions of other creditors. Everyone understands going in that the more areas of disagreement, the greater the legal battles and the higher the legal fees. The money spent on attorneys is money not available for distribution, and all of this reduces the chance for a successful outcome.

If one creditor feels that another creditor is likely to be very aggressive, they may adopt a similar stance to protect their own interests. This could be the beginning of the end. You can't please everyone, and you may not be able to prevent the aggressive action of all creditors. But it is important that you persuade as many of your creditors as you can to give you the opportunity to effect a reorganization.

## Learn What to Do If Your Unsecured Creditors Form a Creditors' Committee

From the beginning of your case, the court will have to notify your 10 largest unsecured creditors of all actions pending before the court. This notice will give them a chance to object if they are opposed to the direction the case is going. In several circumstances, these creditors may form an official committee and hire an attorney to represent their interests. For example, creditors may form a group before a bankruptcy is filed to force a recalcitrant debtor to take action to satisfy debts. Or they may form after a filing is made and after consultation with one another.

Perhaps the most difficult committee to deal with is one formed by an attorney. Some of the more aggressive creditors' attorneys will follow bankruptcy filings; when they find a case that interests them, they will contact the top creditors and offer to form the committee to "protect their rights." What they often neglect to say is that this service can be very costly, and the cost comes out of the money that would be used to satisfy their debts. And, in the end, if there aren't any funds, these creditors may be forced to pay attorneys' fees without even getting any money from the debtor.

You know your creditors; they were your vendors. If anyone can convince them that their cooperation is in everyone's interest, it is you. The caution about making any promises remains but that doesn't mean that you can't communicate. Assure them that you are doing everything you can to turn things around. If you can continue to do business with these vendors, that will be an incentive for them to keep you going. If you can get more than half of these largest creditors on your side, this will minimize the problems you will face.

Don't be afraid to discuss the cost of adversarial litigation with your creditors. Each motion takes the time of at least two attorneys—yours and theirs. Their billable time will include all the preparation of the motion as well as court time, which could be 6 to 8 hours for each attorney for a total of 12 to 16 hours at up to $250 each per hour. That totals $3,000 to $4,000 per motion. It doesn't take much of these costs to destroy any hopes of future success.

In fact, if you are faced with a particularly aggressive creditors' committee, it may be advisable to pursue a sale of assets that will liquidate the company rather than fight this committee ad nauseam.

## Keep in Mind that the Creditors' Committee Can Investigate Many Company Transactions

If the members of the creditors' committee suspect that there has been improper transfers of company assets, they can instigate an investigation. Because many of these vendors may have inside information about the way you operated your business and your personal life-style, be careful about how you operate once you are under their scrutiny. If they are principals in their own companies, the debts you didn't pay may be money out of their pocket, and they may be very interested in finding out if any of this money has flowed to you personally.

## SUBMIT REGULAR REPORTS TO THE COURTS

Once you have filed for bankruptcy, you will be under the supervision of the court. One of the requirements you will have to fulfill will be to submit monthly operating statements to the court. These will also go to certain creditors. This will allow the interested parties to monitor the operating results of your company and alert them to any further deterioration so that they can take action if needed. A sample of the rules from one district is shown in Exhibit 5–2 on page 81.

Under some circumstances, you may be required to submit very detailed reports. One case I reviewed in the Pittsburgh district had the debtor submitting a record of every check issued. Creditors had forced this action to keep the debtor from improperly dispersing funds from operations. Normally your accountant will issue these reports and that will be one more expense of the debtor.

## SUBMIT A PLAN OF REORGANIZATION

The debtor has the exclusive right for 120 days to file a plan of reorganization. After this initial time, the creditors can draft a plan of their own. However, the court can extend this period of exclusivity if the debtor files a motion requesting this extra time. The time to file this motion is not on the 119th day. You will want to sit down with your attorney and decide how long you will realistically need to stabilize your operation and develop a workable plan of reorganization. Before the first 90 days have elapsed, you should have filed your motion for additional time. In all cases, it is best if you take the initiative.

Cases can drag on for years; mine did because we were in the middle of litigation. But don't count on it—be prepared. A sample reorganization plan is included in chapter 11.

Having your creditors submit a plan will be very costly in terms of legal fees. Their ideas of how you should effect a reorganization will usually leave the company with so little cash that it is doubtful you would want to continue to operate it. So it is clearly in your best interest to be the only one to propose the plan.

## SET A BAR DATE FOR ALL CLAIMS
## AGAINST THE DEBTOR

The final date a claim can be filed against the debtor is known as the bar date; the court will set this date. There is no specific timing for the setting of this date, but it will be in advance of any voting on the plan of reorganization.

When you file your original petition, you are required to list all known creditors of your company. Once the bar date has been established, all of these creditors will be notified that they must file a proof of claim by that date. Failure to do so will invalidate any claim they may have. You can expect that a percentage of your unsecured will not take the time and effort to file, thereby reducing this class of debt.

In my case, my plan had only one negative vote, and when I reviewed the valid claims, I discovered that this company hadn't filed one. So their vote was a hollow one, we no longer owed them a cent!

## ALWAYS REVIEW CLAIMS TO MAKE SURE
## THEY ARE VALID

When originally filing your petition, you must list all debts—even those you dispute. If a proof of claim is not filed for these debts, they are automatically canceled. Even if the claim is made you can follow through with the dispute by filing a "motion to disallow" the claim. You present your reasons for the dispute, and the creditor must file a motion in support of his claim. In some cases, the amount isn't worth this additional cost so you will prevail by default. In the cases in which both sides are heard, the judge will decide.

Most amazing to me were several claims made against my case that were in excess of the amount owed. Perhaps it was because of a clerical error, but in some cases it is probably motivated by the feeling that because only a portion will be paid, the creditor may as well inflate the total amount. Take the time to review and dispute these increased amounts.

There is also a deadline for you to file against any claims. This is normally within 60 days after the confirmation of your plan. Most attorneys will not automatically forward claims to you for your review as they are filed. It must be your responsibility to monitor claims on a regular basis. Or you may find yourself trying to research 30 claims 3 days before the deadline. That's what happened to me—I didn't know that I had to create the objections until a few days before the time ran out to file motions.

## Decide Whether to Assume or Reject Contracts and Leases

Suppose your company has been burdened by leases for locations that have not been profitable and are draining cash from the total operation. You may have contracted for supplies at a price or in such quantity that the terms are no longer favorable. It may be a union contract that you have tried to reopen without any cooperation of union leaders. Or you may have bid a job at too low a price and now the losses are mounting.

These are just some of the legal agreements that may be set aside by the action of the court. This topic will be covered in detail in Chapter 7, but it is a topic for early consideration.

Conversely, if you are in arrears in lease payments for property or equipment, the lessor can go to court and force you to pay. If you don't, the lease will be voided, and you will lose the equipment or be forced to leave the property. This is a case that will not be protected by the automatic stay.

## Sell Your Assets If You Have the Permission of the Court

Most businesses have pledged their assets as collateral in any secured lending agreement. To liquidate these secured assets, you will need the approval of your lender and the court. The cash proceeds from such a sale will usually go to the lender to reduce the balance of your loan. However, if you have a good deal and a convincing argument, it may be possible to convince the bank to allow you to use a portion of the proceeds for what will probably be much-needed working capital. These agreements will almost always be accepted by the court.

## File a Disclosure Statement

Once you are ready to present to the court and your creditors your plan of how you expect to repay your debts, you will file a disclosure statement. This topic is covered in greater depth in chapter 11, but for the purpose of understanding the entire chronology of a bankruptcy, you must realize that this happens before a plan is voted on by the creditors. Briefly, this document includes

- A description of the reason for the bankruptcy
- A description of the current financial condition of the company including a current balance statement

- A projection of expected business conditions for the first year or so of the reorganization plan
- A summary of the plan and the reasons that the plan would be more beneficial to creditors than a liquidation

The purpose of this statement is to give the creditors additional information on which to base their decision to vote for or against the plan. The court will hold a hearing on the adequacy of this statement before allowing any voting on the plan. Creditors who believe that more information is required or that the information given is in error may appear before the court to argue their point. The judge will then decide, and if he approves, you will go on to the next step toward success.

## SUBMIT THE PLAN TO CREDITORS FOR THEIR VOTE

The reorganization plan will be sent to all creditors for their review and vote. Each plan will have a ballot attached to it for the purpose of recording the vote. All creditors should be encouraged to vote—particularly those who are likely to vote in favor.

It is possible to negotiate with secured creditors and the taxing bodies in the priority claim class and come to an agreement that will serve as their vote in favor of the plan. You may be conducting these negotiations as an ongoing aspect of your case, and the deadline of the plan will serve as a motivator to conclude them.

The one class that is most difficult to predict is the unsecured creditors, unless they have formed a creditors' committee that has been very active and verbal about their demands. If they have objected throughout, they may attempt to file an opposing plan. This action would require permission of the court.

## CONFIRM A REORGANIZATION PLAN OVER
## THE OBJECTION OF SOME CREDITORS

The easiest and best way for the court to confirm a plan is by obtaining a favorable vote of the creditors from all classes of claims. But when the vote is mixed, it is still possible to have the plan confirmed. The court may overrule the negative vote of one class of creditor if other classes have signified their approval by vote or agreement. The court must be convinced that this class of creditor will receive more under the term of the plan than from a liquidation. The ultimate criteria is the return to the creditor.

At the confirmation hearing, your attorney will read the results of the ballots that have been returned. If the vote is in your favor, the process will be simple. If not, a longer hearing over the benefit of confirmation will be conducted, and the judge will decide. All creditors, regardless of whether they voted for a plan, will be bound by the terms of a plan that has been confirmed.

There are many aspects of a bankruptcy that create stress and bring on some depression. The financial pressures are obvious. But for many it is the loss of control that hits hardest. We sought out our own businesses because we thrived on the independence, and now it feels as if everyone controls our lives and careers but us.

## REGAIN CONTROL OF EVENTS BY UNDERSTANDING THE BANKRUPTCY PROCESS

You have two choices at this point. One, you can let your attorney run the case, and your fate will be decided by the actions of others. Or you can understand that your participation and creativity can impact the course of a case by giving it strong leadership. Seeing you and hearing from you will give your creditors renewed confidence in the potential for success of your reorganization.

In $4^{1}/_{2}$ years, I attended virtually every hearing on my case even when there was agreement in advance so that the motion took only a few minutes to present. My attorney insisted on it, and I'm glad that she did. Too many cases that I observed did not have the principal in attendance.

If you had a meeting with a customer, you would be there. If you had a meeting with your banker, you would be there. Now you have a meeting with the judge that will determine your future, and you should be there. Becoming familiar with the court and its proceedings will help you to regain control of your circumstance as you begin to understand how unintimidating it is in reality. If you observe other cases, you will become aware of how much choice the judge really exercises.

Because the other side files a motion does not mean that they will succeed. If you read about large bankruptcies in the *Wall Street Journal* or your local paper, the most frequent area of conflict between debtor and creditor that you will see is about the "exclusive right" to file a plan. An aggressive creditor's committee may begin to ask for the right to file its own plan within the first 6 months of the case. Several major steel companies fought off these motions for years with the judge deciding in their favor repeatedly. Even when it comes to cash, a compelling argument can win. Fewer than 6 months before they ceased flying, Eastern Airlines was allowed to use cash from an escrow account for one more attempt at a turnaround that would make it into a viable airline. And this occurred over the strenuous objections of creditors who argued that the plan had little chance for success. They were right—the losses continued; in the end, the airline folded and had even less money to distribute to creditors.

The lesson here is that a creative and proactive impression by the business in bankruptcy can be given much latitude and accommodation by the court. From the day you file, your judge will begin to decide how your case will most likely proceed. Every time you appear in front of the judge, your docket (case file) will be there as a reminder. If you file motions with complete documentation attached or appear in court well prepared to present your case, your judge will believe that you have the ability and resolve to see your case to its successful conclusion. And, as a result, the judge will give you a chance to do just that. After all, the entire process is about giving a debtor a second chance.

The judge won't develop this same impression if all he sees is your attorney. You want an experienced practitioner so he will be, by nature of that fact, in front of the judge with some frequency. This will not garner the special interest of the court. Your appearance will make an impression. Make sure your attorney points out your presence.

I recently discussed this theory with an attorney. He agreed that bankruptcy is a business, not a legal issue. He then went on to say that the business owner should run the business and let the lawyer fight the bankruptcy. I couldn't disagree more.

Although it adds an extra burden to your job, you should become knowledgeable, involved, and present as your case progresses. Don't let the judge rule against an absent debtor; instead, make him want to rule in favor of a hardworking business owner who can turn things around. Convince your creditors of that fact along the way, and your chance for success becomes substantial.

## SUMMING UP

Knowing what to expect empowers you to take control. Review the major events of a bankruptcy process carefully, and know what is likely to happen next. You won't be shocked by a filing, and you will be fully prepared to respond.

Exhibit 5–2    Sample Statement for Making Payments and Filing Reports    **81**

**Exhibit 5–2    Sample Statement for Making Payments and Filing Reports to the Court**

---

## IN THE UNITED STATES BANKRUPTCY COURT
## FOR THE WESTERN DISTRICT OF PENNSYLVANIA

RULE 2015.1—DUTY TO MAKE PAYMENTS AND FILE REPORTS IN
        CHAPTER 11 AND 13 CASES

### A. PAYMENTS

The trustee or debtor in possession in a chapter 11 case, and the debtor if engaged in business in a chapter 13 case, shall, unless otherwise ordered or prohibited by the Code:

1. keep current and pay when due any debt which has arisen since the entry of the order for relief, including any debt arising from rentals or other money due on account of real estate leases; provided, however, that any debt for utility service shall be paid within five days of receipt of the bill for such service.

2. submit by the end of the second business day after the payment of wages to employees, an accounting and certified or cashier's check in full payment of the following taxes accrued as a result of the payment of wages, to the local office of the Special Procedures Function of the Internal Revenue Service:

    (a) the employee tax (FICA) withheld under § 3102 of the Internal Revenue Code of 1954, (hereinafter cited as Tax Code);

    (b) the employee tax (FICA) withheld under Tax Code § 3311; and

    (c) the employee income tax withheld under Tax Code § 3402; and

3. submit to the local office of the Department of Revenue of the Commonwealth of Pennsylvania a certified or cashier's check in full payment of the following taxes in the manner hereafter set forth:

    (a) all Pennsylvania sales tax collected pursuant to 72 P.S. 7202 et seq. shall be remitted together with the proper tax returns, no later than the end of the fifth business day following the last day of each month in which such sales taxes were required to be collected; and

    (b) all employer withholding tax (personal income tax) withheld pursuant to 72 P.S. 7316 *et seq.* shall be remitted together with the proper tax returns, no later than the end of the second

**Exhibit 5–2**  *(continued)*

business day after the payment of wages to employees.

4. submit no later than the last day of the month following the end of the quarter to the local office of the
Field Accounting Service of the Commonwealth of Pennsylvania, Department of Labor and Industry, Office of
Employment Security, in accordance with the filing
and payment provisions of the Pennsylvania Unemployment Compensation Law, 43 P.S. §§ 781.4, 784 and 785,
tax returns together with a certified or cashier's
check in full payment of the following taxes:

  (a) employer contributions due pursuant to Section
  305 of the Pennsylvania Unemployment Compensation Law, 43, P.S. § 785; and

  (b) employee contributions withheld pursuant to
  Section 301.4 of the Pennsylvania Unemployment
  Compensation Law, 43 P.S. § 781.4.

**B. REPORTS**

The trustee or debtor in possession in a chapter 11
case, and the debtor if engaged in business in a chapter 13
case, shall:

1. timely file all federal, state and local tax returns
with the applicable taxing bodies during the pen-
dency of the bankruptcy case;

2. file copies of the most recent balance sheet and
profit and loss statement, with the clerk;

3. annually file with the clerk, within ninety (90)
calendar days of the close of the debtor's fiscal
year, an updated balance sheet and profit and loss
statement;

4. file an initial statement of operations, including
but not limited to a report of receipts and disbursements, accrued payables and accrued receivables, for the period commencing with the date of
filing of the petition and ending with the last day
of the month of the filing of the petition. The initial report shall be filed with the clerk on or before the date first set for the meeting of
creditors; and

5. file monthly statements of operations with the clerk
not later than the fifteenth (15th) day of each
month for the statement covering the preceding
month, and serve copies on counsel, if any, for any
appointed committee in a chapter 11 case or the
trustee in a chapter 13 case.

Exhibit 5–2    Sample Statement for Making Payments and Filing Reports    83

**Exhibit 5–2**  *(continued)*

### C. CONTENTS OF REPORTS

1. The initial report filed pursuant to subparagraph B.4., above, shall include a statement of the name and location of each depository or place of investment holding funds of the estate, and the applicable account number or numbers.

2. In addition to the information required by Bankruptcy Rules 2015 (a) (3), all statements of operations shall contain a cumulative list of all debts which have arisen since the order for relief was entered.

### D. NOTIFICATION

Though not a precondition to compliance, a copy of this rule shall be issued by the clerk's office to each debtor in possession in a chapter 11 case, and each debtor if engaged in business in a chapter 13 case, promptly after the commencement of the case.

### COMMENT

1. Substantially all of the obligations conferred by this rule on debtors doing business were contained in orders routinely entered in chapter 11 cases in the past.

2. Subparagraph C.2. requires the development of a cumulative schedule of unpaid debts incurred after the commencement of the case. The development of the cumulative schedule during the case should simplify compliance with Bankruptcy Rule 1019(6), should the case be converted.

cc: Debtor in Possession
    Attorney for Debtor in Possession

A study of companies that have faced enormous financial difficulties and surmounted them without a bankruptcy filing and its accompanying cost will inevitably show a pattern of effective and open communication and the cooperation this inspires. Chrysler Corporation during the early 1980s is a well-known example. The market was rejecting its product, the morale of its employees had seriously deteriorated, the public perception and private assessment of the quality of its automobiles were at all-time lows, and Chrysler's future looked bleak.

# CAN WE TALK?

## OPENING CONSTRUCTIVE LINES OF COMMUNICATION

Lee Iaococa and his candid, sometimes blunt style of communication made the difference. He negotiated for federal loan guarantees in public, as well as in private, increasing the pressure on public officials. Employees, vendors, and even the buying public were challenged to become a factor in the rebirth of "The New Chrysler Corporation." The general rebound of the auto industry, accompanied by the improved image of both the company and its products, brought it back from the brink.

Seizing the initiative and setting the tone of the information is in every company's best interest. The time-consuming process of communicating with creditors, customers, and the public is rewarded by a focus on the positive. This is critical to avoid an informational vacuum that will be filled with uncertainty and rumors. In the normal course of business, you communicate with a wide variety of individuals and other businesses. Once you have filed for bankruptcy, you should put into place a strategy to inform each of these groups and to provide ongoing progress reports to employees, suppliers, customers, and lenders.

## GIVE YOUR EMPLOYEES AS MUCH INFORMATION AS POSSIBLE

The time for a company to develop open lines of communication with its employees is the first day the doors open. Your staff must understand more than the company policy; they must understand the company's mission, its customers, what quality and service is expected from them, and, ultimately, the company's goals. From the way your phone is answered to the way your goods are shipped, every contact the public has with your company builds its image and reputation. Employees who are angry or feel cheated do not treat others very well. Workers who fear for the future of their jobs will let outsiders know this in many ways, and rumors will spread that may undermine your diligent attempt of revitalization outside of a bankruptcy filing.

A bankrupt business's employees are the first to feel it when the business is experiencing problems. Their work loads will reflect the lack of orders, and they may already be on shortened hours or temporary layoff. A company losing money may not be able to purchase all of the necessary inventory and raw material, and machinery and equipment may be left to fall into disrepair and not be replaced as needed. When conditions reach the critical stage, paychecks may be short or nonexistent.

If you explain in vague terms about the "tough times," you may force some extra effort from employees, but the cooperation will be of short duration. Mounting concerns about their own futures will eventually erupt into open frustration, and employees' suspicions will grow. The timing and the manner in which you choose to open communication may vary, but the need to communicate is constant.

If you have one or two key employees, they should be told that you are contemplating a bankruptcy filing as soon as you take it under serious consideration. They may have ideas to help you avoid this action or valuable suggestions about how to preposition your company before any filing is made. You also need to know in advance whether or not the people you depend on most will be willing to stay through the battles ahead.

Avoiding these discussions will do more harm than simply denying your business the potential contributions of these employees. Typically, people look for work within an area or industry where they have had experience. Often it is with the competition. The last problem you need is for all the inside rumor and conjecture to be spread to competitors by your own employees looking for a new job. If you are candid with your key staff, they can answer questions of the people who report to them, and you'll have better control on what information leaks out from within your organization.

In my own case, I had one key manager whose feedback I depended on for several years. I never could have accomplished a reorganization without his support, and it was my job to win his confidence. As soon as I knew trouble was in the horizon, we discussed it, and we both agreed that we wanted to fight through our commercial dispute even if it meant filing a bankruptcy. Our case was more difficult and took longer than either one of us expected, and this manager finally did leave—but not until our litigation was settled, and we were beginning to file our plan of reorganization. His loyalty and help went beyond what anyone could expect, but I believe that it came because he had been part of the decision-making process in the beginning and felt committed to see it to its conclusion. You may be pleasantly surprised at how much your employees are willing to contribute if they feel a part of the process from the beginning.

The Eastern Airlines bankruptcy was, during its 18-month attempt to reorganize, a study in contrast. Eastern began bankruptcy proceedings during a strike by machinists that was honored by others including pilots. It soon required real fortitude to brush past the sometimes aggressive picketers to travel on Eastern. A massive sell-off of assets raised cash, and an extraordinarily cooperative bankruptcy judge permitted the use of that cash to keep the airline flying. It soon became increasingly clear, however, that the company would not be able to reorganize successfully. In a last attempt to save the airline, the bankruptcy court appointed Martin Shugrue as Eastern's trustee.

The trustee began by meeting with all constituencies of the airline, not the least of which were the employees. The traveling public immediately noticed the attitude change he inspired. This, coupled with aggressive marketing plans, finally brought signs of life to Eastern, so that in November 1990, the bankruptcy court approved one more large infusion of cash despite creditors' objections. Shugrue's "hard-hitting television commercials, the pride and morale he infused in Eastern's employees and his efforts to woo frequent flyers were all hailed as innovative," wrote Martin Deutsch, editor and publisher of *Frequent Flyer Magazine* in March 1991.

Although Shugrue's efforts fell short, and the airline shut down in January 1991, many believe that if this had been the approach from the beginning, Eastern would have successfully reorganized.

The lesson: *Key employees must be given complete information as soon as possible.* They will usually welcome candid disclosure and the opportunity to express their concerns as well as participate in creating solutions. Operating under the supervision of the bankruptcy court intensifies the pressure on managers, as well as increases their work loads. Management's sense of control will be greater if key employees are an active part of the "turnaround team."

## Retaining Key Employees: Difficult but Important

Some talented managers may want to leave rather than face the stress of reorganization and the uncertainty of its success. They may feel their association with a company in trouble will reflect on them and make any future job search more difficult. It's your job to convince your managers of the challenge that lies ahead and the reward for accomplishing a successful reorganization. In some cases, above-average performers with confidence in their own abilities may actually welcome the challenge. In fact, the dramatic increase in business bankruptcies is creating a market for this talent. Sandy Sigoloff, who engineered a highly praised turnaround at Wickes, is known as a specialist in this area.

Borderline performers should be given the opportunity to leave as soon as possible. Businesses planning to affect a successful reorganization cannot afford to retain those individuals who may have been part of the problem. You must identify and take action on terminating those whose performance is substandard.

## Begin Regular Face-to-Face Meetings with Employees

A group meeting is the most effective way to communicate with the general employees. Managers should offer all the information that has a direct bearing on how the bankruptcy will affect their employment, and all reasonable questions should be answered candidly. Any changes in operation, such as a short-term closing, should be disclosed as soon as the change is known to management.

Renegotiating the terms of employment may be necessary to cut costs, increase productivity, and generate greater profits for the survival and ultimate reorganization of the business. For the non-union employee, this occurs, of course, at management's discretion. But if management renegotiates arbitrarily and without sufficient explanation, there will be a backlash that might impair the bankrupt business's credibility. No one *likes* to take a pay cut.

## Try to Win Support for Any Employment Changes that Must Be Made

Union contracts may be reopened for negotiation or voided with the approval of the bankruptcy court. Several large companies have rejected union contracts with varying degrees of success. Continental Airlines did so in 1983 with its plan replacing any employees who refused to work under the new contract terms. As a result, the airline was able to resume most of its flights within a matter of weeks of its bankruptcy filing. Wheeling-Pittsburgh Steel Corporation suffered a 98-day strike in 1985 after the court permitted the bankrupt company to reject its workers' union contract. Labor forced the resignation of CEO Dennis Carney, accusing him of bad faith negotiation. New leadership eventually forged a new contract but not without the considerable cost of additional losses that the labor dispute caused.

Laid-off employees should receive their information from management and not secondhand from fellow employees, even if their futures have not been determined. Laid-off employees form a labor pool that may be needed in the future and will not be available if they are allowed to drift away without any continued contact with the company. In addition, current employees will wonder if they, too, are considered expendable if they see others laid off without explanation. Needed and productive employees could leave for lack of communication.

## If Your Retired Employees Will Be Affected, Let Them Know

Filing a Chapter 11 bankruptcy can have great impact on a company's retirees. The 1986 filing of the LTV Steel Corporation was attributed, in part, to a massive pension liability and a large pension fund that the company was unable to satisfy. Once LTV filed the petition, the corporation suspended its retirees' health benefits. Four months later, the Pension Benefits Guaranty Corporation, a quasi-governmental agency that insures pensions, assumed control of the entire LTV pension fund. Immediately lost by this action was the $400-a-month early retirement pension the union negotiated just a few months before the bankruptcy filing. This became a much-publicized story in the areas where LTV had plants. The newspapers and television and radio news carried heart-rending sagas of the fears of these vulnerable former employees. Had LTV been a consumer-oriented company, it would have been a public relations nightmare.

The quality of products and services during bankruptcy is critically important to maintain customer interest and confidence. If employees become angry or disenchanted during bankruptcy, their attitudes can undermine reorganization efforts. If you can motivate your employees to believe in and care about the company's future, however, it can greatly enhance the business's chance for successful reorganization.

## Obtain the Support of Employees and Retirees to Avoid Legal Claims

Disenchanted employees or retirees can also create a legal nightmare for the bankrupt business. Unpaid wages and benefits are debts that make these individuals unsecured creditors. They can form a group and hire legal counsel to protect their rights. The attorney can take an active position in all motions brought before the court regarding the operation of the business. They can also file motions of their own up to and including requesting the liquidation (Chapter 7 conversion) of the business to satisfy the employees' outstanding claims.

Each employee or retiree who has money due constitutes a vote when the reorganization plan is presented to the court. If most of these unsecured creditors vote against the plan, it can prevent it from being approved. Active workers may see the continuation of their jobs as an incentive for cooperation, but the workers who have been laid off or retired will be more concerned with getting what they view as being owed to them.

Although it may be financially impossible for a company to satisfy all the claims, it is critical that you keep past and present employees informed.

## ESTABLISH COMMUNICATION WITH YOUR SUPPLIERS

Purchasing is often overlooked as a key function to the success of any company. The best price, the best quality, and the best delivery directly affect the company's bottom line. To many entrepreneurs and CEOs, however, this does not seem like the most glamorous or challenging function in which to invest effort. Often, the jobs with these important responsibilities are filled with rather average and uncreative individuals.

In good times, this is an unfortunate oversight. But when times get tough, this oversight can escalate to crisis proportions, and the consequences are obvious. During supply shortages, for example, the companies with the most professional buyers will get the supplies that they need; the ones without these individuals won't.

If short-term cash-flow difficulties develop, suppliers should be informed as soon as possible. Unanswered phone calls or promises that can't be kept establish suspicion in the relationship that could blow up into an openly adversarial position should a bankruptcy filing occur.

Few bankruptcies develop overnight, so most suppliers are already aware that a customer is experiencing difficulties. Suppliers see the signs in the ordering levels or the slowness of payments, or both. It is foolish to compound these problems with unanswered phone calls or broken promises. Few suppliers will respond positively to the replacement of a promised payment with a notice from the bankruptcy court.

Several large corporations have learned to develop good vendor relationships the hard way. Once the Federated and Allied Department Stores filed for bankruptcy, their buyers found themselves in the strange position of currying favors with suppliers instead of the courting they were accustomed to. Without goods in the stores, even such venerable, established names as Bloomingdales and Burdines were at the mercy of vendors to extend new credit while waiting for payment of the old.

Steel companies such as Wheeling-Pittsburgh, Sharon Steel, LTV Steel Corporation, and other large buyers of goods and services found fewer vendors bidding on their contracts, and, at times, buyers had to solicit new vendors actively, or pay the price, literally. In a bizarre example, a Presidential Airways pilot paid for aviation fuel with his own credit card. The airline had inadequately informed suppliers at some airports what their intentions were regarding payments during the airline's short and unsuccessful period in Chapter 11 bankruptcy.

## Enlisting the Support of Your Vendors

The best scenario for all businesses requires open and honest lines of communication. If a supplier understands the nature of the problems and the steps taken to correct them, the supplier will be more likely to offer more ongoing cooperation. Even when bankruptcy filing becomes inevitable, the notice of bankruptcy should come first from you rather than the court. If adversarial lines are drawn, they will continue to be a source of legal roadblocks throughout the reorganization proceedings.

Concurrent with your filing but before the notice comes from the court, you should send letters to all of your vendors. They should be addressed to a specific individual, not to the company. A major company such as AT&T or American Express will refer your case to an appropriate department so you won't be able to communicate directly with them. Confine your effort to the vendors that you know. Exhibit 6–1 provides a sample letter informing vendors of a bankruptcy filing.

If you make the first step, these vendors/creditors will be more comfortable opening up to you with their concerns.

Once my own bankruptcy filing became an irrevocable decision, but before the actual filing, I began the difficult process of informing important suppliers. Many suppliers were friends, and this added dimension to the relationships we enjoyed made the task more difficult. For example, many suppliers first expressed concern for my well-being and sympathy for the circumstances in which I found myself battling. The fact remained, however, that we were discussing money that would not be repaid to them even though it was legally and morally owed. In some cases, my company had received greater credit and extended terms because of the personal relationships I shared with suppliers. Knowing this, I heard the disappointment and in some cases, anger behind the kind words. But at the moment, I was too overcome with embarrassment and, quite frankly, the fear of what was ahead to respond to these supplier-friends adequately. Now I know what I could have said and done.

I could have reassured my vendors of my intention to continue in operation while I pursued a legal solution to my problems. As the case progressed, I should have continued updates to those vendors with whom I did not have regular contact. When it was over, a few old vendors expressed surprise that we were still in business. They hadn't heard from me in 4 years!

## Learn How to Win over a Vendor after You've Filed for Bankruptcy

To maintain a positive supplier relationship and to limit the creditors' exposure, it is legally permissible, under some circumstances, to return merchandise and to pay bills incurred within 45 days before the bankruptcy is filed. The debtor's attorney must approve all such returns and payments before they are made.

Most suppliers, old and new, will usually require cash payments in advance after a business files for bankruptcy. This is an added burden on the bankrupt business. However, suppliers may extend credit to major customers whose level of sales or distribution are important, despite the bankruptcy, because the success of the bankrupt business's reorganization serves the supplier's best interests. Through a successful reorganization, the supplier, as an unsecured creditor, will be paid a greater

**Exhibit 6–1    Sample Letter Informing Vendors of a Bankruptcy Filing**

Dear name of Company President:

On January 10, 1991, the XYZ Corporation filed for protection under Chapter 11 of the Bankruptcy Code. We have taken this action to preserve our assets as we begin to reorganize the company to meet current business conditions.

You will be receiving a notification from the court so that you may properly file a claim.

Please be assured that XYZ Corporation has already begun changing our operation by closing a small plant we no longer needed and streamlining our production. We fully expect to be able to file a plan of reorganization by May 20, 1993.

We value our long-standing business relationship and hope it can continue in the future. Please feel free to call on me if you have any questions. If I am unable to answer them, our legal counsel will be happy to accommodate you.

We are working to settle this to everyone's satisfaction as quickly as possible.

Sincerely,

President
XYZ Corporation

portion of the prebankruptcy debt owed by the debtor. In addition, profits from current and future sales to the bankrupt business should also serve as an incentive to suppliers, but the logic of this reasoning does not always prevail. Not all suppliers realize that the debts incurred after filing bankruptcy are priority debts that must be paid before any other unsecured debt.

Finding and keeping a source of supply can be the most difficult problem a small company encounters while operating in Chapter 11. The need to purchase at competitive costs to maintain profitability is critical. The first place to look is existing vendors, even if they are unsecured creditors.

When the shoe store discussed in chapter 1 filed for Chapter 11 reorganization, the inventory level at the store was at an all-time high, but many popular colors and sizes were in limited supply. It would have been impossible to switch to completely different shoe lines, so it was critical for the owner to maintain a cooperative postfiling relationship with his existing suppliers. His offer to return some of his merchandise and to pay the restocking fee would minimize his existing debt. In addition, the store would pay all new shipments cash in advance. These changes required strict attention to inventory levels, which had been lacking in the past at the shoe store, and was the start of a successful new beginning for the company.

Selling existing vendors on the operating company's future prospects is a necessary goal even if they aren't going to be a current supplier, because, at any time during the reorganization, disgruntled unsecured creditors can hinder the debtor's reorganization.

New vendors can be found and it is not necessary to offer the information that a company is operating under court protection, although you cannot actively mislead vendors. They certainly can find out on their own and make independent decisions. If the vendor does not require cash in advance or cash on delivery, you should, of course, promptly pay all debts incurred after bankruptcy.

During the course of my own bankruptcy, I had the occasion to do business with a steel company that was also in reorganization. In fact, our cases were handled by the same judge, and I occasionally waited while large contingents of the company's attorneys went over their contested issues. I was, therefore, amazed when my company's invoice to the steel maker remained unpaid for more than 60 days. After sending a copy of the invoice, and even faxing another copy, my amazement turned to anger, and I threatened to file a motion before "our" judge if payment was not made. My invoice was paid 5 days later.

# Be Willing to Negotiate Additional Protection for Your Important Vendors

Any type of collateral that has not previously been fully secured may be used to secure credit from a supplier. The court will have to grant permission, and other creditors have the right to object to the company's decision to incur secured debt. A good case for the necessity of this action will have to be made to the court and to creditors, and it is your obligation to assist legal counsel to persuade the court and creditors that it is in the creditors' best interests to allow new secured debt.

The use of personal guarantees is another strategy available to a small business owner, although it is a high-risk one. A successful outcome does not create additional problems. If the outcome is less than successful, however, the addition of your personal liability could increase the likelihood of personal bankruptcy following the business bankruptcy.

Many small business owners begin to use their own lines of credit and even personal credit cards to purchase supplies for their companies. Our shoe store owner bought everything from office supplies to light bulbs with his personal credit. The success of his business after reorganization made it all worthwhile because he saved his very livelihood. It is important to emphasize that without prior court approval, these debts are not guaranteed by the company and may never be repaid.

# Know that Unsecured Creditors Will Be Informed by the Court

All unsecured creditors are eligible to serve on a creditors' committee, although the 10 largest creditors are automatically members unless they choose *not* to serve. These creditors receive notice from the court on all matters pertaining to the bankruptcy filing. Even if a committee does not organize formally, these 10 top creditors are notified of all motions before the court and have the opportunity to state any objections.

Within 6 weeks of a bankruptcy filing, a meeting known as a Section 341 meeting of creditors is convened. Although these few, short weeks may be the most traumatic for you, they are also the critical time in which to rebuild any fragmented relationships with creditors.

It is best for any personal questions to be aired and resolved in a private manner between the individuals involved, rather than to be allowed to fester for the 6 weeks before the 341 meeting. Although authorized court personnel conduct the 341 meeting, any creditor in attendance is permitted to raise questions. An acrimonious session in which tempers flare could set the tone for the entire duration of the case.

## Maintain Your Friendships with Your Suppliers

If personal relationships exist, they should be encouraged to continue, if possible. Any bankrupt business must be prepared for some anger and some outright rejections, however. But if you are known as an honorable company or individual, candor about the present and the future plans is required. For more formal relationships, written communication should begin at this time with the letter from you describing in as much detail as possible your company's plans to create the circumstances for a successful reorganization. This intense phase of communication may not prevent a creditors' committee from forming, but it may make it a friendly committee when it does form.

## Avoid Communicating with Your Suppliers Through Attorneys

If your attorney suggests communication with creditors need not continue, you and your attorney should discuss, in detail, why you should not communicate with creditors. Is it because you aren't *required* to communicate with creditors? There may be serious consequences with this approach. Attorneys will often attempt to control the flow of information to creditors, and charge you legal fees for each creditor inquiry and answer. This may be unnecessary and inadvisable. In *A Feast for Lawyers—Inside Chapter 11: An Expose,* Sol Stein, CEO of Stein and Day Publishers, reports his counsel forbade him to talk to creditors during his reorganization, a fact that seems to have worked against him. The friends he had among his creditors never had the opportunity to help because they were not informed that their assistance was needed.

A bankruptcy filed after a series of collection actions by vendors will almost always have an adversarial creditors' committee. Unsecured creditors can organize and hire an attorney to represent them. If they are located out of town, these creditors can convene meetings and bill their travel to the debtor company, as well as all legal fees incurred. But even a single, large unsecured creditor can make any reorganization difficult, if not impossible.

Stein and Day Publishers had one major trade creditor, Bookcrafters, a printer, that objected to every attempt by the publisher to continue any meaningful operations. Through its counsel, Bookcrafters

filed many objections to the motions filed by Stein and Day for operating funds, and, ultimately, the printer filed its own motion to convert the case to Chapter 7 to liquidate all of the publishing firm's
assets.

In his book about the bankruptcy, Sol Stein does not fully explain
what created this animosity, but regardless of the cause, its effects
were devastating. The time and effort consumed by fighting these objections were surpassed only by the enormous legal fees the fight generated to the bankrupt estate. As Stein can attest, these situations almost
always lead to the end of the operating business.

## Solicit Cooperation from Creditors by Asking for It Personally

The best prevention of this costly and damaging situation is to develop
the support of these companies early and keep it throughout the proceedings by voluntarily providing progress reports.

My occasional phone calls to creditors throughout what became a
particularly long bankruptcy case were always well received. The creditors welcomed the fact that my company, through these phone conver-
sations, displayed concern about the debts it incurred and demonstrated
it was attempting to satisfy them.

Eventually, all unsecured creditors will be given the opportunity
to vote on any reorganization plan. They must be convinced that they
are receiving, as settlement on their debt, the largest amount available.
If these vendors see future business and profits, they are more likely to
accept a plan when it is offered.

### COMMUNICATING WITH YOUR BANKER: IMPORTANT BUT DIFFICULT

Secured lenders are usually limited to banks, insurance companies, and
other formal lending institutions. Their loans are backed by an asset
such as real estate or a group of assets, such as machinery, equipment,
or inventory. The secured lenders' positions before and during a
bankruptcy proceeding differs from an unsecured lender. Once a loan
has been made, the proper state forms filed, and nonpayment of the loan
occurs, secured lenders can seize property in which they have a secured
interest. Once a bankruptcy is filed, however, the automatic stay applies
to this type of creditor also. They will normally cease all collection efforts at that time. Because most banks and other commercial lenders

have greater experience with bankruptcy, however, they are aware of their rights and will deal with the debtor through the courts.

In larger bankruptcies, you have more leverage to control the actions of the secured creditor, particularly where the assets are large and difficult to sell. For example, secured lenders have shown little interest in taking over the steel mills operated by Wheeling-Pittsburgh Steel or the LTV Steel Corporation. However, if a company has a single, large asset such as real estate, which can be easily disposed of, the easiest course of action for the lender to take for a quick out is to sell the property to satisfy the loan.

If a loan is adequately secured by collateral, the lending institution will usually not act precipitously against the debtor. A highly leveraged company, however, can expect active attention from their secured lenders unless loan payments are quickly resume. All lenders realize the value of the machinery and equipment in which they hold interest depreciates as time goes on, and that inventory is used, and they will not be patient for long.

If it is at all possible, you should resume making payments on your secured loans. Naturally, this keeps your lender happy because your loan is once again a performing asset and does not have to be written off. If you have been making payments—even reduced ones—your banker is very likely to agree to a negotiated settlement as part of your reorganization plan.

You will be filing monthly operating statements with the bankruptcy court and to each of your secured lenders, but it is also possible to maintain a cordial and cooperative relationship by adding short recaps of the progress you are making toward cutting costs or increasing markets during this period of reorganization. Ask your attorney about the advisability of this contact.

If your secured creditors are not receiving any payments and do not see any progress being made in a turnaround, they most likely will file a motion to convert your case to a Chapter 7 liquidation.

Before they can do this, they must file a motion for relief from automatic stay. Exhibit 6–2 shows a sample motion and the accompanying documents (see page 101).

There are two main criteria for the court to allow a creditor to pursue foreclosure action on the property of a debtor. The first is the lack of "adequate protection." This may mean that the value continues to depreciate, and no payments are being made to creditors so they are becoming "unsecured" in their interest. The second factor is the property is not required by the debtor. The sample motion in Exhibit 6–2 asks for permission to pursue certain personal property of the debtor.

Once conversion to Chapter 7 begins in earnest, you and your attorney will be required to expend energies to fight off this threat—energy much needed to operate and reorganize the business. If you can't get your bank (or other secured lender) on your side, your time may be short until you'll have to file a plan. After the first 120 days—the clock begins to tick.

## COMMUNICATING WITH YOUR CUSTOMERS: THE KEY TO YOUR BUSINESS FUTURE

To operate any business successfully, a company must earn and maintain the confidence of its customers. In a bankruptcy reorganization, this becomes one of the most critical, and at the same time, the most difficult goal to achieve. Your customers may feel that continuing a business relationship may mean putting their money at risk if your company closes.

Anyone who has held a ticket for a future flight on an airline that filed for bankruptcy understands the tough facts—they become an unsecured creditor of the bankrupt airline with little chance of collecting a cent. Deposits on cars, appliances, and even wedding gowns have been lost by customers in a bankruptcy filing, so the perception of risk does have merit.

Eastern Airlines addressed this problem by requesting and receiving permission from the bankruptcy court to establish an escrow account to be used to refund tickets in the event they stopped flying. They promoted this fact to potential customers—particularly travel agents who had become reluctant to issue Eastern tickets. Finding a way to address the concerns your customers may have, either real or imagined, is an important issue in retaining your customer base.

There are other potential changes in your business operation that may concern your customers. Your inventory may be lower than before the filing, or you may have to change credit policies, perhaps requiring cash deposits and no credit cards. Acknowledge these changes—you can't hide them by making excuses.

If your market is retail, your advertising becomes important, particularly when it focuses on the future and inspires confidence such as the campaign Pan Am ran in full-page ads that stated "It's Going to Be Business as Usual during our Financial Reorganization."

Even industrial concerns have used bold advertising to make a statement about their future. Wheeling-Pittsburgh Steel declared on billboards in the areas they operated that they were "Coming Back Stronger"—it was a bold and memorable statement.

With current desktop publishing capabilities, you may be able to create a newsletter to send to your customers. Although the main emphasis should be on new products and services or upcoming events, a progress report of the "restructuring" of your business is a good idea. Even if it's in a letter, word from the head of the company about how you are "streamlining" operations to "become more efficient and productive" leaves a positive impression. You needn't use the term bankrupt—perhaps the euphemism of "securing the future of the company" would be more effective. And always invite further inquiry of your customers about both your business and the current circumstances.

## MAINTAIN SUPPORT OF FRIENDS AND FAMILY

Any discussion of bankruptcy would be seriously flawed if it didn't consider the toll in human terms. A reorganization is a difficult and stressful undertaking that occurs after a prolonged period of very tough business conditions. The owners, managers, and employees are frequently run down by the experience and may believe that they cannot face another hurdle, particularly one this high. Management's confidence may be shaken and its judgment impaired.

It is the time to draw on the support of your family and friends, not the time to withdraw from those who are close. For a business owner, a bankruptcy filing may represent a steep fall and its accompanying injured pride. Confidence is an important asset in a successful reorganization, and confidence can be rebuilt by a show of faith from those who care.

The increased stress and additional work load will be felt throughout the organization. Each worker may have an individual response to the pressure and uncertainty. Great care must be taken that the frustration does not spill over into hostility between fellow workers. Everyone should be encouraged to maintain friendships, even if it requires some professional intervention, either in-house or through an industrial psychologist.

For the entrepreneur, business is an extension of family, and many times family and friends have shared the work, as well as the benefits of the successful business. Conducting the business reorganization as a joint project for all who care is a needed boost for the company, as well as the company's people.

In addition to a support system, friends can provide the benefit of an objective sounding board and a great source of free advice. It may even prove advantageous, from a business standpoint, to be seen as an underdog around whom many may rally. In fact, this could be the sales boost the company may require.

## SUMMING UP

A business exists to perform a function: to provide goods and services to individuals or other companies. This mission continues during a business reorganization. This simple fact is important to keep in focus at all times and to use as a goal to communicate to employees, vendors, customers, creditors, banks, and all individuals involved in the business reorganization. But, most important, the owner or CEO must continue to believe in this mission.

Exhibit 6–2    Sample Motion for Relief to Pursue Foreclosure Action    101

**Exhibit 6–2    Sample Motion for Relief to Pursue Foreclosure Action on the Property of a Debtor**

## In the United States Bankruptcy Court
### for the Western District of Pennsylvania

IN RE:

|                              |                        |
|------------------------------|------------------------|
| Debtors,                     | Bankruptcy No. 9–      |
| Movant,                      |                        |
| vs.                          | Motion No. 9–          |
| Respondents.                 |                        |

### Motion for Relief from the Automatic Stay

NOW COMES, _____, by its attorneys, _____ and files this Motion for Relief from the Automatic Stay based upon the following:

1. This is an action arising pursuant to a case under Title 11 of the United States Code, therefore, the Court has jurisdiction in this matter.

2. Movant is _____ of _____.

3. Respondents are _____ and _____ of _____ having instituted this Chapter _____ case by Voluntary Petition on _____ _____, 19____.

4. Respondent, _____, is the Court appointed Trustee.

5. On or about _____ _____, 19____, the Debtor, _____, entered into a Retail Installment Contract to purchase one (1) 1986 Used Bayliner, 1902 Capri one, (1) 1986 Force 125 HP, and one (1) 1986 Escort. The collateral was purchased from _____, _____. A true and correct copy of the Retail Installment Contract is attached hereto as Exhibit "A."

6. On the same date, _____ assigned its interest in the Contract to the _____. A copy of the Seller's Assignment and Warranty is attached as part of Exhibit "A."

7. As security for repayment of the purchase obligation, the Debtor granted the _____ a security interest in the collateral, as more specifically set forth in Exhibit "A." _____ perfected its interest by having its lien noted on the UCC-1 Financing Statement, a copy of which is attached hereto as Exhibit "B."

**Exhibit 6–2**  *(continued)*

8. The Debtor has defaulted under the terms and conditions of the Retail Installment Contract by failing to make payments when due.

9. There is presently due and owing an unpaid balance of $_____ plus late charges, interest and attorney's fees.

10. The Debtor has indicated his intent to voluntarily surrender the collateral.

11. _____ believes and therefore avers that there is no equity in the boat, motor and trailer and that the property is of no benefit to the estate.

12. _____ is entitled to relief from stay for cause, including lack of adequate protection.

WHEREFORE, _____ respectfully requests this Honorable Court to grant it relief from the automatic stay to proceed against the following collateral: (1) 1986 Used Bayliner, 1902 Capri, (1) 1986 Force 125 HP, and (1) 1986 Escort.

Exhibit 6–2    Sample Motion for Relief to Pursue Foreclosure Action    103

**Exhibit 6–2**    *(continued)*

## Certificate of Service

I, _____, hereby certify that I served a copy of the within Motion for Relief from the Automatic Stay upon the following parties this ____nd day of _____, 19____ by United States mail, first class, postage prepaid, addressed as follows:

_____

**Exhibit 6–2**    *(continued)*

## IN THE UNITED STATES BANKRUPTCY COURT
## FOR THE WESTERN DISTRICT OF PENNSYLVANIA

IN RE:

|                     |                          |
| ------------------- | ------------------------ |
| Debtors,            | Bankruptcy No. 9–        |
| Movant,             |                          |
| vs.                 | Motion No. 9–            |
| Respondents.        |                          |

### Order of Court

AND NOW, this _____ day of _____, 19____, upon consideration of the foregoing Motion, it is ORDERED that _____ is hereby granted relief from the automatic stay to proceed against the Debtor's collateral. The collateral is more specifically described as follows: (1) 1986 Used Bay-liner, 1902 Capri, one (1) 1986 Force 125 HP, and one (1) 1986 Escort.

_____

In the best of all possible worlds, regular performance evaluations should be done by most companies on at least an annual basis. But most of us don't do business in the best of all possible worlds, we do it in the real world. Our lives are too involved in putting out the fires that seem to spring up daily to allow the luxury of review. But once you have gone through a crisis, you realize that this process of analysis is an important tool for survival as well as growth.

A company reorganizing under Chapter 11 bankruptcy *must* take a hard, critical look at itself. It is a twofold process—the first part is an operational review and the second is a market analysis. Operational issues are discussed in this chapter, and the market questions are covered in Chapter 9.

The primary reasons for this review are

1. To determine the factors that brought the company to this point and to correct them
2. To take advantage of the opportunity to void existing contracts and leases
3. To liquidate nonperforming assets to raise cash and reduce debt

# 7

# GREATER THAN THE SUM

## ANALYZING YOUR BUSINESS TO CUT COSTS, INCREASE PROFITS, AND RAISE CASH

A "business-as-usual" attitude during a reorganization is a fast track to failure. Losses must be stopped and replaced by sufficient profits to fund a plan. The turnaround usually involves both a reduction in costs and an increase in prices. Both of these are difficult tasks and involve a great deal of hard work.

## CUT ALL UNNECESSARY COSTS

You must cut all unnecessary costs, including overhead and operating expenses. For example, are you leasing space that is more luxurious than is practical for your needs? When Allegheny International, the parent of Sunbeam-Oster filed for Chapter 11, they were leasing some very visible and costly space in Pittsburgh, which included a main showroom to display their consumer products. After the filing, they gave up these quarters and consolidated in smaller, less expensive space.

Wheeling-Pittsburgh Steel had their operating headquarters in a major office building in Downtown Pittsburgh. During their reorganization process, they moved to Wheeling, West Virginia, a move subsidized by the city because of the jobs it created. Although it inconvenienced some executives by significantly extending their commute, it cut the company's costs substantially.

The perks such as cars and club memberships that were part of the good times have to be sacrificed. This is one of a series of decisions that you will have to make, and you must be objective.

Keep in mind that you are requiring creditors to wait for payments and to take less than they are actually owed. For some of your vendors, this may be money out of their own pockets. It is understandable that they may resent this. If they see you continue to support an extravagant life-style, this can have a damaging effect, and it may make it more difficult to solicit their support. *You must prove to your creditors that you are serious about your reorganization.*

Of equal consideration is the need to continue an image that inspires confidence in your ability to succeed. Looking "down in the mouth" may work against this and turn support into pity, which you don't want. These are judgment calls.

One of the cases I reviewed in my own judicial district was an industrial fabricator whose court-mandated controls were very strict. Each month along with their operating statement, they had to submit a list of each check they wrote and the amount. Their creditors included their union for unpaid pension contributions as well as some employees for unpaid wages. And yet each and every month, checks were written for club dues including airline clubs. If it seemed odd to me, I'm sure creditors might have reacted the same way. Remember that your file is public record and may be reviewed by anyone who takes the time to do so.

Other discretionary costs such as travel must be evaluated. From a marketing and public relations standpoint, it may be more important than ever to call on customers and vendors face to face. First-class travel should be replaced by a more conservative choice of hotels and restaurants. Remember how the press made an issue out of Charles Keating, in the wake of his bankrupt savings and loan, staying in the most expensive hotel in Washington while testifying before Congress. It was just one fact that helped create the very negative image that dogged Keating and made him an unsympathetic character.

## ANALYZE YOUR COSTS AND EXPENSES

The bankrupt company must begin a turnaround once the filing is made. It is crucial that you begin to make the needed profits to fund a plan of reorganization.

An analysis of your past 3 years' operating statements will give you an overview of the problem areas you must begin to deal with immediately. Ask yourself the following questions:

- How do your expenses in each category (wages, material costs, rent, etc.) compare with other companies?
- Are your costs higher than they should be?
- Can your costs be controlled?
- Can you raise your prices to offset your cost structure?
- Can you generate more income while keeping the same overhead?

These are some of the tough questions you should be asking. This is your ship, and you must take the helm. If you started the business, you're the one who knows what it's going to take to cure it. A DIP company is a new legal entity, and you should treat it as a new start, one with opportunities for a second chance. The earliest cost-cutting moves are cosmetic, a sign to all that changes are forthcoming. Now it's time to roll up your sleeves and make substantive corrections.

## Review Every Category of Cost Including Wages

Every company has its own cost structure, which contributes to both the strengths and weaknesses of the business. It would be a mistake to take sudden action without serious consideration.

For example, in a service business, wages are the major costs. On first glance, it may seem only logical to cut wages immediately to save money. However, if your salary structure is low to begin with, further cuts may create such animosity among employees that any savings would be offset by decreased productivity.

The airline industry has struggled with this quandary for years, without great success. Many of the airlines that ultimately filed for Chapter 11 had low wage structures achieved by several rounds of concessions demanded to prevent a bankruptcy. For Eastern, Pan Am, and Continental, it didn't work. After the filing, more give-backs were demanded, and the result was a completely demoralized work force. Passengers were reluctant to continue flying with these airlines.

The savings achieved by these further wage reductions were negated by the loss of revenue owing to lower passenger loads. Eastern Airlines was a prime example. The hostility of many of Eastern employees including those who remained on strike made it very uncomfortable to fly with Eastern. At times, there were picket lines to cross, and the general level of service was very poor. Business travelers could not count on Eastern, and leisure travelers required deep discounting. Revenue miles began a downward spiral to the end; the complete liquidation of the airline was ordered by the court in early 1991.

## Explain the Facts and Promote the Long-Term Goal If Salary Cuts Are Required

It is possible to make across-the-board salary and benefit cuts on nonunion employees without any consultation. It is also possible to ask the bankruptcy court to invalidate an existing union contract. Although both acts may save money, they involve risks that could involve wholesale resignations of needed managers or union strikes that could damage your customer relations.

In the stress of the surrounding events, it is easy to lose sight of the pressure that is being felt by other employees of your company. Their jobs may be in jeopardy, and they have personal financial obligations to worry about. Most expect cuts in personnel and understand that their own incomes may be cut. If you had the distance to be objective, you would probably agree that the prospect of lower wages for an increased work load doesn't seem fair. And the longer it goes on without resolution, the more the tension grows.

If the clear indication is that a cut in salaries will be a critical factor in your business turnaround, determine the needed amounts and the length of time before the cuts may be restored and sit down face to face with those who will be affected. Selling this sacrifice is very difficult, but your non-union employees deserve a chance to discuss their concerns and thoughts with you face to face.

## Learn that the Contract Can Be Voided by the Court If Negotiations with a Union Are Not Successful

Unions are in business to collect dues and in return to secure the highest wages and benefits for their members. It is very unpopular and damaging public relations to preside over contract negotiations that conclude with give-backs. Expect the union representative that you deal with to resist your attempts at bringing labor costs down even when the company's survival is at stake. Businesses, large and small, have collapsed because of acrimonious labor relations. I still remember that on the day Eastern Airlines stopped flying, several striking mechanics put a sign up on an abandoned gate saying, "We won." It can be almost impossible to negotiate with that type of intransigence.

Before asserting your toughest legal rights, you should attempt an amicable resolution. If your employees believe in the seriousness of the situation and generally want to see the company continue, they may be willing to make concessions under their existing contract. An increase in productivity may be the equivalent of wage cut and result in the needed profits with a satisfied work force.

*If your business volume has dropped, your costs must be reduced in proportion.* The obvious administrative cuts in perks and travel are first as well as all office expense. Can you rent cheaper yet serviceable quarters? Even if you have a lease on your current building, you can request court permission to vacate that lease. Do you have excess support staff? Is it possible to replace a receptionist with a voice mail system to answer phones and take messages when no one is available?

Be more careful when you begin cutting closer to the bone in the area of sales, marketing, and advertising. Customers are a key to your future success so you must continue to attract, serve, and retain them.

## Ask the Court to Invalidate Supply Contracts that You No Longer Wish to Continue

At a time when natural gas prices were dropping, Columbia Gas was obligated to purchase gas at prices too high to pass on to customers. After repeated unsuccessful attempts at negotiating lower prices, Columbia filed for Chapter 11 protection and had the court cancel their supply contract. The losses that Columbia suffered endangered their ability to meet debt load and other financial commitments so they found themselves in bankruptcy court. The suppliers who refused to settle their dispute amicably now found themselves forced to accept lower prices and went unpaid for purchases made before the filing. Chances are that they will accept less than 50% of what is owed so it is difficult to imagine why this couldn't be settled out of court.

If you have committed to transactions that, if completed, would jeopardize your company, you might want to have the court invalidate the contracts. This doesn't mean that the supplier can be forced to sell to you at a lower price or even sell to you at all. But it does mean that you can look for an alternative supplier that may prove more advantageous. Consider what alternatives you may have before proceeding against any contractual relationship. Will other vendors be wary of dealing with you? How many choices do you have? But if this is a critical problem for your company, you may have to take that risk.

## Determine Whether Your Leased Equipment and Vehicles Are Still Needed

The next phase of your business analysis is to consider the value of all leases you maintain on machinery, equipment, and vehicles. You may have taken on the equipment over the years or at a time when you were gearing up for an expansion that is no longer a reality.

Do you still need to have company cars? Are the vehicles too pricey for your current situation? Do you still require as many trucks? Now is the time to cut back because the court will allow you to reject any existing leases. The sacrifices that you make now may be the ones that allow you to reorganize your company successfully, and eventually you can replace what you are currently giving up. Hanging on to a luxurious company car now can be foolish—if you lose the company, you lose the car.

You should also review all other machinery and equipment that your company leases. You want to trim but not cut back to the bone. If your business level is low now but you expect to be able to revitalize your sales effort, don't give up the equipment you'll need to fulfill new orders. Remember that as a bankrupt company, it may be difficult to replace the equipment.

There isn't any legal reason that a company can't lease equipment to a business reorganizing under bankruptcy laws, but few will be willing to do so—particularly in the early months after the filing. Eventually you will establish new business relationships to replace any existing ones that may have been damaged. But this takes time so don't give up equipment you may need.

**Terminate equipment leases.**    Once you have decided to terminate a lease, you will file a motion with the court. This is a relatively straightforward procedure and will be easily accomplished. Your attorney will prepare a motion documenting the items in question and who was the original lessor and the terms of the lease. Your motion will simply state that you wish to reject the lease and return the property to its original owner. It is possible that the judge will sign the order without a hearing but even if a hearing is required, there is little chance that it will be more than perfunctory. You may even be able to ship the equipment in question back to its owner collect, which will help during this time of great financial strain.

The lessor may then turn around and file these charges associated with the return as an administrative charge against the case, which must be paid at the time of reorganization. At least you will have additional time, and the fact is that few companies will take the time and effort to file for these charges.

## Reject Real Estate Leases

You may file a motion to reject real estate leases as excessive overhead costs. If excessive overhead costs created your financial problems, you can use the same procedure to reject any lease you wish to break. Take the time now to consider your real estate needs not just for the immediate time but over the next year or so. Are you going to be shrinking your company further in the near term? If so, now is the time to give up the space when you can break a lease without penalty.

Conversely, if you expect to use additional space as you begin to recover, it is prudent to hold on to the property now if you can manage it. It can be very difficult to lease real estate during a bankruptcy proceeding. Most landlords are not willing to rent to a bankrupt company.

My case lasted more than 4 years because of other legal proceedings. After a while, I almost forgot about it. We rented space in a deteriorating building, and we wanted to move. I found more appropriate space and negotiated a lease. I did not disclose that we were in Chapter 11; I wasn't thinking about it, and it is not required by any law. When the landlord found out, he was very angry and refused to consider us as tenants.

Our new rent would have been less than the one we were meeting regularly so it would have been no problem for him. His space remained vacant for more than a year, and we stayed in business long beyond the 3-year lease I wanted. It was his loss, but now looking back, I wish I would have had a more open negotiation and could have moved at that time.

The reaction of the landlord is typical, and you should consider this when you project your needs over the next few years. It may be difficult to keep the exact amount of space you need, but it is worthwhile to attempt just that.

## CONSIDER SELLING EXCESS ASSETS TO RAISE CASH

The ultimate goal of a Chapter 11 proceeding is to reduce debt and debt payment. To that end, selling assets to pay down your existing debt is a good idea. All of the same cautions stated earlier in this chapter regarding leased equipment should apply.

Do you need this asset for the current level of your business? Will you need it in the short-term or midterm future to revive your business? If the answer to these questions is no, then you can proceed with a sale of assets. If yours is a retail or consumer company, it is important that it doesn't begin to look as if you are liquidating the company because you may lose the confidence of your customers and that could further damage the company.

## Consider Selling Real Estate

Does your company own real estate that has appreciated in value and might be easily sold to an investor? It is likely that you have borrowed against this property, and it may be these payments that have created part of your financial problems.

Even if your company wants to remain in the property, it may be possible to sell it to an investor and lease it back for your use. Remember that the secured creditor will get the proceeds of the sale, but this will reduce your obligation to this creditor; once the reorganization is complete, your debt service will be smaller. If the property is no longer worth the balance of the loan, the remaining debt will become unsecured and be paid along with all unsecured creditors for a fraction of the original amounts.

The process you use to accomplish the sale of any asset is the same. Your attorney will file a motion with the court seeking approval of the sale. The motion will include all pertinent information about the transaction beyond the name of the buyer and the selling price. Other issues to be disclosed will be:

- All terms of the sale
- What your company may be doing in lieu of the property sold such as leasing it back
- Where the proceeds of the sale will be applied
- What effect, if any, their transaction will have on your reorganization

Once the motion is filed, the various groups, such as secured creditors and the committee of unsecured creditors, are notified that this action is about to occur. If there isn't a creditors committee then the 10 largest unsecured creditors will be sent notice. They will be given a period of several weeks to file any objections with the court before a hearing. Also in most cases a public notice in the paper is required to solicit any higher or better offers.

Motions objecting to the sale may be filed for reasons other than the price of the asset. Objecting motions may relate how the distribution of the proceeds of the sale or the company plans to continue to the point of their official reorganization.

The court will set a hearing date of the original motion and at that time will hear objections. A copy of a motion for a "proposed sale" is shown in Exhibit 7–1 (see page 118).

*The prospect of available cash will activate attorneys looking for fees.* Many bankruptcies continue on for years, and attorneys representing both the debtor and the creditors may not get paid for a long period if at all. So it is not surprising that fee petitions may surface after an asset is sold, and cash will become available. Creditors' attorneys (creditors not entitled to the proceeds of the sale) may make noises about objecting to the transaction for a variety of reasons. This threatened delay could ultimately ruin the sale so you'll want to avoid it. Don't be surprised if a simple solution is achieved, which includes using some money to pay legal fees. This will have an impact on you so you should be aware of what's being negotiated.

If you have a $100,000 loan securing a building and you manage to sell it for $80,000, the value of your secured loan is established at the actual selling price. If the attorneys carve out $20,000 in fees, you will be left with the debt in the amount of the $20,000 deduction and no asset. A bankruptcy will bring several of these painful realities to bear, but you should not feel that you do not have the right to object. You are the debtor "in possession," and your attorney should be representing your best interest. There comes a time when some lawyers protect each other to the potential detriment of their client. Consider this carefully.

## SELL OTHER ASSETS IN THE SAME MANNER
## AS THE REAL ESTATE TRANSACTION

Any equipment or vehicles you might have that are excess to your usage may be sold with the permission of the court. If you have a secured loan covering these items, the proceeds will be treated as in the previous real estate transaction.

If the assets are not covered by any security agreement, there is room for creative negotiation. An active creditors' committee will make demands that proceeds go to an escrow account, which will ultimately be distributed to them. The court has latitude in deciding these issues.

If you can develop a compelling argument, you may be able to convince your judge to release a large portion of the proceeds to your company as working capital. Eastern Airlines sold planes, landing rights, and airport gates in the earlier days of their Chapter 11 stay. The funds were put into an escrow account in part to be used to fund a plan of reorganization. Because of continuing losses, however, Eastern went to court repeatedly to dip into these funds, always over the strenuous objections of their creditors. Each time, the company came prepared with a plan and projections that showed how the cash would be used to fund a turnaround into a profitable airline. And each time, Eastern management prevailed.

In almost all cases, a profitably operating company is preferable to a liquidation because it will pay more to the creditors over a period. In addition, an operating company saves jobs and contributes to the local economy and tax base. Many judges take this into consideration when making their decision. The purpose of the law was to "allow a company to rehabilitate itself," and if this is your theme, it won't fall on deaf ears in front of the court. Your serious and earnest efforts at a turnaround will be rewarded by the cooperation of the court.

It is a good idea to keep some of the funds in hand to use as a part of your reorganization plan. All categories of debt can be paid off in a period of up to 6 years, but you will find a plan will receive better acceptance if it includes an up-front payment as a sweetener. The chance of receiving some of the debt on confirmation can motivate the unsecured creditors to vote in favor of the plan even if they have little faith in the prospect of the company; a liquidation would pay all of the proceeds to administrative, priority, and secured creditors, and leave nothing for distribution to the unsecured (or their attorneys).

Many attorneys representing unsecured creditor committees get agreement with their clients that if there aren't funds available in the end, legal fees will be paid by creditors. So creditor companies stand not only to lose the amount of the debt, they may also have to pay legal fees. The counsel representing these companies appreciate a plan that has funds to pay these fees.

## FIND HIDDEN ASSETS THAT CAN BE TURNED INTO CASH

Do you have inventory that hasn't moved in a long time? First call your customers and offer discount for immediate sale. Then try your competitors—they may have markets that you lost. In addition, try salvage dealers, but don't expect to get anything over 10 cents on the dollar. If you've been in business for any length of time, you would be surprised at the accumulation you may have that can be turned into cash. A word of caution: Don't liquidate yourself to a dangerous level; realize that replacements may be difficult to find.

There are assets you may have that you haven't even considered. What about the rights to a trademark name or logo that has customer recognition? These may be in an area where your company is no longer active. Perhaps a friendly competitor would value these rights as well as a customer list for the product line.

Do you have one location that you can sell to an entrepreneur who could then operate it more profitably than you are doing at this time? Perhaps you are paying others to work the shop, and a new owner is willing to invest sweat equity.

There are an unlimited number of possibilities, and you must allow yourself to consider them. Your goal is to reduce debt and consolidate operations into a profitable entity. I was surprised that airlines could sell landing rights and gate space. They were not assets in the traditional sense but worth something nevertheless.

Your DIP company is a new legal entity—make it into a new venture, and you will begin the process you need to effect a successful restructuring.

## CONSIDER SELLING THE ENTIRE COMPANY OR A MAJOR PART OF IT

When a very weakened Pan Am Airlines filed a Chapter 11 petition in early 1991, few gave the company much chance at a successful reorganization. In the months that followed the filing, evidence mounted that the problems faced by Pan Am were too complicated to solve, particularly in an overall weak economy. Their route structure was insufficient to feed enough of a load factor for profitable operations.

Whereas Eastern Airlines had begun to carve itself up early on by selling off assets piecemeal, Pan Am management focused on keeping the airline intact and finding a buyer for the entire operation. The Eastern strategy failed, but Pan Am succeeded in selling the bulk of the airline to Delta including the shuttle between Boston-Washington and most of their foreign routes. And there will remain a small South American carrier still called Pan Am. Because many employees will keep their jobs, this appears to be a good solution.

## Two Ways to Sell a Company—as a Going Concern or as an Asset Sale

If you find a buyer who sees real possibility of a good future for your business, perhaps with some additional working capital to upgrade operations or inventory, you may be able to sell it intact. You would most likely not be paid for the assets; instead, all cash would be used to fund a plan. But you would be out from any personal liability or personal guarantees. And it is possible that your services would be required during the transition and perhaps beyond—you may even continue to manage the company for an absentee owner. These can be tough decisions because of the traumatic nature of the entire bankruptcy process.

You may be able to find a partner to put in money to fund your plan if you give him or her a percentage of the ownership. The format of negotiations for a deal at this phase is very straightforward much as it would be if there weren't any bankruptcy involved. It's what happens before the deal is consummated that is different. You must file a motion and proceed with notice to creditors and a hearing on the deal before you can complete it.

A good deal in the eyes of the creditor is one that makes them whole again, but they are very likely to accept less if the new company seems secure to them. Be sure that any potential buyer understands the possibility of delay—if everything goes smoothly, it will take 60 to 90 days to close the deal. Any objections could add as much as 2 to 3 months to this process.

*Keep in mind that an asset sale does not assume existing debt.* Just as in any sale of assets, the buyer is purchasing one item or a series of items free and clear of all debt. Even if you are selling every machine, vehicle, and inventory that is involved in your business, the money proceeds that comes from this sale goes into a pot that is disbursed to creditors according to their standing depending on any security agreements that cover what is being sold. It is possible to end up this type of a sale with some liability still existing. Moreover, you may not be able to discharge this liability except with a personal bankruptcy filing. Be careful about securing releases from creditors for the amounts they are accepting in full settlement of debt.

## Beware of Vultures that Circle a Bankruptcy Looking for a Distress Sale

There will come a day when the stress becomes overwhelming, and all you think about is making everything go away. You think you will accept any offer just to get on with your life. You should be aware that there are people (call them investors if you must) that look around for just such a distress sale. They have no intention of playing completely fair—they want to take advantage of your desperation.

Mine came in the form of an attorney (who turned out to be disbarred) and his business partner. We met several times before they made an offer, and as I reviewed this offer in a quiet moment, it became evident that they would get the assets and I would get the debt.

There are some who might be tempted to try to negotiate with these characters, but I don't recommend it. They aren't interested in the real value of your business that may be there. The professional "bone picker" won't pay that price—they thrive on the deals they can make with an eye to turning a quick profit.

## SUMMING UP

A major overhaul is needed if your company is to streamline enough to continue in profitable operation. Leave no stone unturned as you review operations and use of available assets. Clean house of every unnecessary cost to produce all available profits needed to fund a plan of reorganization. Sell assets no longer needed to reduce overall debt and create a reserve of money needed to pay creditors at confirmation.

**Exhibit 7–1    Sample Motion for Sale of Property**

IN THE UNITED STATES BANKRUPTCY COURT
FOR THE WESTERN DISTRICT OF PENNSYLVANIA

IN RE:

Bankruptcy No. 91–
Chapter
Motion No. 91–

Debtor(s)

Movant.

### Motion for Sale of Personal Property Free and Clear of Liens, Claims and Encumbrances

NOW COMES, _____, trustee, by and through his counsel, _____ and files this Motion for Sale of Personal Property Free and Clear of Liens, Claims and Encumbrances based upon the following:

1. These proceedings were commenced by the filing of a Voluntary Petition on _____ _____, 19____.

2. The case was subsequently converted to proceeding under Chapter _____ and on _____ _____, 19____ _____ was appointed as the Chapter _____ Trustee.

3. Among the assets of the Debtor's estate are vehicles and equipment more particularly described as follows:

    a. 1975 International flatbed dump truck
    b. 1972 White triaxle truck
    c. 1977 Ford tractor
    d. Yale 4,000 lb. forklift
    e. storage trailer

4. The trustee has obtained an offer of $_____ from _____ located at _____ for the above referenced property. The trustee is holding hand money from the offeror in the amount of $_____.

5. To the best of the trustee's knowledge and information there are no lines on the personal property which is the subject matter of this sale.

6. All creditors will be given notice of the sale and any existing liens and encumbrances shall be divested and shifted to the balance of the net proceeds derived from said sale.

7. The assets are being sold without warranty by the trustee, "as is" and the purchaser shall be required to pay

Exhibit 7-1    Sample Motion for Sale of Property    119

**Exhibit 7-1**  *(continued)*

100% of the sale price within five (5) days of the entry of an Order confirming said sale.

    8.   The trustee believes that this sale is in the best interest of the estate.

    WHEREFORE, _____, trustee, respectfully requests this Honorable Court to enter its Order confirming the sale of the above-described property to _____ or such persons or entities making a higher or better offer on the date of sale.

**Exhibit 7–1**  *(continued)*

## Certificate of Service

I, _____, hereby certify that I served a true and correct copy of the within Motion for Sale of Personal Property Free and Clear of Liens, Claims and Encumbrances upon the following parties this _____ day of _____, 19___ by United States mail, first class, postage prepaid, addressed as follows:

_____

Exhibit 7–1     Sample Motion for Sale of Property     **121**

**Exhibit 7–1**  *(continued)*

## IN THE UNITED STATES BANKRUPTCY COURT
## FOR THE WESTERN DISTRICT OF PENNSYLVANIA

IN RE:

|                | Bankruptcy No. 91– |
|                | Chapter |
|                | Motion No. 91– |

Debtor(s)

Movant.

### Order of Court

AND NOW, this _____ day of _____, 19____ at
_____, _____, upon consideration of the Trustee's Mo-
tion for Sale of Personal Property Free and Clear of Liens,
Claims and Encumbrances, it appearing that an appropriate
Notice of Sale has been transmitted to all creditors and
parties-of-interest, and that advertisement has been
waived, after hearing upon said Motion, it is Ordered that
the property of the Debtor consisting of:

  a. 1975 International flatbed dump truck
  b. 1972 White triaxle truck
  c. 1977 Ford tractor
  d. Yale 4,000 lb. forklift
  e. storage trailer

is hereby sold free and clear of liens to _____ for a total consideration of $_____.

It is further Ordered that the trustee make, execute and
deliver to the purchaser above named, the necessary documents required to transfer title to the property purchased
upon compliance with the terms of sale.

_____

The two goals of a reorganization are, first, to restructure your debt and, second, to have a profitable going concern that can retire the debt. Much of the focus of this book has been on the first task because the bankruptcy scenario is unfamiliar and needs a great deal of explanation.

Critical to the success of your reorganization is the second piece of the puzzle—the ongoing concern. This fact is ignored by many attorneys involved in the proceedings as they make demands on your time and financial resources that threaten the entire business. And it is easy for you and your other managers to get so caught up in the proceedings that you lose sight of the business itself.

# 8
# KEEP YOUR EYE ON THE BALL

## RUNNING YOUR COMPANY AS A VIABLE CONCERN

This is the beginning of a new life for your company, and you must show employees, managers, customers, and vendors that you believe in your joint future. And the fact is that you do have a new chance to have a future.

It is frequently asserted that few companies make it through the Chapter 11 bankruptcy process as if this proves that the task is virtually impossible. That isn't true—it is possible to reorganize successfully if you equip yourself with knowledge of the process and keep your operating company as your top priority.

Eastern Airlines entered bankruptcy in the midst of a strike, deeply in debt, and with a poor public image. The adversarial groups that formed immediately were as active as any case might ever have to face. And if all of these negative factors weren't enough, the general economic condition for the airline industry was poor. And yet, Eastern almost made it! Rather than using this as evidence that it is almost impossible to negotiate a Chapter 11 successfully, it should be viewed as a tribute to the very real chance that a business has to right itself and get on with its business life.

The reason that Eastern came close to a turnaround had to do with new leadership that turned its attention and focus to the airline business and not the bankruptcy. Late in the case, the judge appointed Martin Shugrue as the trustee of Eastern taking the airline away from the control of Continental Airlines. Shugrue spent his early days winning over employees and then devised a plan to win back its customer base. The airline upgraded its service and lowered prices for business travelers, and its passenger loads began to grow. When Shugrue went to court to seek additional time and release of funds for operating capital, his tactic was not legal maneuvering but rather to point out the progress of the operating company. The judge responded favorably to this progress and allowed Shugrue much time to effect the change. In the end, however, it didn't happen in part because the "company recovery" process began too late and in part because the Gulf War was battering healthy airlines, giving little chance for the weak ones.

## LEARN TO REFOCUS ON YOUR COMPANY'S MISSION

A company exists to produce goods or provide a service to its customers. And to make a profit. That is the reason that you went into business and the reason that you should stay in business. Whatever the cause of the financial problems that required you to file for Chapter 11 protection, it is your business that must return to financial viability so that once you have achieved your reorganization plan, the company can meet its new obligations.

Whether the company is very small with only one or two employees, or it has multiple locations with hundreds of employees, each worker is a key factor in the future. You are not alone in experiencing the stress of the filing; it effects everyone associated with the company. Your employees must believe that the main goal will remain the product or service that they have been involved in producing, selling, or servicing. They may have additional work required by the bankruptcy filing, but their main job will continue to be the work of the company itself. And the quality of the work has never been more important than it is now. And the reemphasis of what your company does best will improve the attitude of everyone including your customers who have never been more important than they are at this time.

## MAKE SURE THAT YOUR CUSTOMERS BELIEVE THAT YOU'RE STILL IN BUSINESS

Just a decade ago, the filing of a bankruptcy petition was viewed as the end of a business. The airline industry is a good example of how the public perception has changed. When Braniff Airlines filed (the first time) it ceased flying in advance of a court appearance, to protect its planes from being repossessed. The airline never got back off the ground because banks were uncooperative, and customers refused to purchase tickets. Customers who hold unfulfilled contracts with a company such as deposits or tickets for flights become unsecured creditors of the bankruptcy and seldom recover any of their money. This is a difficult if not impossible market to win back.

Eastern Airlines also stopped flying after they filed their petition for protection, but the reason was an employee strike rather than the bankruptcy. Within a week, the airline had begun limited operation, and within a few months they were back to a fully expanded company, although smaller than previously. Eventually, Eastern began to win back their passengers in part because it became a better airline and in part because it created a way to guarantee its customers money in the event of a total failure.

Currently, the public hardly reacts to Chapter 11 with the view that this is the beginning of the end. TWA announced a planned filing 6 months in advance with hardly a ripple.

You know your customers, and you know your industry. If bankruptcy has become a fact of life, as it has in retailing, you may not face adverse reactions. But if it is an unusual occurrence in your market or if you are in a very small town, you may face more adverse reactions from customers.

Regardless of the initial attitude you face, your task and the task of all of your employees is to work hard to maintain the confidence of existing customers as well as to win over new ones.

## CREATE NEW WAYS TO PROMOTE YOUR BUSINESS

At a time when your financial resources may be very limited, you need to increase the ways you promote your business, and its product or service. Holding a series of sales can be a very risky way to accomplish this goal. First, you need to keep all of the operating margins you can, and deep discounting works counter to this end. Second, an aggressive sale promotion could take on the look of a "going-out-of-business" sale and that is just the type of event you want to avoid. Even if it becomes necessary to liquidate inventory to raise cash, birthday sales and holiday sales project a better message.

## Increase Your Visibility in the Business Community

Looking for free promotion can be an important contribution to your success at this time. Getting the name of your company in front of the public is a factor in the strategy of your belief in the future. Do you do volunteer work or sit on boards? Now is the time to be seen, not to hide. What has happened to your company does not make you less of a valuable contributor to your community. Every time you appear at a meeting or an event, the name of your company is visible, and the exposure is free.

The year before my filing, I was elected to a very senior nonprofit board of directors in Pittsburgh. It was a group of very high-ranking corporate executives. I felt a bit sheepish when I attended my first meeting after my company went into bankruptcy reorganization. It is normal to experience a loss of confidence in your own ability. My own history had been full of volunteer activity including other board participation, and I soon became comfortable again. I wasn't able to provide much in the way of financial support, but I was still able to contribute.

There are many community activities that beg for support, and it may be that you, along with your managers and employees, could volunteer. You could form a bowling team in a charity match or have a company entrant in a corporate Olympics. What better way to give and get at the same time! Customers will respect you for making the effort, and your group will be proud of itself. So, in addition to the free press, this can be an important first step in regaining your confidence.

My company responded in other ways to the needs we saw. Times have been generally tough in the metal industry, and when one of our smaller customers experienced their own financial distress and could no longer buy our products, I looked around for any excess inventory and sent it to them with a note wishing them well. I still have the thank you note that described us as "a special group of people." At that time we didn't feel special but the note helped.

## Contribute Products (or Services) to Charity Auctions for the Free Advertising

Most public television stations have an annual auction to raise operating funds for the station. Because most older inventory brings only pennies on the dollar, you should use it to bring greater advantage. It may be worth a more substantial contribution depending on how the station potentially reaches your market.

At one time you may have been able to spend liberally for advertising and promotion and perhaps you didn't give each expenditure thoughtful consideration, but those days are gone. Money can be replaced by creativity and resourcefulness. In the end, your focus will be concentrated on your target market by necessity, and the reality is that you will get bigger bang for lesser dollar.

Perhaps as important is the change in perception that happens when you begin to look beyond your own problems and consider the situation of others. What happens to anyone going through the stress of bankruptcy is loss of control, fear of the unknown, and a dose of self-pity. The way to gain control is to learn about and control the process, and it is difficult to feel sorry for yourself if you change your focus to the really tough situations others may face.

## Make Sure All Promotions Project Confidence in the Future, Not Preparation for Failure

The ongoing goodwill and patronage of your existing customer base is critical to your success. You need to focus your limited resources of time and money to finding new customers to build on your existing base. Serve that base with confidence in the future.

For example, a frequent buyers club that offers rewards for purchasing now gives the message that you expect to be around. Also, if yours is an older established company, publicizing that history makes the tradition seem strong enough to transcend the current difficulty.

My manufacturing company sells to distributors that work on annual contracts. They have committed to a stable price and delivery source for their customers. If they lost faith in our ability to deliver, it would be foolhardy for them not to seek to replace us as a vendor. During some very tough periods, we had to struggle and work exceptionally hard to maintain that business. It was critical to our plan to reorganize successfully.

### LOOK FOR NEW MARKETS WHERE THE PROFIT MARGINS ARE BETTER

A turnaround means that you convert a loss into a profit. Part of this can be achieved by the cost-cutting techniques described in Chapter 7 of this book. Much of the savings will flow directly to your bottom line. You may also have to absorb some increased costs, however, because of your status as a Chapter 11 bankruptcy case.

In many cases, your credit will be limited or nonexistent. You will buy supplies, material, or product in smaller quantities. This may raise your unit cost as well as the freight and handling involved. Pay attention to all of the changes in direct operating costs so that they stay in control.

If your existing product or service sales are not going to provide the increased profits you require, then explore new products or services that do have potential. Do not view your business from the perspective of a caretaker merely preventing any further damage. Look at the future from the standpoint of its possibilities, and try to exploit the opportunities.

Enlist your customers as well as your vendors in the task of revitalizing your company. It is in their best interest to retain a dependable source of supply or a good customer, and it is your job to convince them that you will continue to serve in that role.

If your customers realize how committed your entire company is to serving their needs, they may bring new opportunities to your operation and allow you the chance to increase both revenue and profits. After my filing, I began to ask for additional business more aggressively than I had previously, and my efforts were rewarded with new orders with higher profit margins.

I worked to design new products with better material use and that also added directly to my bottom line. These projects required closer work with our suppliers, and although they were also creditors of our bankruptcy, the effect of this association was positive. First, they did assist in my task to improve the results of my operation. Second, these creditors became positive about our chances of success and voted in favor of our plan of reorganization. Finally, the improved relationship resulted in my company getting a new line of open credit after the plan was approved.

## DEVELOP NEW SOURCES OF SUPPLY

Even if your existing vendors are reluctant to continue to do business with you, that doesn't mean that your company can't effect a successful turnaround. As you continue to try to win back these suppliers, you can begin to find new ones to replace them. Perhaps you will find better material or products at more favorable pricing. You will be a new customer to these vendors, and they will work to get and keep your business. New lines can energize an existing business into a more active marketing effort so this may be just what is needed to kick start a "second chance."

You do not have to disclose to your new vendor that you are operating under Chapter 11 protection. You can't deny it if asked, but you aren't required to volunteer the information. New suppliers make their own decisions about credit granting, and because the information about your legal status is public knowledge, any credit reporting agency will include it in their data. The responsibility belongs to the creditor, not you.

However, it is usually valuable to be candid because a vendor who finds out *after* they've shipped you an open account may feel that you did have an obligation to disclose, and they may shut down a promising business relationship. Your checks will most likely say "debtor in possession" after your name (or at least DIP) so your legal status is evident to anyone. My company was solicited by a new material supplier after we went into Chapter 11, and we began purchasing small quantities of material on open account. We wrote our "DIP" checks for payment and nothing was said for 3 years. Literally 1 week after our plan was approved, and we were about to emerge from bankruptcy, this company noticed and questioned me on this fact. I treated their concern seriously, but I must admit to being amused by it.

## PLAN AHEAD FOR THE DAY YOU WILL EMERGE FROM BANKRUPTCY

Your financial distress is the disease, a Chapter 11 reorganization is the treatment, and your emergence is the cure. Perhaps you will only need a mild course of rest and medication, or you may need very radical surgery. Anyone who has faced medical problems knows how tough it can be to get better. But you should also remember that the day comes when recovery is complete, and the pain is all but a memory. Then you begin to live your life in a normal way again.

Your bankruptcy will also end—it is hoped with a restructured business still in operation. Neither one of you will be exactly the same again. Keep your faith in this future, and make plans for how you will operate when the day comes. It is a good goal.

During the years we were under court protection, we operated in a deteriorating building in a deteriorating neighborhood. My plan was to move as soon as it appeared that our plan would be approved. And I should have followed that plan! I didn't because it took 6 months for me to believe that it really was over. We are now in a much-improved environment—it is a warmer, safer, and more productive setup. It is an appropriate reward for all the hard work. Plan on one for your company.

## SUMMING UP

Even though the bankruptcy adds to your work load, you must take the time and effort to keep your business going in the right direction. Make sure what you are fighting to save continues to be worth the battle. Life will return to normal when the case is concluded.

# III

## THE
## REORGANIZATION

### A CHANCE TO START OVER

From the day your company seeks protection from the Bankruptcy Court, the clock begins ticking toward the day that you must file your plan of reorganization. For the first 120 days, you have the exclusive right to file your plan. If there are no extraordinary events in your case, the court will most likely grant an additional 60 days on your request. You should begin to think about what repayment terms you might be able to offer as soon as it is possible.

There are several classes of creditors to be considered, although members of each class must be treated equally, you may make different arrangements with each class. For example, if you offer 30% to holders of unsecured claims, all such claims will receive that amount; you can't pay more to one creditor than another in that same category. But you may pay 100% to priority claims and only 30% to unsecured claims.

There are four broad categories of creditors. Some are acquired during the course of the case, and the amounts may change from the filing of the petition to the filing of the plan. The primary categories are as follows:

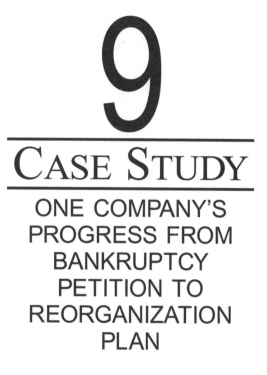

# 9

# CASE STUDY

## ONE COMPANY'S PROGRESS FROM BANKRUPTCY PETITION TO REORGANIZATION PLAN

1. *Administrative*—These are professional fees and other debts acquired after the filing of the case.

2. *Priority unsecured claims*—These are normally certain unpaid wages, and all government taxes due and owing.

3.  *Secured claims*—These are all debts that are secured with property equal or greater to the value of the claim.
4.  *Unsecured claims*—These are all debts that are uncovered by any type of security.

For the purpose of following how a company's numbers change from one phase of the process to the next and finally to the reorganized phase, I have chosen the automotive supplier described in chapter 1 as an example. Many of the numbers have been streamlined for purposes of clarity. The goal is to understand how the numbers move from a generalized profit and loss statement and balance sheet to a bankruptcy petition and then on to the plan of reorganization.

Exhibit 9–1 is a 2-year operating statement, and Exhibit 9–2 is a balance sheet for the XYZ Industrial Supply. The problems this company faced were typical of those in the "rust belt" with sales dropping, overhead remaining as a higher proportion of costs, and losses mounting. The figures on the balance sheet show a deficit net worth—and the deficit would be even greater if the inventory were priced at a liquidation value that would reduce it by two-thirds. So keep in mind that most of these numbers are subject to interpretation.

Exhibit 9–3, on page 140, is the complete bankruptcy filing of the XYZ Corporation, which explains how the operation is described in a petition. All debts are now categorized as priority unsecured, secured, and unsecured without priority. At the time of this filing, XYZ numbers were

| | |
|---|---|
| Priority claims | $ 42,450 |
| Secured claims | 171,000 |
| Unsecured claims | 304,000 |

The total debt at this point is $517,000, which would be impossible for this company to retire even over an extended period. Substantial restructuring must be done for the plan of reorganization to be feasible and approved.

Exhibit 9–1    Sample Operating Statement    135

**Exhibit 9–1    Sample Operating Statement**

| XYZ Industrial Supply<br>Dearborn, Michigan: Profit and Loss | | |
|---|---|---|
| | **1989** | **1990** |
| Income | | |
| Sales | $1,600,000 | $1,100,000 |
| Less returns | 163,000 | 147,000 |
| Disc. | 31,460 | 8,600 |
| Net sales | 1,405,540 | 944,400 |
| Expenses | | |
| Cost of goods | | |
| Material | 800,000 | 510,000 |
| Direct labor | 131,000 | 120,000 |
| Delivery | 13,000 | 12,000 |
| Inbound freight | 7,200 | 5,400 |
| Total | 951,200 | 647,400 |
| Gross profit | 454,340 | 297,000 |
| Administrative | | |
| Salaries | 188,000 | 145,000 |
| Mortgage | 34,800 | 34,800 |
| Utilities | 19,000 | 19,000 |
| Office expense | 9,600 | 9,600 |
| Legal and accounting | 10,000 | 10,000 |
| Travel | 22,500 | 18,000 |
| Entertainment | 36,000 | 27,000 |
| Debt service | 18,000 | 18,000 |
| Taxes | 21,000 | 19,000 |
| Employee benefits | 28,000 | 24,000 |
| Total | 386,900 | 324,400 |
| Net before tax | 67,440 | (27,400) |

**Exhibit 9–2   Sample Balance Sheet**

**XYZ Industrial Supply,
Dearborn, Michigan: Balance Sheet—1989**

| | | |
|---|---:|---:|
| Cash in bank | $ 27,000 | |
| Accounts receivable | 63,400 | |
| Inventory | 476,000 | |
| Real estate | 150,000 | |
| Vehicles | 27,000 | |
| | 743,400 | |
| Accounts payable | | $363,000 |
| Withholding taxes | | 29,000 |
| Real estate loan | | 115,000 |
| Short term loan | | 35,000 |
| Vehicle loan | | 21,000 |
| Note payable stockholder | | 85,000 |
| | | 648,000 |
| Net worth | 95,000 | |

**Balance Sheet—1990**

| | | |
|---|---:|---:|
| Cash in bank | 21,000 | |
| Accounts receivable | 47,265 | |
| Inventory | 342,000 | |
| Real estate | 150,000 | |
| Vehicles | 24,000 | |
| | 584,265 | |
| Accounts payable | | 304,000 |
| Withholding taxes | | 21,000 |
| Real estate loan | | 105,000 |
| Short-term loan | | 35,000 |
| Vehicle loan | | 18,000 |
| Note payable stockholder | | 101,000 |
| | | 584,000 |
| Net worth | 265 | |

## REDUCE DEBT BEFORE YOU REORGANIZE

At the time of the filing, XYZ had only $8,000 per month available to retire any debt plan it might propose. It would be imprudent to commit more than half of that amount to servicing the debt they had incurred. Interest alone on $517,000 at 9% would have been over that amount. There were two critical tasks to accomplish in advance of any plan. The first was to trim overhead, and the second was to sell assets to reduce debt. The following steps were taken:

1. XYZ sold the owned building to an investor for $134,000—less than the listed value but sufficient to pay off the mortgage. This sale had two benefits: it reduced debt and overhead. XYZ then rented the building at $1,500 month on a 5-year lease. This resulted in the following positive changes:

   reduced priority debt to $35,650

   reduced secured debt to $56,000

   increased monthly cash excess to $9,790

   increased available cash by $12,000, which the bank allowed XYZ to keep as working capital. Most banks have cross-collateralization clauses on loans, which would allow them to apply any overage to other loans. This bank released the excess funds to help in the reorganization.

2. XYZ sold excess inventory with a book value of $118,000 in one lump sum to a competitor for $42,000, which was placed in an escrow account for the purpose of funding the reorganization plan. This reduced the book value inventory to approximately $260,000.

3. XYZ reduced annual salaries (including direct wages) by $24,000, thereby increasing available excess cash to approximately $12,000 per month with $6,000 a safe amount to commit to the plan.

In addition to these positive steps, some debt was incurred because of the increased fees for an outside accountant required to draw monthly statements. This was required by the court, and the cost was $800 per month, which was an administrative debt of $4,800 at the time the plan was filed. There were also additional legal fees of $1,900, making the total in this class $6,700.

Therefore, at the time of the reorganization plan, the financial position of XYZ Corporation looked something like this:

| | |
|---|---:|
| Available cash | $ 42,000 |
| Monthly available cash | 6,000 |
| | |
| New debt claims | |
| Administrative | 6,800 |
| Priority unsecured | 35,650 |
| Secured claims | 56,000 |
| Unsecured claims | 304,000 |

## HOW TO BEGIN A PAYMENT PLAN FOR CREDITORS

Typically, administrative debts are paid at confirmation, and the others will have a payout of up to 6 years at a negotiated interest rate. A walk-through of the process of how you could arrive at a feasible plan would be done by taking your available cash and applying it class by class to determine how much would be available to offer to the unsecured creditors. For the XYZ Corporation, the steps would be

1.  Pay to administrative claims $6,800 on confirmation—available cash now reduced to $35,200.
2.  Pay to priority claims 25% on confirmation ($8,912.50) and the balance of $26,737.50 over 48 months at 8% interest. Monthly payments will be $668.00 ($111.00 interest and $557.00 principal.) Available cash is now reduced to $26,288.00.
3.  Pay to secured creditors 20% of their claims ($11,200.00) on confirmation and the balance of $44,800.00 over 48 months at 9% interest. Payments will be $1,269.00 ($336.00 interest and $933.00 principal.) Cash is reduced to $15,088.

XYZ has now committed $26,912.50 of the original $42,000 cash fund to the first three categories. They have also agreed to payments of $1,937 monthly to priority and secured creditors. There is $15,000 in cash and $4,000 per month available for distribution to the unsecured creditors. Their claims total $304,000, so a conservative approach would be to offer them 25% on $76,000 with 10% of it up front ($7,600.00) and the balance over 48 months at 9% interest ($495.00 interest and $1,375.00 principal) for a total payment of $1,870 per month.

It is not prudent to commit all of your cash in your plan because it may take months for the confirmation to be complete, and the professional fees will increase. There is also the need for working capital, so keep some in reserve.

Payments must be reasonable enough to be met even during downturns or temporary cash flow problems because a default is very serious and could result in a conversion to liquidation.

As for the XYZ Industrial Supply Corporation, the reorganization afforded by Chapter 11 has allowed them to reduce a debt of more than $500,000 to one of $175,000 payable over 4 years. Their overhead is manageable even with the debt repayment offered by their plan.

Once this schedule has been conceived, a disclosure statement will be filed (Chapter 10) and a plan of reorganization (Chapter 11) will be sent to creditors along with a ballot on which to record their vote.

## SUMMING UP

First you must determine the amount of debt you have in each class of creditor, then you begin to allocate your resources starting with the administrative debt. Be conservative but fair as you allocate your resources, and remember that you must have some balance left to offer the unsecured creditors. The typical range in a tight case is from 10% to 30%.

**Exhibit 9–3    Sample Bankruptcy Petition, XYZ Industrial Supply**

## UNITED STATES BANKRUPTCY COURT
## NORTHERN DISTRICT OF MICHIGAN

### Voluntary Petition

IN RE _____    NAME OF JOINT DEBTOR

**XYZ Industrial Supply**

ALL OTHER NAMES _____    NO JOINT DEBTOR

SOC. SEC./TAX I.D. NO. _____

**00-000000**

STREET ADDRESS OF DEBTOR _____

**100 First Street**
**Dearborn, MI 33104**

COUNTY OF PRINCIPAL PLACE OF BUSINESS

**Dearborn**

MAILING ADDRESS OF DEBTOR _____

**100 First Street**
**Dearborn, MI 33104**

LOCATION OF PRINCIPAL ASSETS OF BUSINESS DEBTOR

### Venue

Debtor has had its principal place of business in this District for 180 days immediately preceding the date of this petition.

### Information Regarding Debtor

| | |
|---|---|
| TYPE OF DEBTOR<br>**Corporation Not Publicly Held**<br>NATURE OF DEBT<br>**Business**<br>A. TYPE OF BUSINESS<br>**Retail/Wholesale**<br>B. BRIEFLY DESCRIBE NATURE OF BUSINESS<br>**Sale of tools, bearings**<br>**and general industrial supplies**<br>STATISTICAL/ADMINISTRATIVE INFORMATION<br>Debtor estimates that there will be funds available for distribution to unsecured creditors. | CHAPTER OF BANKRUPTCY CODE UNDER WHICH THE PETITION IS FILED<br>**11**<br>FILING FEE<br>Filing fee attached |
| | ATTORNEY NAME AND ADDRESS<br>**Michael L. Martin, Esquire**<br>**204 Craig Street**<br>**Dearborn, MI 33104** |

| | RANGE | (SARD CODE) | ATTORNEYS DESIGNATED TO REPRESENT DEBTOR |
|---|---|---|---|
| NO. OF CREDITORS | 16-49 | (2) | |
| ASSETS (thousands) | 500-999 | (4) | THIS SPACE FOR COURT USE ONLY |
| LIABIL. (thousands) | 500-999 | (4) | |
| NO. OF EMPLOYEES | 08 | (2) | |
| EQUITY SEC. HOLDERS | 1-19 | (2) | |

Exhibit 9–3    Sample Bankruptcy Petition, XYZ Industrial Supply    141

Name of Debtor: **XYZ Industrial Supply**
  Case No.:

---

Debtor intends to file a plan within the time allowed by statute, rule, or order of the court.

### Prior Bankruptcy Cases Filed within Last 6 Years

NONE

### Pending Bankruptcy Case Filed by Partner or Affiliate

NONE

### Request for Relief

Debtor requests relief in accordance with the chapter of title 11 United States Code specified in this petition.

### Signatures
### Attorney

---

**Michael L. Martin, Esquire**            Date

---

### Partnership or Corporate Debtor

I declare under penalty of perjury that the information provided in this petition is true and correct, and that the filing of this petition on behalf of the debtor has been authorized.

---

**Joe Johnson**                    Date
**President**

### Exhibit A

Exhibit A is attached and made a part of this Petition.

**Exhibit 9–3**   *(continued)*

| SCHEDULE A—REAL PROPERTY | |
|---|---|
| Description and location of property | Current market value of debtor's interest in the property without deducting any secured claim |
| Nature of debtor's interest in property | Amount of secured claim |

18,000 sq. feet warehouse/office building

Debtor's interest:    **150,000.00**
Total debt on property:    **115,000.00**

Location: 100 First Street, Dearborn, Michigan
33104
Secured creditor(s): Michigan Savings Bank
Possession: In debtor's possession.

Total:    **150,000.00**

Exhibit 9–3    Sample Bankruptcy Petition, XYZ Industrial Supply    143

**Exhibit 9–3**  *(continued)*

## SCHEDULE B—PERSONAL PROPERTY

| Type of property<br><br>Description and location of property | Current market value of debtor's interest in property without deducting any secured claim |
|---|---|

1. Cash on hand.
   NONE

2. Checking, savings, or other financial accounts, cer-
   tificates of deposit, or shares in banks, savings and
   loan, thrift, building and loan, and homestead associa-
   tions, or credit unions, brokerage houses, or coopera-
   tives.
   **Michigan Savings Bank**
   **212 Grant Street**
   **Lansing, MI 33102**

   Debtor's interest:    **21,000.00**
   Total debt on property:    **0.00**

   Possession: **In debtor's possession.**

3. Security deposits with public utilities,  telephone
   companies, landlords, and others.
   **$70.00—Allied Electric Company**
   **$75.00—Dearborn Gas Company**
   **$85.00—Dearborn Light Company**

   Debtor's interest:    **230.00**
   Total debt on property:    **0.00**

   Possession: **In debtor's possession.**

4. Household goods and furnishings, including audio,
   video, and computer equipment.
   NONE

5. Books, pictures, and other art objects, antiques,
   stamp, coin, record, tape, compact disc, and other collections or collectibles.
   NONE

6. Wearing apparel.
   NONE

7. Furs and jewelry.
   NONE

8. Firearms and sports, photographic, and other hobby
   equipment.
   NONE

9. Interests in insurance policies.
   NONE

**Exhibit 9–3**   *(continued)*

---

10. Annuities.
    NONE

11. Interests in IRA, ERISA, Keogh, or other pension or profit sharing plans.
    NONE

12. Stock and interests in incorporated and unincorporated businesses.
    NONE

13. Interests in partnerships or joint ventures.
    NONE

14. Government and corporate bonds and other negotiable and non-negotiable instruments.
    NONE

15. Accounts receivable.
    NONE

16. Alimony, maintenance, support, and property settlements to which the debtor is or may be entitled.
    NONE

17. Other liquidated debts owing debtor including tax refunds.
    NONE

18. Equitable or future interests, life estates, and rights or powers exercisable for the benefit of the debtor other than those listed in Schedule of Real Property.
    NONE

19. Contingent and noncontingent interests in estate of a decedent, death benefit plan, life insurance policy, or trust.
    NONE

20. Other contingent and unliquidated claims of every nature, including tax refunds, counterclaims of the debtor, and rights to setoff claims.
    NONE

21. Patents, copyrights, and other intellectual property.
    NONE

22. Licenses, franchises, and other general intangibles.
    NONE

23. Automobiles, trucks, trailers, and other vehicles or accessories.

    **3  1970 Mac trucks**
    **1   88 Ford Tempo**
    **1   86 Buick Regal**

|  | |
|---|---|
| Debtor's interest: | **24,000.00** |
| Total debt on property: | **21,000.00** |

Exhibit 9–3    Sample Bankruptcy Petition, XYZ Industrial Supply    145

**Exhibit 9–3**   *(continued)*

---

Location: **In debtor's possession.**
Secured creditor(s): **Michigan Savings Bank**

24. Boats, motors, and accessories.
   NONE
25. Aircraft and accessories.
   NONE
26. Office equipment, furnishings, and supplies.
   NONE
27. Machinery, fixtures, equipment, and supplies used in business.
   NONE
28. Inventory.
   **Tools, bearings, and industrial supplies.**
   Debtor's interest: **342,000.00**
   Total debt on property: **269,060.00**

Location: **In debtor's possession.**
Secured creditor(s): **Triple A Tools—$186,400.00**
**Capital Bearing Co.—$31,465.00**
**Colonial Products—$14,230.00**
**Carlton Industrial Supply—$36,965.00**

29. Animals.
   NONE
30. Crops—growing or harvested.
   NONE
31. Farming equipment and implements.
   NONE
32. Farm supplies, chemicals, and feed.
   NONE
33. Other personal property of any kind not already listed.
   NONE
   Total: **387,230.00**

**Exhibit 9–3** *(continued)*

## SCHEDULE C—PROPERTY CLAIMED AS EXEMPT

Debtor selects the exemptions to which debtor is entitled under:

NONE

Exhibit 9–3    Sample Bankruptcy Petition, XYZ Industrial Supply    **147**

**Exhibit 9–3**   *(continued)*

| SCHEDULE D—CREDITORS HOLDING SECURED CLAIMS | |
| --- | --- |
| Creditor's name and complete mailing address including zip code | Amount of claim without deducting value of collateral |
| Date claim was incurred, nature of lien, and description and market value of property subject to the lien | Unsecured portion, if any |

Account no.:
**Michigan Savings Bank**
**212 Grant Street**
**Lansing, MI 33102**

Amount of claim:   **115,000.00**
Unsecured:          **0.00**

Incurred: **12/1/87**
Nature of lien: **Mortgage on business property.**
Claim is: **Fixed and liquidated.**
Collateral description: **18,000 sq. feet warehouse/office building.**
Collateral market value: **150,000.00**

Account no.
**Michigan Savings Bank**
**212 Grant Street**
**Lansing, MI 33102**

Amount of claim:   **35,000.00**
Unsecured:          **0.00**

Incurred: **12/01/89**
Nature of lien: **Line of credit-working capital.**
Claim is: **Fixed and liquidated.**
Collateral description: **Accounts receivables, inventory and equipment.**
Collateral market value: **100,000.00**

Account no.:
**Michigan Savings Bank**
**212 Grant Street**
**Lansing, MI 33102**

Amount of claim:   **21,000.00**
Unsecured:       **3,000.00**

Incurred: **1988–89**
Nature of lien: **Vehicle loans.**
Claim is: **Fixed and liquidated.**
Collateral description: **3   1970 Mac trucks**
**1   1988 Ford Tempo**
**1   1986 Buick Regal**
Collateral market value: **18,000.00**

Subtotal this page:   **171,000.00**
Total:   **171,000.00**

**Exhibit 9–3**  *(continued)*

## SCHEDULE E—CREDITORS HOLDING
## UNSECURED PRIORITY CLAIMS

### TYPES OF PRIORITY CLAIMS:

Wages, Salaries, and Commissions

Wages, salaries, and commissions, including vacation, severance, and sick leave pay owing to employees, up to a maximum of $2000 per employee, earned within 90 days immediately preceding the filing of the original petition, or the cessation of business, whichever occurred first, to the extent provided in 11 U.S.C. sec. 507(a)(3).

Contributions to Employee Benefit Plans

Money owed to employee benefit plans for services rendered within 180 days immediately preceding the filing of the original petition, or the cessation of business, whichever occurred first to the extent provided in 11 U.S.C. sec. 507(a)(4).

Certain Farmers or Fishermen

Claims of certain farmers or fishermen, up to a maximum of $2000 per farmer or fisherman, against the debtor, as provided in 11 U.S.C. sec. 507(a)(5).

Deposits by Individuals

Claims of individuals up to a maximum of $900 for deposits for the purchase, lease, or rental of property or services for personal, family, or household use, that were not delivered or provided. 11 U.S.C. sec. 507(a)(6).

**X** Taxes and Certain Other Debts Owed to Governmental Units

Taxes, customs duties, and penalties owing to federal, state, and local governmental units as set forth in 11 U.S.C. sec. 507(a)(7).

Exhibit 9–3    Sample Bankruptcy Petition, XYZ Industrial Supply    **149**

**Exhibit 9–3**  *(continued)*

| SCHEDULE E—CREDITORS HOLDING UNSECURED PRIORITY CLAIMS | |
|---|---|
| Creditor's name and complete mailing address including zip code | Amount entitled to priority |
| Date claim was incurred and consideration for claim | Total amount of claim |

1. Wages, Salaries, and Commissions.
   NONE
2. Contributions to Employee Benefit Plans.
   NONE
3. Certain Farmers or Fishermen.
   NONE
4. Deposits by Individuals.
   NONE
5. Taxes and Certain Other Debts Owed to Governmental Units.

| | |
|---|---|
| Account no.: **Dearborn County Tax** Dearborn County Court Dearborn, MI 33103 | Priority amount: **6,800.00** Amount of claim: **6,800.00** |

Incurred: **1988–90**
Consideration for claim: **Real Estate Tax.**
Claim is: **Fixed and liquidated.**

| | |
|---|---|
| **Dearborn County Sheriff Dearborn County Court Dearborn, MI** | DUPLICATE LISTING OF DEBT— COLLECTION AGENCY OR ATTORNEY FOR: **Dearborn County Tax** |

| | |
|---|---|
| Account no.: **State of Michigan Bureau of Employment Lansing, MI 33102** | Priority amount: **14,050.00** Amount of claim: **14,050.00** |

Incurred: **1989–90**
Consideration for claim: **Unemployment tax**
Claim is: **Fixed and liquidated.**

Subtotal this page: **20,850.00**

**Exhibit 9–3**   *(continued)*

**State Attorney General**          DUPLICATE LISTING OF DEBT—
**Lansing, MI 33102**              COLLECTION AGENCY OR ATTORNEY
                                     FOR:   **State of Michigan**

Account no.:                       Priority amount: **21,600.00**
**U.S. Government**                 Amount of claim: **21,600.00**
**Internal Revenue**
**District Director**
**Detroit, MI 33101**

                    Incurred: **1988–90**
Consideration for claim: **Withholding tax.**
             Claim is: **Fixed and liquidated.**

**U.S. Attorney**                   DUPLICATE LISTING OF DEBT—
**Internal Revenue**               COLLECTION AGENCY OR ATTORNEY
**District Director**                   FOR:   **U.S. Government**
**Detroit, MI 33101**

                              Subtotal this page: **21,600.00**
                                       Total: **42,450.00**

Exhibit 9-3    Sample Bankruptcy Petition, XYZ Industrial Supply    151

**Exhibit 9-3**   *(continued)*

| SCHEDULE F—CREDITORS HOLDING UNSECURED NONPRIORITY CLAIMS | |
| --- | --- |
| Creditor's name and complete mailing address including zip code | Amount of claim |
| Date claim was incurred and consideration for claim. If claim is subject to setoff, so state. | |

Account no.:                                    Amount of claim:    **7,600.00**
**A T & T**
**P.O. Box 41005**
**Dearborn, MI 33104**

Incurred: **1990**
Consideration for claim: **Long distance telephone service.**
Claim is: **Fixed and liquidated.**

**A B C Collections**              DUPLICATE LISTING OF DEBT—
**889 Adams Street**              COLLECTION AGENCY OR ATTORNEY
**Dearborn, MI 33104**          FOR: **A T & T**

Account no.:                                    Amount of claim:    **2,420.00**
**Allied Electric**
**P.O. Box 72365890**
**Lansing, MI 33102**

Incurred: **1990**
Consideration for claim: **Electric service.**
Claim is: **Fixed and liquidated.**

Account no.:                                    Amount of claim:    **12,400.00**
**American Express**
**P.O. Box 7784**
**Phoenix, AZ 89770**

Incurred: **10-11/90**
Consideration for claim: **Misc. charges incurred for**
                                          **business expenses.**
Claim is: **Fixed and liquidated.**

Account no.:                                    Amount of claim:    **31,465.00**
**Capital Bearing Co.**
**4487 Washington Street**
**St. Louis, MO 88702**

Incurred: **1990**
Consideration for claim: **Purchase of bearing inventory.**
Claim is: **Fixed and liquidated.**

**Exhibit 9–3**    *(continued)*

---

Account no.:                          Amount of claim:    **36,905.00**
**Carlton Industrial Suppl**
**9741 Monroe Drive**
**Flint, MI 33105**

Incurred: **10/30/90**
Consideration for claim: **Purchase of inventory items.**
Claim is: **Fixed and liquidated.**

Subtotal this page:    **90,790.00**

Account no.:                          Amount of claim:    **14,230.00**
**Colonial Products**
**8890 Jefferson Street**
**Dearborn, MI 33104**

Incurred: **2/10/90**
Consideration for claim: **Purchase of inventory items.**
Claim is: **Fixed and liquidated.**

**Bob Kennedy, Esquire**          DUPLICATE LISTING OF DEBT—
**5874 Madison Ave.**            COLLECTION AGENCY OR ATTORNEY
**Dearborn, MI 33104**          FOR: **Colonial Products**

Account no.:                          Amount of claim:    **1,500.00**
**Dearborn Gas Company**
**P.O. Box 889742**
**Dearborn, MI 33104**

Incurred: **1990**
Consideration for claim: **Gas service.**
Claim is: **Fixed and liquidated.**

Account no.:                          Amount of claim:    **1,400.00**
**Dearborn Light Company**
**P.O. Box 6894**
**Dearborn, MI 33104**

Incurred: **1990**
Consideration for claim: **Electric service.**
Claim is: **Fixed and liquidated.**

Account no.:                          Amount of claim:    **3,950.00**
**Granger Supply**
**897 Harrison Street**
**Detroit, MI 33101**

Incurred: **1989–90**
Consideration for claim: **Purchase of inventory items.**
Claim is: **Fixed and liquidated.**

---

Exhibit 9–3    Sample Bankruptcy Petition, XYZ Industrial Supply    153

**Exhibit 9–3**   *(continued)*

---

Account no.:                              Amount of claim:    **3,200.00**
**Michigan Bell**
**P.O. Box 485293**
**Lansing, MI 33102**

                          Incurred: **1987–90**
Consideration for claim: **Telephone service.**
              Claim is: **Fixed and liquidated.**


      Subtotal this page:                          **24,280.00**

Account no.:                              Amount of claim:    **2,530.00**
**Travel Go Round**
**P.O. Box 9508**
**Columbus, OH 42588**

                          Incurred: **1990**
Consideration for claim: **Travel expense incurred by XYZ**
                          **Representatives in the course of**
                          **business.**
              Claim is: **Fixed and liquidated.**

Account no.:                              Amount of claim: **186,400.00**
**Triple A Tools**
**445 Market Street**
**Chicago, IL 44510**

                          Incurred: **1/18/90**
Consideration for claim: **Purchase of tool inventory.**
              Claim is: **Fixed and liquidated.**
   Claiming setoff of: **2,300.00**

   **John Smith, Esquire**        DUPLICATE LISTING OF DEBT—
   **789 Lincoln Street**         COLLECTION AGENCY OR ATTORNEY
   **Chicago, IL 44510**          FOR: **Triple A Tools**




                          Subtotal this page: **188,930.00**
                                       Total: **304,000.00**

---

**Exhibit 9–3**   *(continued)*

| SCHEDULE G—EXECUTORY CONTRACTS AND UNEXPIRED LEASES | |
|---|---|
| Name and mailing address, including zip code, of other parties to lease or contract. | Description of contract or lease and nature of debtor's interest. State whether lease is for nonresidential real property. State contract number of any government contract. |

CONTRACTS TO MICHIGAN SAVINGS BANK FOR PURCHASE OF VEHICLES

Exhibit 9–3    Sample Bankruptcy Petition, XYZ Industrial Supply    155

**Exhibit 9–3**  *(continued)*

| SCHEDULE H—CODEBTORS | |
| --- | --- |
| Name and address of codebtor | Name and Address of creditor |
| NONE | |

**Exhibit 9–3** *(continued)*

## CURRENT MONTHLY INCOME AND
## EXPENDITURES OF BUSINESS DEBTOR

CURRENT MONTHLY INCOME

    Source:      Total Current Monthly Income:   91,666.66
    **XYZ sales and accounts receivable**

CURRENT MONTHLY EXPENSES

| | |
|---|---|
| 1. Rent/mortgage payment | 2,900.00 |
| 2. Repair/upkeep | 800.00 |
| 3. Electricity and heating fuel | 1,171.00 |
| 4. Water and sewer | 212.00 |
| 5. Telephone | 750.00 |
| 6. Garbage | 70.00 |
| 7. Security | 0.00 |
| 8. Other utilities: | |
|    None | |
| 9. Insurance | 1,130.00 |
| 10. Taxes: | |
|    Taxes | 1,583.33 |
| 11. Installment payments on equipment: | |
|    None | |
| 12. Rental/lease payments: | |
|    None | |
| 13. Maintenance of equipment: | |
|    None | |
| 14. Advertising | 160.00 |
| 15. Bank service charges | 0.00 |
| 16. Interest | 0.00 |
| 17. Depreciation | 0.00 |
| 18. Office expenses | 800.00 |
| 19. Dues and publications | 0.00 |
| 20. Laundry or cleaning | 0.00 |
| 21. Supplies and materials | 350.00 |
| 22. Freight | 450.00 |
| 23. Travel and entertainment | 3,750.00 |
| 24. Wages and salaries | 12,083.33 |
| 25. Commissions | 0.00 |
| 26. Employee benefit programs | 2,000.00 |
| 27. Pensions/profit-sharing plans | 0.00 |

Exhibit 9–3    Sample Bankruptcy Petition, XYZ Industrial Supply    157

**Exhibit 9–3**   *(continued)*

28. Production costs:

| | |
|---|---|
| **Cost of goods** | 42,500.00 |
| **Direct labor** | 10,000.00 |
| **Delivery** | 1,000.00 |
| **Debt service** | 1,500.00 |

29. Other expenses:

None

Total Current Monthly Expenses    83,209.66
Excess of Income over Expenses     8,457.00

(The penalties for making a false statement or concealing property is a fine of up to $500,000 or imprisonment for up to 5 years or both.—18 U.S.C. secs. 152 and 3571.)

## Declaration

**I, Joe Johnson, president** for **XYZ Industrial Supply** named as the debtor in this case, declare under penalty of perjury that I have read the foregoing **Summary and Schedules**, consisting of 17 sheets, and that it is true and correct to the best of my information and belief.

Signature: _____          Date: _____

    **Joe Johnson**
    **president**

**Exhibit 9–3**    *(continued)*

# UNITED STATES BANKRUPTCY COURT
## FOR THE NORTHERN DISTRICT OF MICHIGAN

## Summary of Schedules

| Schedule Name | No. Sheets | Assets | Liabilities | Other |
|---|---|---|---|---|
| X (mark if attached) | | | | |
| —— A—Real Property | 1 | 150,000.00 | | |
| —— B—Personal Property | 3 | 387,230.00 | | |
| —— C—Property Claimed as Exempt | 1 | | | |
| —— D—Creditors Holding Secured Claims | 1 | | 171,000.00 | |
| —— E—Creditors Holding Unsecured Priority Claims | 3 | | 42,450.00 | |
| —— F—Creditors Holding Unsecured Nonpriority Claims | 3 | | 304,000.00 | |
| —— G—Executory Contracts and Unexpired Leases | 1 | | | |
| —— H—Codebtors | 1 | | | |
| —— Current Income of Corporate Debtor | N/A | | | 91,666.66 |
| —— Current Expenditures of Corporate Debtor | 2 | | | 83,206.66 |

| | | | | |
|---|---|---|---|---|
| Summary Sheet | 1 | * * * * * * * * * * * * * * * * * * * * * * * * * * * | | |
| Total No. Sheets | 17 | * * * * * * * * * * * * * * * * * * * * * * * * * * * | | |
| Total Assets → | | | 537,230.00 | * * * * * * * * |
| Total Liabilities → | | | 517,450.00 | * * * * * * * * |
| Total No. of Creditors → | | | 18 | * * * * * * * * |
| Excess Income (if any) → | | | | 8,457.00 |

Exhibit 9–3    Sample Bankruptcy Petition, XYZ Industrial Supply    159

**Exhibit 9–3**  *(continued)*

Michael L. Martin, Esquire
MARTIN & MARTIN
204 Craig Street
Dearborn, MI 33104
Attorney for the Petitioner

### UNITED STATES BANKRUPTCY COURT
### FOR THE NORTHERN DISTRICT OF MICHIGAN

IN RE                                    Case No.:
**XYZ Industrial Supply**
Debtor                                   **Exhibit A**
Debtor's Employer's Tax
Identification No.: **00-000000**        Chapter **11**

1. Debtor's employer identification number is: **00-000000**
2. If any of debtor's securities are registered under section 12 of the Securities and Exchange Act of 1934, the SEC file number is:
3. The following financial data is the latest available information and refers to debtor's condition on:
   a. Total assets: **537,230.00**
   b. Total liabilities: **517,450.00**

|  |  | Approximate number of holders |
|---|---:|---:|
| Fixed, liquidated unsecured debt: | **171,000.00** | **3** |
| Contingent secured debt: | **0.00** | **0** |
| Disputed secured claims: | **0.00** | **0** |
| Unliquidated secured debt: | **0.00** | **0** |

|  |  | Approximate number of holders |
|---|---:|---:|
| Fixed, liquidated secured debt: | **346,450.00** | **15** |
| Contingent unsecured debt: | **0.00** | **0** |
| Disputed unsecured claims: | **0.00** | **0** |
| Unliquidated unsecured debt: | **0.00** | **0** |
| Number of shares of preferred stock: |  |  |
| Value: | **0.00** |  |
| Number of shares of common stock: |  |  |
| Value: | **0.00** |  |

Comments, if any:
NONE

**Exhibit 9–3** *(continued)*

4. Brief description of debtor's business:
   **Sale of industrial supplies.**

5. List the name of any person who directly or indirectly owns, controls, or holds with power to vote, 20% or more of the voting securities of debtor:

   NONE

6. List the names of all corporations, 20% or more of the outstanding voting securities of which are directly or indirectly owned, controlled, or held, with power to vote, by debtor:

   NONE

Exhibit 9–3    Sample Bankruptcy Petition, XYZ Industrial Supply    **161**

**Exhibit 9–3**   *(continued)*

Michael L. Martin, Esquire
MARTIN & MARTIN
204 Craig Street
Dearborn, MI 33104
Attorney for the Petitioner

## UNITED STATES BANKRUPTCY COURT
### FOR THE NORTHERN DISTRICT OF MICHIGAN

IN RE                                    Case No.:

**XYZ Industrial Supply**
Debtor                                   **List of Creditors**
Debtor's Employer's Tax                  **Holding the 20**
Identification No.: **00-000000**        **Largest Unsecured Claims**
                                         Chapter **11**

Following is the list of the debtor's creditors holding the
20 largest unsecured claims. This list is prepared in accordance with Fed. R. Bankr. P. 1007(d) for filing in this chapter 11 case. This list does not include (1) persons who come
within the definition of insider set forth in 11 U.S.C. sec.
101(30), or (2) secured creditors unless the value of the
collateral is such that the unsecured deficiency places the
creditor among the holders of the 20 largest unsecured
claims.

| Name of creditor and complete mailing address including zip code | Name, telephone number, and complete mailing address including zip code of employee, agent, or department of creditor familiar with claim who may be contacted | Amount of claim |
|---|---|---|
| Nature of claim (trade debt, bank loan, type of judgment, etc.) | | Value of security |
| Indicate if claim is contingent, unliquidated, disputed, or subject to setoff | | |

**Exhibit 9–3**    *(continued)*

```
Creditor:              Contact person:      Claim:    7,600.00
A T & T                A T & T
P.O. Box 41005         P.O. Box 41005
Dearborn, MI 33104     Dearborn, MI 33104

    Nature of claim: Long distance telephone service.
          Claim is: Fixed and Liquidated.
Claiming setoff of:      0.00


Creditor:              Contact person:      Claim:    2,420.00
Allied Electric        Allied Electric
P.O. Box 72365890      P.O. Box 72365890
Lansing, MI 33102      Lansing, MI 33102

    Nature of claim: Electric service.
          Claim is: Fixed and Liquidated.
Claiming setoff of:      0.00


Creditor:              Contact person:      Claim:   12,400.00
American Express       American Express
P.O. Box 7784          P.O. Box 7784
Phoenix, AZ 89770      Phoenix, AZ 89770

    Nature of claim: Misc. charges incurred for business
                     expenses.
          Claim is: Fixed and Liquidated.
Claiming setoff of:      0.00


Creditor:              Contact person:      Claim:   31,465.00
Capital Bearing Co.    Capital Bearing Co.
4487 Washington St.    4487 Washington St.
St. Louis, MO 88702    St. Louis, MO 88702

    Nature of claim: Purchase of bearing inventory.
          Claim is: Fixed and Liquidated.
Claiming setoff of:      0.00


Creditor:              Contact person:      Claim:   36,905.00
Carlton Industrial     Carlton Industrial
  Suppl.                 Suppl.
9741 Monroe Drive      9741 Monroe Drive
Flint, MI 33105        Flint, MI 33105

    Nature of claim: Purchase of inventory items.
          Claim is: Fixed and Liquidated.
Claiming setoff of:      0.00
```

Exhibit 9–3    Sample Bankruptcy Petition, XYZ Industrial Supply    163

**Exhibit 9–3** *(continued)*

Creditor:                    Contact person:        Claim:  **14,230.00**
**Colonial Products    Colonial Products**
**8890 Jefferson St.    8890 Jefferson St.**
**Dearborn, MI 33104   Dearborn, MI 33104**

     Nature of claim: **Purchase of inventory items.**
           Claim is: **Fixed and Liquidated.**
  Claiming setoff of:     **0.00**


Creditor:                    Contact person:        Claim:   **6,800.00**
**Dearborn County Tax  Dearborn County Tax**
**Dearborn County      Dearborn County**
  **Court                Court**
**Dearborn, MI 33103   Dearborn, MI 33103**

     Nature of claim: **Real Estate Tax.**
           Claim is: **Fixed and Liquidated.**
  Claiming setoff of:     **0.00**


Creditor:                    Contact person:        Claim:   **1,500.00**
**Dearborn Gas Co.     Dearborn Gas Co.**
**P.O. Box 889742      P.O. Box 889742**
**Dearborn, MI 33104   Dearborn, MI 33104**

     Nature of claim: **Gas service.**
           Claim is: **Fixed and Liquidated.**
  Claiming setoff of:     **0.00**


Creditor:                    Contact person:        Claim:   **1,400.00**
**Dearborn Light Co.   Dearborn Light Co.**
**P.O. Box 6894        P.O. Box 6894**
**Dearborn, MI 33104   Dearborn, MI 33104**

     Nature of claim: **Electric service.**
           Claim is: **Fixed and Liquidated.**
  Claiming setoff of:     **0.00**


Creditor:                    Contact person:        Claim:   **3,950.00**
**Granger Supply       Granger Supply**
**897 Harrison St.     897 Harrison St.**
**Detroit, MI 33101    Detroit, MI 33101**

     Nature of claim: **Purchase of inventory items.**
           Claim is: **Fixed and Liquidated.**
  Claiming setoff of:     **0.00**

**Exhibit 9–3**  *(continued)*

Creditor:                Contact person:         Claim:    **3,200.00**
**Michigan Bell**          **Michigan Bell**
**P.O. Box 485293**        **P.O. Box 485293**
**Lansing, MI 33102**      **Lansing, MI 33102**

Nature of claim: **Telephone service.**
        Claim is: **Fixed and Liquidated.**
Claiming setoff of:     **0.00**


Creditor:                Contact person:         Claim:    **3,000.00**
**Michigan Savings**        **Michigan Savings**
  **Bank**                   **Bank**
**212 Grant Street**       **212 Grant Street**
**Lansing, MI 33102**      **Lansing, MI 33102**

Nature of claim: **Vehicle loans.**
        Claim is: **Fixed and Liquidated.**
Claiming setoff of:     **0.00**
        Collateral
        description: **3 1970 Mac trucks**
                     **1 1988 Ford Tempo**
                     **1 1986 Buick Regal**
    Collateral value:     **18,000.00**


Creditor:                Contact person:         Claim:    **14,050.00**
**State of Michigan**       **State of Michigan**
**Bureau of**              **Bureau of**
  **Employment**            **Employment**
**Lansing, MI 33102**      **Lansing, MI 33102**

Nature of claim: **Unemployment tax.**
        Claim is: **Fixed and Liquidated.**
Claiming setoff of:     **0.00**


Creditor:                Contact person:         Claim:    **2,530.00**
**Travel Go Round**        **Travel Go Round**
**P.O. Box 9508**          **P.O. Box 9508**
**Columbus, OH 42588**     **Columbus, OH 42588**

Nature of claim: **Travel expense incurred by XYZ**
                 **Representatives in the course of**
                 **business.**
        Claim is: **Fixed and Liquidated.**
Claiming setoff of:     **0.00**

Exhibit 9–3    Sample Bankruptcy Petition, XYZ Industrial Supply    **165**

**Exhibit 9–3**   *(continued)*

---

Creditor:                Contact person:        Claim: **186,400.00**
**Triple A Tools**       **Triple A Tools**
**445 Market Street**    **445 Market Street**
**Chicago, IL 44510**    **Chicago, IL 44510**

   Nature of claim: **Purchase of tool inventory.**
          Claim is: **Fixed and Liquidated.**
  Claiming setoff of: **2,300.00**


Creditor:                Contact person:        Claim:   **21,600.00**
**U.S. Government**       **U.S. Government**
**Internal Revenue**     **Internal Revenue**
**District Director**    **District Director**
**Detroit, MI 33101**    **Detroit, MI 33101**

   Nature of claim: **Withholding tax.**
          Claim is: **Fixed and Liquidated.**
  Claiming setoff of: **0.00**


(The penalties for making a false statement or concealing
property is a fine of up to $500,000 or imprisonment for up
to 5 years or both.—18 U.S.C. secs. 152 and 3571.)

### Declaration

**I, Joe Johnson, president** for **XYZ Industrial Supply** named as
the debtor in this case, declare under penalty of perjury
that I have read the foregoing **List of Creditors Holding 20
Largest Unsecured Claims,** consisting of 7 sheets, and that
it is true and correct to the best of my information and
belief.


Signature: _____    Date: _____
        **Joe Johnson**
        **President**

---

**Exhibit 9–3** *(continued)*

Michael L. Martin, Esquire
MARTIN & MARTIN
204 Craig Street
Dearborn, MI 33104
Attorney for the Petitioner

### UNITED STATES BANKRUPTCY COURT
### FOR THE NORTHERN DISTRICT OF MICHIGAN

| | |
|---|---|
| IN RE | Case No.: |
| **XYZ Industrial Supply** | |
| Debtor | Statement of Financial |
| Debtor's Employer's Tax | Affairs |
| Identification No.: **00-000000** | Chapter **11** |

1. Income from employement or operation of business.

   State the gross amount of income the debtor has received from employment, trade, or profession, or from operation of debtor's business from the beginning of this calendar year to the date this case was commenced. State also the gross amounts received during the two years immediately preceding this calendar year.

   |  |  |  |  |
   |---|---|---|---|
   | This year: | **January** 1990 | Amount: | **1,100,000.00** |
   | Source: | **XYZ Industrial Supply** | | |
   | Last year: | **January** 1989 | Amount: | **1,600,000.00** |
   | Source: | **XYZ Industrial Supply** | | |
   | Previous year: | **January** 1988 | Amount: | **1,760,000.00** |
   | Source: | **XYZ Industrial Supply** | | |
   | Previous year: | **January** 1987 | Amount: | **0.00** |
   | Source: | | | |

2. Income other than from employment or operation of business.

   State the amount of income received by the debtor other than from employment, trade, profession, or operation of the debtor's business during the two years immediately preceding the commencement of this case.

   |  |  |  |  |
   |---|---|---|---|
   | This year: | **January** 1990 | Amount: | **0.00** |
   | Source: | | | |
   | Last year: | **January** 1989 | Amount: | **0.00** |
   | Source: | | | |
   | Previous year: | **January** 1988 | Amount: | **0.00** |
   | Source: | | | |
   | Previous year: | **January** 1987 | Amount: | **0.00** |
   | Source: | | | |

Exhibit 9–3    Sample Bankruptcy Petition, XYZ Industrial Supply    **167**

**Exhibit 9–3**  *(continued)*

---

3. Payments to creditors.
   a. List all payments on loans, installment purchases of goods or services, and other debts, aggregating more than $600 to any creditor, made within 90 days immediately preceding the commencement of this case.
      NONE

   b. List all payments made within one year immediately preceding the commencement of this case to or for the benefit of creditors who are or were insiders.
      NONE

4. Suits, executions, garnishments, and attachments.
   a. List all suits to which the debtor is or was a party within one year immediately preceding the filing of this bankruptcy case.

   Status: **Lawsuit went to judgment.**
   **Complaint filed and judgment entered in favor of Plaintiff, Colonial Products and against Defendant, XYZ Industrial Supply on February 15, 1991 at Case No. 91-245 in Mag. District 04-2-06 by Honorable District Justice Martin J. Keith.**

   Status: **Lawsuit is pending.**
   **Suit filed 10/21/91 in Dearborn County.**

   **$18,000.00 collection against _____ Machine Company. Complaint filed in Court of Common Pleas of Dearborn County—Civil Division by XYZ Industrial Supply, Plaintiff against ____ Machine Company, Defendant on May 7, 1990 at Case No. 90-636 before Judge Henry Joseph.**

   b. Describe all property that has been attached, garnished, or seized under any legal or equitable process within one year immediately preceding the commencement of this case.

   Creditor:  **Dearborn County Tax**
              **Dearborn County Court**
              **Dearborn, MI 33103**

   Tax lien recorded:  **1989/1990—$6,800.00 lien**
                       **recorded.**

   Creditor:  **State of Michigan**
              **Bureau of Employment**
              **Lansing, MI 33102**

   Tax lien recorded:  **1990—$9,000.00 lien recorded.**
                       **1989—$5,050.00 lien recorded.**

**Exhibit 9–3**   *(continued)*

Creditor:   **U.S. Government**
            **Internal Revenue**
            **District Director**
            **Detroit, MI 33101**

Tax lien recorded:   **1991—Notice of Intention to**
                     **Levy.**
                     **1990—$4,800.00 lien recorded.**
                     **1989—$3,000.00 lien recorded.**
                     **1988—$7,000.00 lien recorded,**
                     **$3,500.00 paid against lien.**

5. Repossessions, foreclosures, and returns.

   List all property that has been repossessed by a creditor, sold at a foreclosure sale, transferred through a
   deed in lieu of foreclosure or returned to the seller,
   within one year immediately preceding the commencement
   of this case.

   **2 GMAC trucks repossessed in 1989 by Northern Bank of**
   **Michigan.**

6. Assignment and receiverships.
   a. Describe any assignment of property for the benefit
      of creditors made within 120 days immediately pre-
      ceding the commencement of this case.
      NONE

   b. List all property which has been in the hands of a
      receiver or court-appointed official within one
      year immediately preceding the commencement of this
      case.
      NONE

7. Gifts.

   List all gifts or charitable contributions made within
   one year immediately preceding the commencement of this
   case except ordinary and usual gifts to family members
   aggregating less than $200 in value per individual fam-
   ily member and charitable contributions aggregating
   less than $100 per recipient.

   **$2,500.00 to United Way in 1990.**

8. Losses.

   List all losses from fire, theft, other casualty or gam-
   bling within one year immediately preceding the commencement of this case or since the commencement of this
   case.

   **$162,000.00 bad debt write-off—1989.**

Exhibit 9–3    Sample Bankruptcy Petition, XYZ Industrial Supply    **169**

**Exhibit 9–3**  *(continued)*

9. Payments related to debt counseling or bankruptcy.

   List all payments made or property transferred by or on behalf of the debtor to any persons, including attorneys, for consultation concerning debt consolidation, relief under the bankrutpcy law or preparation of a petiton in bankruptcy within one year immediately preceding the commencement of this case.

   **MARTIN & MARTIN**
   **204 Craig Street**
   **Dearborn, MI 33104**

   Filing fee: **$600.00**
   Attorney's fees: **10,000.00**
   Source was: **Debtor's earnings**
   Date(s) of payment: **10/13/90 and 11/11/90**

10. Other transfers.

    List all other property, other than property transferred in the ordinary course of the business or financial affairs of the debtor transferred either absolutely or as security within one year immediately preceding the commencement of this case.

    NONE

11. Closed financial accounts.

    List all financial accounts and instruments held in the name of the debtor or for the benefit of the debtor which were closed, sold, or otherwise transferred within one year immediately preceding the commencement of this case.

    NONE

12. Safe deposit boxes.

    List each safe deposit box or other box or depository in which the debtor has or had securities, cash, or other valuables within one year immediately preceding the commencement of this case.

    NONE

13. Setoffs.

    List all setoffs made by any creditor, including a bank, against a debt or deposit of the debtor within 90 days preceding the commencement of this case.

    NONE

14. Property held for another person.

    List all property owned by another person that the debtor holds or controls.

    NONE

**Exhibit 9–3**  *(continued)*

15. Prior address of debtor.

    If the debtor has moved within the two years immediately preceding the commencement of this case, list all premises which the debtor occupied during that period and vacated prior to the commencement of this case.

    Beginning date at present location: **1979**
    Prior locations:

16. Nature, location, and name of business.
    a. For individuals, list the names and addresses of all businesses in which the debtor was an officer, director, partner, or managing executive of a corporation, partnership, sole proprietorship, or was a self-employed professional within the two years immediately preceding the commencement of this case, or in which the debtor owned 5 percent or more of the voting or equity securities within the two years immediately preceding the commencement of this case.

       N/A

    b. If the debtor is a partnership, list the names and addresses of all businesses in which the debtor was a partner or owned 5 percent or more of the voting securities, within the two years immediately preceding the commencement of this case.

       N/A

    c. If the debtor is a corporation, list the names and addresses of all businesses in which the debtor was a partner or owned 5 percent or more of the voting securities, within the two years immediately preceding the commencement of this case.

       NONE

17. Books, records, and financial statements.
    a. List all bookkeepers and accountants who within the six years immediately preceding the filing of this bankruptcy case kept or supervised the keeping of books of account and records of the debtor.

       **Alice Smith—Controller**
       **Jones & Co.—Accountants**

    b. List all firms or indivudals who within the two years immediately preceding the filing of this bankruptcy case have audited the books of account and records, or prepared a financial statement of the debtor.

       **There have been no audits.**

Exhibit 9–3    Sample Bankruptcy Petition, XYZ Industrial Supply    **171**

**Exhibit 9–3**  *(continued)*

c. List all firms or individuals who at the time of the commencement of this case were in possession of the books of account and records of the debtor.

IN DEBTOR'S POSSESSION

d. List all financial institutions, creditors, and other parties, including mercantile and trade agencies, to whom a financial statement was issued within the two years immediately preceding the commencement of this case by the debtor.

NONE

18. Inventories.
   a. List the dates of the last two inventories taken of your property, the name of the person who supervised the taking of each inventory, and the dollar amount and basis of each inventory.

Date of last: **12/31/89**
   Specifics: **Value at cost $476,000.00, at liquidation $100,000.00.**
Date of prior: **12/31/88**
   Specifics: **Value at cost $634,000.00, at liquidation $150,000.00.**

   b. List the name and address of the person having possession of the records of each of the two inventories reported in a., above.

Date of last: **12/31/89**
   Custodian: **Alice Smith**
Date of prior: **12/31/88**
   Custodian: **Alice Smith**

19. Current Partners, Officers, Directors, and Shareholders.
   a. If the debtor is a partnership, list the nature and percentage of partnership interest of each member of the partnership.

N/A

   b. If the debtor is a corporation, list all officers and directors of the corporation, and each stockholder who directly or indirectly owns, controls, or holds 5 percent or more of the voting securities of the corporation.

Title: **Office, Director, and Stockholder.**

**Joe Johnson**
**655 Forest Drive**
**Dearborn, MI 33104**

Nature and percentage of interest:
**90% owner**

**Exhibit 9–3**   *(continued)*

---

**Alice Smith**
**856 Brookline Ave.**
**Dearborn, MI 33104**

Nature and percentage of interest:
**10% owner**

20. Former partners, officers, directors, and shareholders.
   a. If the debtor is a partnership, list each member who withdrew from the partnership within one year immediately preceding the commencement of this case.
   N/A

   b. If the debtor is a corporation, list all officers or directors whose relationship with the corporation terminated within one year immediately preceding the commencement of this case.
   NONE

21. Withdrawals from a partnership or distributions by a corporation.
   If the debtor is a partnership or corporation, list all withdrawals or distributions credited or given to an insider, including compensation in any form, bonuses, loans, stock redemptions, options exercised and any other perquisite during one year immediately preceding the commencement of this case.
   NONE

(The penalties for making a false statement or concealing property is a fine of up to $500,000 or imprisonment for up to 5 years or both.—18 U.S.C. sec. 152 and 3571.)

### Declaration

I, **Joe Johnson, president** for **XYZ Industrial Supply** named as the debtor in this case, declare under penalty of perjury that I have read the foregoing **Statement of Financial Affairs**, consisting of 7 sheets, and that it is true and correct to the best of my information and belief.

Signature: _____     Date: _____
**Joe Johnson**
**President**

Exhibit 9–3    Sample Bankruptcy Petition, XYZ Industrial Supply    173

**Exhibit 9–3**  *(continued)*

```
Michael L. Martin, Esquire
MARTIN & MARTIN
204 Craig Street
Dearborn, MI 33104
Attorney for the Petitioner
```

UNITED STATES BANKRUPTCY COURT
FOR THE NORTHERN DISTRICT OF MICHIGAN

| | |
|---|---|
| IN RE | Case No.: |
| **XYZ Industrial Supply** | |
| Debtor | **Rule 2016(b)—Statement** |
| Debtor's Employer's Tax | **of Attorney Compensation** |
| Identification No.: 00-000000 | |
| | Chapter 11 |

Pursuant to 11 U.S.C. sec. 329 and Rule of Bankruptcy Procedure 2016(b), the undersigned, attorney for the debtor in this case, makes this statement setting forth the compensation paid or agreed to be paid to the undersigned for services rendered or to be rendered in contemplation of and in connection with the case by the undersigned, and the source of such compensation.

1. Prior to the filing of this disclosure statement, the debtor in this case has paid to the undersigned the sum of **$10,000.00** plus **$600.00** for the filing fee in this case. The source of the PAID sum was: **Debtor's earnings**

2. In addition, the debtor has agreed to pay the following: $175.00 dollars per hour for all services performed and approved by the Court.
   The source of the TO BE PAID sum will be:
   Company earnings.

3. The undersigned has not shared or agreed to share any portion of such compensation with any other person who is not a member or regular associate of the undersigned's law firm.

4. The undersigned has not received any other payment in this case, and has no other agreement, except as set out herein.

Signature: _____  Date: _____

        **Michael L. Martin,**
        **Esquire**

**Exhibit 9–3** *(continued)*

Michael L. Martin, Esquire
MARTIN & MARTIN
204 Craig Street
Dearborn, MI 33104
Attorney for the Petitioner

## UNITED STATES BANKRUPTCY COURT
## FOR THE NORTHERN DISTRICT OF MICHIGAN

| | |
|---|---|
| IN RE | Case No.: |
| **XYZ Industrial Supply** | |
| Debtor | **List of Equity Security** |
| Debtor's Employer's Tax | **Holders** |
| Identification No.: 00-000000 | Chapter 11 |

The following is the list of the equity security holders of the debtor, including the last known address and number and kind of interests registered in the name of each holder.

| Registered name of equity security holder and last known address or place of business | Type of interest registered and number of shares or other interest registered |
|---|---|
| **Joe Johnson**<br>**655 Forest Drive**<br>**Dearborn, MI 33104** | STOCKHOLDER<br>90% owner |
| **Alice Smith**<br>**856 Brookline Ave.**<br>**Dearborn, MI 33104** | STOCKHOLDER<br>10% owner |

(The penalties for making a false statement or concealing property is a fine of up to $500,000 or imprisonment for up to 5 years or both.—18 U.S.C. sec. 152 and 3571.)

### Declaration

I, **Joe Johnson, president** for **XYZ Industrial Supply** named as the debtor in this case, declare under penalty of perjury that I have read the foregoing **List of Equity Security Holders**, consisting of 1 sheet, and that it is true and correct to the best of my information and belief.

Signature: _____        Date: _____
              **Joe Johnson**
              **President**

Exhibit 9–3    Sample Bankruptcy Petition, XYZ Industrial Supply    **175**

**Exhibit 9–3**    *(continued)*

Michael L. Martin, Esquire
MARTIN & MARTIN
204 Craig Street
Dearborn, MI 33104
Attorney for the Petitioner

# UNITED STATES BANKRUPTCY COURT
## FOR THE NORTHERN DISTRICT OF MICHIGAN

IN RE                                         Case No.:
**XYZ Industrial Supply**
Debtor                                        **Numbered Listing of**
Debtor's Employer's Tax                       **Creditors**
Identification No.: **00-000000**             Chapter **11**

| CREDITOR NAME AND MAILING ADDRESS | CATEGORY OF CLAIM | AMOUNT OF CLAIM |
|---|---|---|
| 1. A T & T<br>P.O. Box 41005<br>Dearborn, MI 33104 | Unsecured claims | 7,600.00 |
| 2. Allied Electric<br>P.O. Box 72365890<br>Lansing, MI 33102 | Unsecured claims | 2,420.00 |
| 3. American Express<br>P.O. Box 7784<br>Phoenix, AZ 89770 | Unsecured claims | 12,400.00 |
| 4. Capital Bearing Co.<br>4487 Washington Street<br>St. Louis, MO 88702 | Unsecured claims | 31,465.00 |
| 5. Carlton Industrial Suppl<br>9741 Monroe Drive<br>Flint, MI 33105 | Unsecured claims | 36,905.00 |
| 6. Colonial Products<br>8890 Jefferson Street<br>Dearborn, MI 33104 | Unsecured claims | 14,230.00 |
| 7. Dearborn County Tax<br>Dearborn County Court<br>Dearborn, MI 33103 | Priority claims—<br>taxes and other<br>debts owed to gov-<br>ernmental units | 6,800.00 |
| 8. Dearborn Gas Company<br>P.O. Box 889742<br>Dearborn, MI 33104 | Unsecured claims | 1,500.00 |
| 9. Dearborn Light Company<br>P.O. Box 6894<br>Dearborn, MI 33104 | Unsecured claims | 1,400.00 |

**Exhibit 9–3**  *(continued)*

| CREDITOR NAME AND MAILING ADDRESS | CATEGORY OF CLAIM | AMOUNT OF CLAIM |
|---|---|---|
| 10. Granger Supply<br>897 Harrison Street<br>Detroit, MI 33101 | Unsecured claims | 3,950.00 |
| 11. Michigan Bell<br>P.O. Box 485293<br>Lansing, MI 33102 | Unsecured claims | 3,200.00 |
| 12. Michigan Savings Bank<br>212 Grant Street<br>Lansing, MI 33102 | Secured claims | 115,000.00 |
| 13. Michigan Savings Bank<br>212 Grant Street<br>Lansing, MI 33102 | Secured claims | 35,000.00 |
| 14. Michigan Savings Bank<br>212 Grant Street<br>Lansing, MI 33102 | Secured claims | 21,000.00 |
| 15. State of Michigan<br>Bureau of Employment<br>Lansing, MI 33102 | Priority claims—taxes and other debts owed to governmental units | 14,050.00 |
| 16. Travel Go Round<br>P.O. Box 9508<br>Columbus, OH 42588 | Unsecured claims | 2,530.00 |
| 17. Triple A Tools<br>445 Market Street<br>Chicago, IL 44510 | Unsecured claims | 186,400.00 |
| 18. U.S. Government<br>Internal Revenue<br>District Director<br>Detroit, MI 33101 | Priority claims—taxes and other debts owed to governmental units | 21,600.00 |

(The penalties for making a false statement or concealing property is a fine of up to $500,000 or imprisonment for up to 5 years or both.—18 U.S.C. secs. 152 and 3571.)

## Declaration

**I, Joe Johnson, president** for **XYZ Industrial Supply** named as the debtor in this case, declare under penalty of perjury that I have read the foregoing **Numbered Listing of Creditors**, consisting of 3 sheets, and that it is true and correct to the best of my information and belief.

Signature: _____    Date: _____

**Joe Johnson**
**President**

Beginning with your first Section 341 meeting, you will have several opportunities to deal with your creditors both in the court proceedings and outside of the formal legal structure. Regardless of whether the relationship has been cooperative, acrimonious, or even nonexistent, you will have one last and critically important reason to open a constructive negotiation with these creditors. You can forge agreements in advance of creating and filing a plan of reorganization.

There are several different positions that you can adopt when offering the terms to restructure your debt. One tactic is to determine exactly what you are able to offer your creditors, put these numbers in a plan, and submit it for a vote on a "take-it-or-leave-it" basis. There are reasons to make your offer this way.

# 10

# LET'S MAKE A DEAL

## NEGOTIATING PAYMENT TERMS WITH YOUR CREDITORS

- You have few creditors.
- There are no disputes over the amount of the debt.
- You have little room to increase the amount and the terms of any payback.

This may work when your only other alternative is to liquidate, and your creditors understand these clear choices. It is not a good technique when the desired result is to find a compromise that will end with an approved plan of reorganization. The less room you give yourself to negotiate, the less likely you are to succeed.

A second tactic that may have been used in the course of your case leading up to the filing of the plan is to employ every legal maneuver available to secure additional time to file and to reduce debt to the lowest level, making sure, if any portion of a debt is unsecured, that it is removed to an unsecured status and forcing all concessions possible.

Either the debtor or a creditor can request an action to determine the secured status of any loan. Exhibit 10–1 shows a sample motion filed by a creditor to determine secured status (see page 189). This example illustrates an adversary proceeding filed in my case in which one secured creditor believed he held a first lien position, and another creditor also believed he held first position. This came up as a result of our disclosure statement and plan, and the issue had to be settled before the process continued. The parties agreed between themselves, and we filed an amended plan.

If you have had an active creditors' committee, you may be forced into an aggressive defense against its actions and an offense of your own to gain any edge you can. These events will be very time-consuming and will inevitably lead to high legal costs, which means less cash available to fund your plan. From day 1 you should be avoiding these confrontations if at all possible. But if they begin, you must be prepared to respond.

## CREATE A DEBT PAYMENT PLAN

For the many bankruptcy cases that are relatively uneventful, a reorganization plan can be negotiated with creditors. Typically, when you read about a bankruptcy, you will see that a "plan has been filed"; little description will be given about the process. One of my greatest frustrations during the long period I spent under bankruptcy protection, was not understanding exactly how I could create a plan of reorganization. I repeatedly asked my attorney to explain how we would determine payback terms, and the answers were never sufficient. Finally we began a series of meetings with our secured creditors, and things began to fall into place. These negotiations ultimately fixed the amounts and terms of one major category of debt, and we created the balance of the plan around these financial parameters.

Don't attempt to create your own plan in a vacuum, and don't let your attorney create one without you. Insist that your lawyer work with you to come to agreement with as many creditors as possible. You are offering a finite amount of financial resources, and once you have allocated all of your available funds, you will be left with few alternatives. If any creditors balk at the amount you are offering, you won't be able to increase that offer without taking away from the other creditors. While it would be possible to withdraw a plan and file an amended version, you could be falling into a morass of conflict. Consequently, it isin your best interest to forge as much agreement in advance of your filing as you can accomplish.

# ASSESS YOUR COMPANY'S FINANCIAL STATUS BEFORE YOU BEGIN NEGOTIATING WITH CREDITORS

If you have worked diligently on taking an analytical view of your business and making the necessary changes to improve performance, you will understand the realities of your company better than ever before. It is this critical knowledge that you must draw on when determining how much of a debt load your operation can sustain and what cash you can generate from operations to service that debt. The number must be generous enough to serve as an incentive to your creditors to approve your plan, yet realistic enough to pay out on a regular basis.

Once you have come up with the amount and terms, think about how you will allocate this money among the various class of creditors. Once you have a tentative plan in mind, you are ready to create a negotiating strategy.

## Determine Which Class of Creditor Will Be the Toughest

There are many reasons you might have found it necessary to file for bankruptcy protection. Chances are you've experienced across-the-board financial difficulties, and owe money to both secured and unsecured creditors. You may also owe back taxes, which are in the priority unsecured category. The last category is administrative, which involves debts acquired after the filing, and includes legal and accounting fees as well as some back wages, rents, and payments to trade creditors.

The most typical place to start paying off debt is with your secured lenders, usually your bank. They own rights to most of what you need (property, equipment, and inventory, etc.) to continue as an operating business. You must pay back any secured loan at the full value of the security. If the value of your assets has diminished, part of the loan may be unsecured. This is one of several items that is up for negotiation, so there is a reason to open a dialogue. The problem is that you may not be negotiating with the bank but rather with their outside legal counsel. In this case, it will probably be done in court between attorneys. If you think that you have a good working relationship with your banker, you might try making contact to set up a face-to-face meeting with their "special loans" or "workout" department.

Unfortunately, these days there is also the possibility that your bank is in trouble and has been taken over by the Resolution Trust

Corporation. This government agency has little in the way of personnel willing and able to renegotiate the terms of a loan. If they hold any of your secured debt, it is likely you will have to get current on the loan and keep current or face foreclosure. Your time would be better spent in replacing the property they hold as collateral.

Even if you are not successful at achieving an agreement with one class of creditor, you should still go on to the next. The more firm numbers you have before writing your plan, the stronger the document and more likely its approval.

## Understand the Rights Regarding Each Class of Creditor

All creditors have the right to vote on a plan of reorganization, and all votes in one class are counted to determine approval or rejection of the plan. Each class is counted separately, and it requires votes representing two-thirds of the dollar amount and one-half of the number of claims of all *voters* to determine the outcome. Any creditor who does not vote is not counted.

As the debtor, you can create subclasses within a class to stack the vote. Your secured creditors can be divided into subclasses differentiated by each separate loan, or by whether the loan is completely or only partially secured. Unsecured creditors can be divided by the amount of their claim (i.e., all under $100 in one class, under $1,000 in another, and over $1,000 in a third). If you have a few strong dissenters, this may be a way to isolate their vote in a class in which you have many supporters.

The amount of debt owed to any creditor will be established by your disclosure statement, and you have the right to challenge the value of assets securing any loan that will determine if a portion of the loan is unsecured. By the same token, you also can stipulate that a loan is fully secured, and this is a serious point for negotiation.

A single creditor (unless they represent most of a class) cannot vote down an entire class. In addition, if all classes but one vote in favor, the plan can be confirmed over the objection of the one class. Any class that is completely unimpaired (they will be paid back in full), will be counted in favor of the plan, and any class that will not be paid at all will be counted as opposed.

The rules governing the voting on a plan can be complicated, but there is also such an infinite variety of possibilities that the best prepared negotiator and strategist has a real advantage.

## Consider What Would Happen to Each Creditor If You Liquidate

The bottom line for your company as well as for your creditors is that if you aren't able to forge a plan of reorganization, your company will be liquidated. The proceeds will be disbursed to creditors according to their position as a creditor. Any asset that serves as collateral for a loan will be liquidated for the creditor holding the security. Then and only then will funds be disbursed to the other category of creditors including those who are unsecured. And *before* any of this occurs, the trustee will deduct their own fees, costs, and attorney's fees.

There are several reasons that most creditors will receive less under most liquidations, and you should be familiar with all of them before you meet with creditors.

1. Assets sold in liquidation bring far less than true value. Whether sold as part of an auction or by private sale, they may only bring 10% to 30% of their worth. Deduct any fees, and a secured creditor will find a return far less than the value of the loan.
2. In Addition to the trustee's fee, other costs will also be deducted from the proceeds. These costs include the cost of rent for space to store items to be sold, the cost of moving goods into storage, and any advertising or mailing fees needed to conduct the sale.
3. Other professional costs such as an accountant or additional attorneys will add to existing administrative costs.

Unless your company has assets vastly in excess of its liabilities (in which case a reorganization is highly likely), the reality for your creditors, regardless of their class, is that a liquidation will bring very little return. In most cases, the unsecureds will receive nothing on their claims. Your plan of reorganization will offer more than a liquidation, and if you are able to meet with creditors to negotiate an agreement in advance of your plan, you should know how substantial this increase in payout will be. This benefit should be stressed in your meeting.

## Know Which Issues You Can Negotiate with Your Creditors

There are several items that are possible areas for agreements that you may make with your creditors. Basically, they are

- Amount of payback
- Type of payback
- Terms of payback

**Negotiate the amount of payback.** Any debtor's claim can be disputed as to the amount, and you can ask the court to disallow the claim up to 60 days after a plan is confirmed. For an unsecured creditor, it may be as a result of a disagreement over the quantity or quality of goods that were covered by these outstanding debts. It may also be a question of whether the goods or services were ever authorized. For example, I disputed a claim for advertising that I did not agree to before it was run in the periodical. If you file a motion against any claim, the creditor will have to submit its own documentation of the validity of the claim and may have to hire an attorney to represent the claim in court. The legal fee could exceed the return!

If your case involves many small unsecured creditors, you could agree not to dispute any individual claims in return for the creditors' support for your plan.

There may be various disagreements with secured lenders over the amount of their claim, which may not be secured by the current value of your assets. If your machinery, vehicles, or inventory had to be sold at liquidation, they would bring only cents on the dollar, and you could claim that lowered amount as their true value. Perhaps in return for not challenging the secured nature of a loan, your banker will allow generous repayment terms and lowered interest rates to make the monthly cost lower.

**Negotiate the type of payback.** You may not have to make a payback in cash alone. Although it is a relatively sophisticated move for a small, closely held company, there are still circumstances in which stock or notes convertible to stock or deferred cash can be used in the place of cash alone. As an example, if you have one large unsecured creditor who may have an interest in ownership of your company, perhaps they would accept company stock in lieu of cash payments. This may be a possibility if you are a large distributor for a particular product line, and the manufacturer has an interest in your continuing to sell their product. Perhaps your location is a critical one, or you have a long-standing relationship with an important customer. You don't know until you ask, and you can't ask unless you meet with creditors.

Your secured lenders will probably not be very flexible about what compensation they receive (they want cash). But they may be willing to take back an asset in return for a reduction of a part of the debt owed. The asset would have to be easily saleable. As an example, if your company owned several different properties and did not sell off any during the course of the case, the bank may be willing to take title to one that would reduce debt and lower cash payback. Again, discuss it and you may uncover some advantageous possibilities.

**Negotiate the time and terms of payback.** As a standard course, most plans allow for a payout period of 6 years or fewer. You may pay small claims at confirmation or during the first year, and larger claims may take the full time allowed. Within these guidelines, however, there is no reason that your payments can't be less in the early years of the plan and increase as time goes on when, it is hoped, your company continues to grow stronger. You may be able to offer lower payments over the entire term of the plan with a single balloon payment at the end. And at that time you may be able to restructure the balloon into a payout.

During the course of a bankruptcy, many creditors begin to doubt that they will ever see any return on the debt owed to them. The longer it goes on, the lower their expectation. When the case finally gets to the point where a repayment offer is being made, you may find a very receptive audience for the possibility of creative terms.

## NEGOTIATE YOUR PAYMENT PLAN WITH YOUR CREDITORS

By the time you are ready to present a plan to your creditors, you should be getting over the initial shock of finding yourself in these proceedings. And you should point out to the creditors you meet with that you are making a personal commitment to work to see that at least a portion of the debt owed to them is paid back. By this time, you have come to realize that you will probably be working harder for less money, and you are still making the effort at doing the "right thing." If you had been intent on running up debts and not paying them, you would have walked away. Working through this process takes courage and honor, and you should be respected for this effort.

The rest of this chapter provides tips for convincing your creditors to accept and support your payment plan.

## Negotiate Directly with Principals and Not Secondhand Through Attorneys

I have suggested strongly throughout this book that you continue to communicate with your business associates even if they have now become creditors of your bankruptcy. And I understand completely why this contact can be very difficult. The stress of pressing financial problems and the inability to pay your bills is a painful issue to discuss with creditors. But it is in the best interest of all concerned for you to let them have regular, firsthand information from you and not just notices from the bankruptcy court.

If your unsecured creditors form a creditors' committee, you should still try to have personal contact with those members with whom you have good working relationships. If they take all of their advice from the attorney representing the committee, they may end up driving up their (and your) legal costs and undermining any potential reorganization plan. Your message throughout this process is that there is a finite amount of money which can either be used to finance a plan and pay back creditors, or paid to everyone's attorney. Don't be shy about this fact—after all it is a fact, and it may not be stressed by the attorney representing the committee. Few lawyers even discuss their fee.

If you have been successful at avoiding a formal creditors' committee, each unsecured creditor will be sent a ballot to vote on your plan. For most companies, the number of creditors is far too great to forge any agreement in advance. If you can convince your largest unsecured to support your plan, however, there is a good chance that you will receive the approval of this class. The formal voting rules will prevent you from soliciting votes during the confirmation process, but you can do all the communicating you wish before the plan and the ballots go out. Let your vendors know when the plan will be ready, what percentage you expect to pay, and how the payments will be structured.

This informal and acceptable manner of negotiating may bring an important side benefit. At this point you are dividing the available cash and future profits. After conversation with your creditors/vendors, you may find one or two who are willing to accept the stock or notes discussed earlier in this chapter. If these terms are acceptable, you can find a way to divide these creditors into a subgroup with the differentiated terms. The major criteria is that their total payout must *only* be equal to the others in their class.

## Don't Promise More than You Can Deliver When Negotiating with Creditors

While your company was in its struggle before filing for protection, you may have made promises for payments that were backed more by good intention than reality. You may have hoped to make a payment in the near future while knowing that it would take almost a miracle to have the funds available.

There is no place in a plan of reorganization or in the negotiations leading up to such a plan for anything but a realistic view of what operating results you expect and what excess cash will be available for debt service. You will be closely watched by the court (as long as it retains jurisdiction) and your creditors to make sure that you make all promised payments. Although you can go back and amend your plan if unforeseen circumstances arise, your creditors also have the right to convert your Chapter 11 reorganization into a Chapter 7 liquidation if you find it difficult to meet the terms of your plan.

When planning strategy with your attorney for any negotiations with your creditors and ultimately in writing your plan, you should be the one who determines what finances can be committed to this debt service. You are the one running the business, not your lawyer. You know what problems might confront you and what is a realistic offer. Attorneys often will suggest you attempt figures virtually out of the question to make agreements with the other side go easier. Stand your ground, and explain the facts of business life if you must.

Frankly, at this point, there is another feature of your relationship with your lawyer that could be coming into play. If your case has gone on for a while, your lawyer may be getting bored and not want to go through monumental struggles involved for your company to secure the best possible deal for a feasible restructuring. You are living with this situation, and your survival depends on it. Be vigilant about each deal that is made with any creditor.

This is not a criticism about the legal profession—it is rather a comment about the nature of many business relationships. Most of us pay less attention to our longer-term customers than we do to our newer ones. Sometimes we take existing business relationships for granted, and the fact is that the practice of law is a business. Each day brings new cases for a lawyer, some more interesting than the others. About the time your company is committing to the plan for a possible rebirth, you may have become just one more law client. This is an important phase and the beginning of a second chance for your company. I am cautioning you not to let up at this point.

## Try to Give Your Creditors What They Need

It is an oversimplification to think that all creditors need the same type of return. Depending on the nature of the organization to whom you owe a debt, its needs may vary, and your offers can also vary. Institutions including banks and government agencies need a recovery of as much debt as possible, but the payback time can be stretched out relatively substantially. The parties negotiating for these institutions can accept or sell to their principals a long-term payout with variable interest.

In the case of your vendors who are your unsecured creditors, they may need a return as soon as possible. If they are also small or midsize businesses, your unpaid debt is a loss that may have created cash problems for their business, and they would welcome cash on confirmation and a short-term payout. Most unsecureds will accept less if it is paid quickly. As proof of this attitude, there are several speculators who buy up debt from unsecured creditors at 10% to 30% of face value in return for immediate payment. They are often successful at this purchase even when there is a plan out for voting that will pay twice as much over a longer period. It is the "bird-in-the-hand" theory, which has some merit given the number of reorganizations that do not make it to completion.

## Monitor the Financial Commitments You're Making to All Creditors

You should keep the entire picture in mind as you try to forge agreements with the various classes of creditors. If you have accrued funds that can be paid out at confirmation, use them as incentive to encourage acceptance. In the early stages of negotiation, don't offer out more than a small portion of these funds—you will need them to pay administrative costs and having some money in reserve may be just what you need to finish an important agreement. Don't forget to keep funds to use as working capital.

Continually monitor the monthly commitments that you are making so that you don't find yourself burdened by the total of payments you've proposed. Also consider any quarterly or other periodic payments as part of your total obligation.

### Repay Administrative Debts—Taxes, Wages, and Professional Fees

Administrative debt is all debt incurred after the date of a bankruptcy filing. This can include but is not limited to taxes, trade credit, unpaid wages, and professional fees. As a general rule, most administrative debt is due on confirmation of your plan of reorganization. Actually, the payment date is the effective date, which is 60 days after the confirmation—these 60 days are for the purpose of appeal by any interested party.

The taxes must be paid at confirmation, and your trade credit will be retired according to the terms agreed to with your vendors. Other administrative creditors may agree to more flexible terms of repayment, however.

## Negotiate Payment of Wages to Employees

It is possible that you have not been able to pay full wages to yourself or other employees during the early days after your filing. It is hoped these full payments get restored quickly as your operations stabilize. Any of these unpaid wages that remain are an administrative debt of the bankrupt company. If you are the majority stockholder and primary manager, and are owed a substantial amount for unpaid wages, there is a good chance that one of your creditors will object to a large lump sum payment to you at the time of confirmation. They may require that you accept a payout that doesn't jeopardize the payments they are accepting.

Conversely, if your company owes wages to other employees who have stayed with the company and are also committed to the reorganization process, those wages may be paid by any agreement acceptable to both parties. You may be willing to use stock in the reorganized company in lieu of cash, and a way of rewarding loyalty and, at the same time, lowering the cash demands required at confirmation. If your employees accept this, it is acceptable to the courts. If they want cash but are willing to accept a payout over several years, that will also be acceptable to the court. Any combination of stock and cash, payable in part on confirmation and in part deferred, can also be negotiated. If you have been communicating effectively with the affected employees, you should have a good idea of what terms could be included in an agreement.

## Negotiate Payment to Professionals Working on Your Bankruptcy Case

Payments to the professionals involved in your bankruptcy case may be handled in a variety of methods. For the most part, the professionals are your attorney and your accountant. Your attorney probably had a retainer that he used to offset his initial charges. The same case may be true of your accountant. If your case has gone on for a while, either one or both may have filed for interim payments. At the time you are creating your plan, they will be submitting bills for their work up until that point. You should know these numbers *before* you start negotiating withother creditors because these professionals may demand their payment in full at the effective date and that will deplete other cash available.

If you have developed a good working relationship with your professional advisers and you have made a nice contribution to their incomes, you may be able to negotiate some deferment of their fees. Remember that they have had an inside seat as your case has unfolded so if there is any doubt that you can successfully restructure your company, they would be in a position to know. You don't know how flexible these advisers can be unless you ask, and it is certainly worth a serious conversation.

## SUMMING UP

The key to negotiation is flexibility and preparation. Learn all you can about the rights and possibilities of all creditors, and then try to work out a mutually satisfactory agreement. It will dramatically increase your chance for approval of your plan as well as the successful completion of your reorganization.

Exhibit 10–1    Sample Motion to Determine Secured Creditor Status    189

**Exhibit 10–1    Sample Motion to Determine Secured Creditor Status**

IN THE UNITED STATES BANKRUPTCY COURT
FOR THE WESTERN DISTRICT OF PENNSYLVANIA

IN RE:

| | |
|---|---|
| PITTSBURGH GLOVE MANUFACTURING COMPANY, Debtor | NO. _____ |
| SMALL BUSINESS ADMINISTRATION Plaintiff | |
| vs. | ADV. NO. |
| PITTSBURGH GLOVE MANUFACTURING COMPANY, Defendant | |

### Complaint to Determine
### Secured Status

AND NOW COMES the Small Business Administration (here-inafter SBA), an Agency of the United States of America, by and through its attorney, _____, Special Assistant to the United States Attorney for the Western District of Pennsyl-vania, and files the following Complaint to Determine Se-cured Status to enter an Order determining SBA's secured status in its collateral in accordance with 11 U.S.C. 506 and 510 of the Bankruptcy Code and in support thereof states the following:

1. SBA is a secured creditor of the Debtor and has a per-fected lien in Debtor's accounts receivable and inventory and other business assets.

2. On May 11, 1990, Debtor filed an Amended Disclosure Statement which lists _____, as having secured claims in the approximate amount of _____, with a lien for $10,000 in the business inventory and receivables, and lists the SBA as having a secured claim in the amount of _____ with a lien in the amount of $24,112.55.

3. The Debtor's designation of _____ as a prior se-cured lienholder to SBA is based upon a letter from SBA to _____ dated August 6, 1980, agreeing to subordinate SBA's lien position in inventory, raw leather goods, goods in pro-cess or finished goods to a purchase money security interest in these same items up to the amount of _____ and in addi-tion to subordinate SBA's first lien position on accounts

**Exhibit 10–1**  *(continued)*

receivable up to the amount of $10,000 to a _____ lien securing the same loan which was not to exceed _____.

4. Said SBA letter specifically referred to _____ letter of July 28, 1980 wherein _____ requested SBA to release its accounts receivable and inventory lien for a 6-month period for a _____ loan in receivables and inventory up to _____. Copies of both letters are attached hereto as Exhibits A and B.

5. The two letters together created the subordination of SBA's receivables lien for a 6-month period up to a total amount of $10,000 and a subordination of SBA's lien on inventory, raw leather goods, goods in process, and finished goods purchased with or proceeds of the _____ loan for a 6-month period up to a total amount of _____.

6. Debtor, having received only the second letter, was not aware of limitation on said subordination agreement, and set forth in the Disclosure Statement that SBA had subordinated its position, thereby listing _____ as having a first position in the receivables and inventory in the amount of $10,000.

7. Said 6-month period ceased to exist in the beginning of 1981 and was no longer valid at the time the bankruptcy was filed.

8. The Disclosure Statement should be corrected since both the classification and disbursement are affected by placing _____ in first lien position for $10,000 and any hearing on said Disclosure Statement should be postponed until a hearing takes place on this Complaint for Determination of Secured Status.

WHEREFORE, SBA prays that this Honorable Court will postpone the date for the hearing on the Disclosure Statement until a hearing is had on this Complaint for Determination of Secured Status pursuant to 11 U.S.C. 506 and 510; SBA requests that this Honorable Court determine that the Subordination Agreement has expired; that SBA has a lien prior to _____ and that _____ is an unsecured creditor.

SMALL BUSINESS ADMINISTRATION

_____

Special Assistant to U.S. Attorney

The plan of reorganization is actually a two-part document. Along with the plan, you are required to file a disclosure statement. The first action of the court will be to hold a hearing on the adequacy of your disclosure; if it is approved, the court will allow voting to begin on the plan.

The disclosure statement, although required by the Bankruptcy Code, does not have a very specific requirement as to what information is included or how it is formatted. You will most likely find out that your attorney has a format in his word processor based on one that has been used before and approved. On first glance, this previous success may seem desirable, but closer consideration shows that the specifics of your own case should be highlighted and detailed in a custom disclosure statement. The warning is that if you want a custom job you will probably have to do it yourself.

# THE FIRST STEP OUT OF BANKRUPTCY

## FILING A DISCLOSURE STATEMENT

At this point you probably still can't determine exactly what a disclosure statement is and that is completely understandable. The more formal, albeit very nebulous, description of what this statement must contain is "information which is adequate for a creditor to decide whether to vote for the plan." For virtually every bankruptcy, the information required would be slightly different, which is why I have recommended that your disclosure be tailored to the specifics of your case.

## Write Your Disclosure Statement

Your disclosure statement should resemble a business plan or prospectus. It should include a brief history of your company as well as some information regarding the reasons behind your bankruptcy filing. The main focus, however, is the financial information that will convince your creditors that their return will be greater from a reorganized company than from a liquidation.

At some point you will include a synopsis of your plan—either in the very beginning or just before the specific financial data. A second goal of the disclosure is to show that your company is likely to have the means to be able actually to meet the obligations set forth in the plan of reorganization.

Because you are not permitted to solicit support from creditors after the plan is out for voting, the accompanying disclosure statement should make your compelling case for approval, and you should take the time to accomplish this task.

Your disclosure statement should include the following information:

- Summary of your reorganization plan
- Background information on your bankruptcy case
- Current state of your company's financial affairs
- Liquidated value of your company
- Your business projections
- Effect of Chapter 7 liquidation
- Your recommendations for implementing your reorganization plan

The following sections describe each part of the disclosure statement in detail.

Exhibit 11–1, on page 198, is a sample disclosure statement for XYZ Industrial Supply based on information supplied in their petition in Chapter 9.

## Write a Summary of Your Reorganization Plan

You won't list each creditor by name or subclass, just a general statement of how each class will be treated. The percentage of return and the term of repayment are the two critical items.

## Describe Your Bankruptcy Case Background

This section can include both a history of your business and an overview of what brought it into bankruptcy. This is one place to make a good public relations case for your business, emphasizing any historical success, length of operation, and market identification. If the cause of your filing was an unexpected disruption or disaster, point out this extraordinary circumstance, which is not likely to be repeated. You have control of what is written, so put the best spin on it. You want those who take the time to read this document to feel confident about the future of your company.

## Describe the Current State of Your Company's Financial Affairs

At the time of filing, you included all pertinent financial information, but your situation most likely has changed during the course of your case. For example, you may have sold real estate or other assets, and also reduced your secured debts. The cash collateral including the value of your receivables may have been confiscated by your secured lender. Any number of line items may have changed, and you have to advise your creditors what has transpired. This section of the disclosure statement will help to explain how you arrived at the plan you are now proposing.

## State the Liquidated Value of Your Company

The Bankruptcy Code requires that a plan offer more to creditors than a liquidation would achieve. This section is key to your presentation of that fact, and you should be as candid as you can be. Any distress sale of assets brings only pennies on the dollar, and that is how you should value the property, equipment, and inventory of your company. In this section you will establish how little will be available for distribution, and in a later section you will discuss the added cost of a liquidation.

## Describe Your Business Projections

Now that you have begun the warning to your creditors of just how little they would benefit in a liquidation, you want to show them how you could return a far greater amount as a working business. Even though your plan may offer a payback of 6 years in duration you do not need to do projections that go beyond a year or 2. Be realistic but try to project the good results of lower costs. You may include a pro-forma statement in this section or as an exhibit attached to the document.

# Explain the Disadvantages
# of Chapter 7 Liquidation

This is the section to contrast what return creditors could expect from the reorganized business compared with the return of a liquidation. You should explain to those creditors who may not be aware that a liquidation would increase the administrative costs that have to be paid by the debtor's funds (if there are any). Some of these costs would be payments to the trustee and to any attorney the trustee may employ. Any case with available cash assets can start a real feeding frenzy among those who serve in this role. You might find it difficult to state this fact clearly and then have your attorney file it because most lawyers don't like to be accused of this behavior. But don't neglect to mention that these fees can get quite large.

Additional costs that can deplete any available funds are the cost of maintaining real estate or equipment, perhaps moving and storing inventory and the cost of a sale. Needless to say, if you were to review many cases, you would find that few liquidations return *anything* to the unsecured creditors. If you believe that this would be the case for your unsecured creditors, make that point.

# Make Your Recommendations
# for Implementing Your Reorganization Plan

This is the time for you to make the final case for approval of your plan of reorganization. Take your best shot as to the reasons why your creditors would receive a greater return than if the case were converted to a Chapter 7 liquidation. You may even want to toss in the fact that your reorganized company will continue to do business with these creditors.

## DETERMINE HOW MUCH FINANCIAL INFORMATION TO DISCLOSE

Your disclosure statement should be as complete as you can make it, and you should restate some of the financial information several times if it is critical to making your case for approval. It is better to give too much information than too little in a disclosure statement.

If your company has the real possibility of returning to profitable operations (or already has during the course of the case), you will want to drive that fact home to your creditors. These profits can be allocated to debt service, and makes their return higher and increases the chance for successfully reaping that return. Most companies will not return any money to the unsecured creditors under a liquidation, but that doesn't always influence this class of creditor to vote in favor of the plan of reorganization. Their negative vote may be as a result of the belief of many that most bankrupt companies won't make it through the reorganization process long enough to pay anything back. It also may be the influence of the attorney representing any creditors' committee for the purpose of forcing a higher percentage of distribution. Your disclosure statement must show any and all creditors that your company is making as high a payback distribution as is prudent for the ongoing operation of your business. The pro-forma statements are meant to show just that scenario.

Your disclosure statement also should reflect any changes in assets or operations since the initial filing. For the XYZ Industrial Supply, the two main post-filing transactions to be reported were the sale of their building and the liquidation of certain inventory. Although both of these actions were done with approval of secured lender, this establishes the change in the asset picture for the unsecureds and explains the apparent shrinkage in the total inventory value.

Your company may have continued losses for some time after the filing; although you have filed operating statements with the court and certain secured creditors, your other unsecureds may no longer have any idea of the asset-liability situation of your business. The disclosure will give then a picture of your current circumstance and you control what this "snapshot" looks like—take advantage of this privilege.

## ASSESS THE ADEQUACY OF YOUR DISCLOSURE STATEMENT—AND HANDLE DISPUTES WITH CREDITORS

Depending on the case load of your assigned judge, a hearing will be scheduled in 4 to 6 weeks on the "adequacy" of your disclosure statement. Your creditors will be permitted to determine whether or not the information contained in the statement is sufficient to make a determination whether or not to vote for a plan. If any objections are filed to your statement, you have the right to file an amended statement in response to a specific question that will satisfy that objection. The problem here gets to be one of time. Each time you make an amended filing, a new hearing will be put on the court calendar, and these delays could take months from the initial date. If you are looking for extra time, this may be a way to get it.

When your plan and its accompanying disclosure statement go out to creditors, it may bring up issues that must be settled before the plan can be submitted for a vote. The two main issues would be whether or not a lender is fully secured by the current value of your collateral and what creditor may have first lien on assets, which also will affect their level of security. These issues may be decided in negotiation before a plan is filed. Or it may be that the dispute develops after these creditors see your plan for the first time and realize that their claim is impaired by their lack of adequate collateral. The creditors who think they have not been positioned properly will ask the court to postpone any further action on your statement and plan until they can file motions to determine the status of their secured claim. This will create further delays and may require a whole new set of documents before the process can begin again. It is not unusual for months to go by after your first filing before the process actually goes into motion.

Now you get into the various issues that may get involved in serious disputes when it comes to the adequacy of your disclosure statement. Two of the most frequent items are the disposition of certain assets and the expected payments made during the course of reorganization.

**Resolve disputes over assets.**    If you have assets that have been sold or otherwise disposed of during the course of your case, you must be prepared to explain to whom they were sold, what was received in the sale, and whether the sale was reasonable. These assets could be vehicles, equipment, or inventory that may not be security for any loan. If the asset did secure a loan, using the proceeds to pay that loan may not be sufficient to avoid scrutiny if the sale was made for a below-market price. The level of scrutiny will usually be in direct correlation to the amount of animosity that has developed during the time leading up to the plan.

There are good reasons for some questions about these transactions. It is to prevent you from selling off company assets preferentially to a buyer at below-market prices. But most sales made to raise quick cash will be done at distressed prices, and you should keep good records and detail any of these types of transactions voluntarily in your disclosure statement.

**Resolve disputes over payments.**    The second area of dispute over disclosure is payments to individuals during the case and scheduled after confirmation. This may include wages for principals or special consultants employed by your company. It is always safer to get approval of the court in advance of hiring any extraordinary personnel or professionals, and it is always prudent to make full disclosure of your own salary and benefits. The court can disallow unreasonable payments but is usually realistic about what is required to retain effective management.

**Resolve other disputes.**    There are other items that can come into dispute regarding a disclosure statement, some critical to the decision process and some very petty. Each case is different because the exact nature of each business is different. If you have been communicating with your creditors during your case, you should be able to anticipate any items that may be of concern and you should voluntarily address these issues in your disclosure. The only caution would be that these statements are widely circulated and are public record so be careful of giving up too much competitive information.

## OBTAIN APPROVAL OF YOUR DISCLOSURE STATEMENT

At some point, the hearing will be held regarding the material contained in the disclosure statement. If there have been objections raised that you think are frivolous, you can wait until the hearing and allow the judge to decide the point. He may require your company to amend your statement to include the information requested by the creditor making the objection, or he may decide to approve your statement as it stands. If it is accepted, then the balloting will begin on approval of your plan. The next hearing scheduled will be on the confirmation of the plan.

## SUMMING UP

The format of your disclosure statement is very flexible, but this may be a critical document for you to develop and file along with your plan. You are in control of what information is included and how it is presented. This may be the information some of your creditors are waiting for to make a decision about their intention to support your plan of reorganization; if you can motivate some of the key players, you may be able to get the majority you need for approval. Take the time to discuss your strategy with your lawyer, and then go to work on a persuasive document.

**Exhibit 11–1   Sample Disclosure Statement**

## In the United States Bankruptcy Court
## Northern District of Michigan

RE: XYZ INDUSTRIAL SUPPLY                          Chapter 11
                                                  Case XX-XXXX

### Disclosure Statement

The debtor provides this Disclosure Statement to all
its known creditors in order to disclose information
deemed by the debtor to be material, important and necessary for its creditors to arrive at a reasonably informed
decision in exercising the right to vote for acceptance of
the Plan of Reorganization filed with this Honorable
Court.

No representations concerning the debtor are authorized
by the debtor other than as set forth in this statement. Any
representations made to secure your acceptance which are
other than as contained in this statement, should not be re-
lied upon by you in arriving at your decision and such additional representations and inducements should be reported
to counsel for the Debtor, who in turn, shall deliver such
information to the Bankruptcy Court for such action as may
be deemed appropriate.

### I.   Summary of the Plan

The plan of Reorganization in this case will be funded by
the Debtor's cash on hand of $42,000 and Debtor's income
from operations.

All allowed expenses of Administration including professionals will be paid in full on the Plan's effective date
or will be paid by prior agreement with the parties.

The Priority Unsecured Claims of the Internal Revenue
Service and the State of Michigan will be paid in deferred
cash payments over 48 months after an initial payment of 25%
of the principal to each. This is in accordance with agreement with debtor.

The Secured Claims of Michigan Savings Bank will be paid
in deferred cash payments over 48 months after an initial
payment of 20% of the principal.

The Unsecured Creditors will receive the sum of
$76,000, a distribution of 25% of their claims. Ten per-
cent of this amount will be paid on the effective date and
the balance will be paid in 48 monthly payments along with
interest of 9%.

Exhibit 11–1 Sample Disclosure Statement    199

**Exhibit 11–1**  *(continued)*

The Equity security holders shall retain their shares in the Debtor.

The Plan discharges the Debtor from all of its debts upon confirmation of the Plan and vests all property in the Debtor.

## II.  Case Background

XYZ Industrial Supply has been in operation continuously in the State of Michigan since 1957. It has been operating at its current location since 1968. This company showed steady growth and profitable operations until 1985 and over the past 3 years has had a revenue decrease of 35%. However, its inventory management system is integrated with three large automotive plants and it continues to sell tools and general industrial supplies to these customers as well as new accounts XYZ has recently developed. The business is very cyclical.

The secured debt in this case was initially incurred to purchase a building, vehicles and to finance inventory purchases.

This Debtor has operated in seriously deteriorating market conditions for several years and the losses it has experienced have mirrored the substantial losses of the automotive industry that it supplies. Several disruptions in its cash flow forced this Debtor to fall behind in payments to its secured creditors and its trade vendors. It became necessary to reorganize under Chapter 11 of the Bankruptcy Code in order to restructure debt and reduce overhead expense.

Since the initial filing, XYZ Industrial Supply has stabilized its operation and began limited re-expansion of its marketing. In addition, the Debtor sold its warehouse, retired its mortgage, and negotiated a lease that allows it to utilize the same building for less cost. A substantial amount of inventory was liquidated at a one-time write down and the proceeds are currently in escrow for use to fund the Plan of Reorganization.

**Exhibit 11–1**  *(continued)*

## III.  Current States of Financial Affairs

| | |
|---|---:|
| Current Assets of Debtor | |
| Cash on Hand-Escrow | 42,000.00 |
| General Bank Accounts | 26,400.00 |
| Accounts Receivable | 32,450.00 |
| Inventory | 230,000.00 |
| Equipment and Vehicles | 16,000.00 |
| Total Assets | 346,850.00 |
| | |
| Liabilities of the Debtor | |
| Administrative Expense | |
| Legal and Accounting | 6,800.00 |
| Priority Unsecured | 35,650.00 |
| Secured Claims | 56,000.00 |
| Unsecured Claims | 304,000.00 |
| | 402,450.00 |

For the 1991 calendar year, operating results were as follows:

| | |
|---|---:|
| Sales | 981,600.00 |
| Less Returns and Discounts | 46,000.00 |
| Net Sales | 935,600.00 |
| | |
| Direct Expense | |
| Material | 440,000.00 |
| Direct Labor | 108.000.00 |
| Delivery | 9,000.00 |
| Inbound Freight | 7,000.00 |
| Total | 564,000.00 |
| Gross Profit | 371,600.00 |
| | |
| Administrative | |
| Salaries | 145,000.00 |
| Rent | 18,000.00 |
| Utilities | 24,000.00 |
| Office Expense | 20,800.00 |
| Legal and Accounting | 18,650.00 |
| Travel and Entertainment | 26,000.00 |
| Taxes | 34,000.00 |
| Employee Benefits | 32,500.00 |
| Debt Service | 12,000.00 |
| Total Expense | 330,950.00 |
| Net Before Taxes | 40,050.00 |

Exhibit 11–1 Sample Disclosure Statement    201

**Exhibit 11–1**   *(continued)*

## IV.  Liquidated Value of Company

   The following is the Debtor's estimate of the value of its assets if sold at liquidation. A percentage of its accounts may prove to be uncollectible. In addition, it is expected that an inventory liquidation would bring a very small return as a portion of that inventory is obsolete.

| | |
|---|---:|
| Cash on Hand-Escrow | 42,000.00 |
| General Bank Account | 26,400.00 |
| Accounts Receivable | 27,600.00 |
| Inventory | 21,000.00 |
| Equipment and Vehicles | 2,500.00 |
| | 119,500.00 |

## V.  Business Projections

   The Debtor expects relatively low growth over the next several years. Having reduced their break even point by 30%, the company is able to generate sufficient profit to service the debt payout being offered by their current Plan of Reorganization. The current monthly projected expenses are as follows:

| | |
|---|---:|
| Rent | 1,500.00 |
| Utilities | 2,000.00 |
| Salaries | 12,000.00 |
| Office Expense | 1,800.00 |
| Legal and Accounting | 1,475.00 |
| Travel and Entertainment | 2,200.00 |
| Employee Expense | 2,000.00 |
| Insurance (Employee) | 900.00 |
| Taxes | 2,800.00 |
| Debt Service | 3,800.00 |
| | 30,475.00 |

   Attached hereto as Exhibit "A" is a pro-forma statement for the years of 1992 and 1993. Income projections are based on contract estimates Debtor has received from current customers and may change if general economic conditions. All direct expenses are variable and based on the level of business activity.

## VI.  Chapter 7 Liquidation

   The projected net proceeds from a liquidation of the company's assets will generate approximately $119,500. This amount will be sufficient to retire the Debtor's secured

**Exhibit 11-1** *(continued)*

debt which is currently $56,000 plus any additional inter-
est which has accrued and is owing. There is currently an
amount of $6,800 of administrative debt owing for profes-
sional fees and this will continue to increase by $2,000 per
month while this case remains open and may be expected to exceed $15,000 at the time voting is completed on this Plan.
The residual amount would be approximately $48,000, all of
which would go to the priority unsecured creditors which are
taxing bodies in the State of Michigan and the Internal Revenue Service.

A Chapter 7 liquidation would add substantial administrative costs to this case including the continuing rental
payments to store inventory prior to any auction or sale as
well as the cost of conducting such a sale. A fee will be paid
to the trustee and the trustee's counsel. It is likely that
these costs would substantially erode the assets of this
Debtor to the degree that Priority Claims would not receive
the full amount of their claims. Under these circumstances,
the general unsecured creditors would receive nothing in a
Chapter 7 liquidation.

## VII.  Recommendation

Conversion to a Chapter 7 liquidation will serve no valid
purpose for priority unsecured creditors or general unsecured creditors. It is likely that the priority claims will
not be paid in full in a liquidation and the general unsecured claims would receive no return while the plan has offered a payment of 25% on this class of claim. In fact, the
initial payment to the general unsecured creditors will exceed their return in a forced liquidation. The priority
creditors will receive 100% of their claims under the plan
which they put at risk in a forced conversion. No creditor
will do better in a liquidation than the proposed Plan. The
Plan will derive the maximum return for all classes of creditors of this estate, therefore, the Plan is obviously in
the best interest of creditors.

Respectfully submitted,
XYZ Industrial Supply

Dated _____     by _____
                                       Joe Johnson, President

Michael L. Martin, Esquire
Martin & Martin
204 Craig Street
Dearborn, MI 33104
Attorney for Debtor-in-Possession

You have filed for bankruptcy to seek protection from your creditors until you have a chance to reorganize your debts. By the time you file your plan of reorganization, this phase is almost anticlimactic. Your filing put your creditors on notice that you were unable to retire your debts as previously agreed. You may have spent some time determining exactly what is the true balance of your legal debts. And before you begin to write a plan, you may have been negotiating with various groups of creditors working out a repayment plan. So instead of some type of mysterious document, a plan of reorganization is just a formal statement of these facts.

# 12

# YOUR BEST OFFER

## FILING YOUR PLAN OF REORGANIZATION

However, once a plan is confirmed, it becomes a binding agreement that has somewhat greater impact than the original debts of the company. Before the filing, if your company failed to make a payment, a creditor had to pursue you through several legal steps that took time and cost money. Once you have gone through the process of bankruptcy, the court can be asked to convert your case to a liquidation if you fail to abide by the terms of your plan. It could be a one-stroke deal, and you could be out of business. Keep that in mind as you commit your repayment offers to your plan. There is a way to modify a plan at a later date if your circumstances change and prevent you from following the original one. This is covered in Chapter 13.

Your plan will be filed along with your disclosure statement. Once the hearing has been held and the disclosure has been accepted, both will be sent to each creditor along with a ballot for voting. After the time has elapsed for ballots to be returned, the results are tabulated and reported at a confirmation hearing.

## WRITE YOUR PLAN OF REORGANIZATION

Unlike the disclosure statement, the rules governing the plan of reorganization are relatively specific (although no two lawyers write documents in the exact same way). Although many cases have situations unique to their set of circumstances, the sections of a plan are relatively standard and easy to write. Your attorney will have the basics in a "boiler-plate" style, and you can assist in customizing it to meet your needs. You needn't get involved in the writing of the plan as long as you understand all the implications and obligations that the plan creates. The following sections describe the usual items covered by the plan; Exhibit 12–1 (see pages 211) shows a sample reorganization plan for XYZ Industrial Supply Co.

## Article I:
## General Conditions and Terms

These are the legal definitions and assumptions that will be used throughout the plan. This section specifies how entities will be referred to and what if any conditions will apply to all classes (or claimants) through the reorganization process.

## Article II:
## Classification of All Claims and Interests

In simplified terms, the four major classes of creditors are administrative, secured, unsecured, and priority unsecured. There are also equity holders; bond holders; and in the case of larger, publicly traded companies, other debt holders.

Each class may then have subclasses that may have to do with the nature of their claim or the size of it. This is where you can, under the rules, wall off troublesome creditors into subclasses of their own or into groups where you are certain the majority will vote in favor.

## Article III:
## Treatment of Unimpaired Claims

All claims that will be paid the full value of their claim are considered unimpaired. In this section, you will describe how these claims are to be paid (i.e., the term and interest rate of repayment). Also if you are exchanging debt for an interest in equity, you will include that under this section.

# Article IV:
# Treatment of the Impaired Classes

Impaired claims are those that will not be paid the full amount of their claim. For the most part, this will be your unsecured creditor. You will specify what percentage their dividend will be and over what time payments will be made.

# Article V: Means for Execution

This section specifies who you expect to accomplish the payments set forth in the plan. Are there funds to be disbursed at acceptance? Will your company sell a major asset such as a division or plant and use the proceeds to fund the plan? Will you be issuing stock? Or will it be funded from ongoing operations? In addition to establishing that your company has the means to complete your plan, you also establish any dramatic changes in the assets of your business. An approved plan protects you if a creditors' committee goes after these questions.

# Article VI: All Special Terms

You might be able to limit your own special circumstances to one article but if your case has been complicated, there will be several special sections. In my case, there was a loan from me to the company, and I agreed to convert most of that claim to working capital and (in other words) to give the note. A small balance may be paid after other terms are completed.

Some items that may be covered separately may be the rejection of any leases or executory contracts. Perhaps you expect a consolidation of your operation on acceptance of your plan. You may be selling inventory or assets of a location to fund the plan. At that point, you would want to reject your lease if your plan was accepted.

Are there any outstanding lawsuits that if settled would bring additional assets or cost the company money?

This is just a sample of the types of issues that would fall under one or more special sections.

# Article VII: Jurisdiction

This section defines the specific areas in which the court retains jurisdiction over your case. In a case in which the largest payments are made at confirmation or shortly thereafter (if substantial assets are being liquidated), court jurisdiction may only be required for a short time. The main purpose for most cases will be to settle any claims that are in dispute. There are bound to be clean-up issues to be decided even if a plan is approved unanimously.

If your plan is a complicated one that requires payments made to a variety of creditors, perhaps through the U.S. Trustee as a dispersing agent, the court will retain jurisdiction for a longer period not only to settle disputes but also to oversee the completion of the plan.

In most cases it is desirable to leave the jurisdiction of the court as soon as possible because you will no longer have to incur legal expense associated with further court appearances.

## LEARN WHAT TO DO IF YOUR CREDITORS FILE A COMPETING PLAN

If you have filed a plan in the first 120 days and if you have received court permission to extend the exclusive period, then your plan will be the only one filed. If the exclusive period has run out and you neglected to ask the court to extend it or the court refused, however, then several different creditors' groups can file a plan of their own. The most likely candidate for this difficult turn of events is the creditors' committee.

It is not surprising that the key feature of most competing plans is that they give a higher return to the group that is doing the filing. There are several reasons that these demands are made in the form of a competing plan. One possible explanation is that this work is done by the lawyer representing the creditors; if it is the formally approved committee, these legal fees are charged to the debtor and become an administrative debt. Although the attorney may be trying to benefit the unsecured creditors, he is also benefiting his own law practice. This type of active lawyer is found in cases in which there will be cash available after the plan has been confirmed. If you have sold part of your business to create funds to effect a reorganization, what you might find is some very active lawyers circling your case. If you are communicating with members of this committee, you should be recommending the negotiation suggested in Chapter 10 rather than two competing plans. It could bring about the same result at far less the cost.

The other issue that may bring about a competing plan from creditors is if they think their return is not very likely from an operating company, and they demand a liquidating plan. That is when all assets are sold to satisfy claims. A liquidating plan may also be championed by one or more members of the creditors' committee that do not want to see you continue in business. Their reasons may be vindictive or they may even be competitive.

If the two plans that are filed are relatively close in nature, try to arrange some sort of negotiation to seek a compromise. Rather than have two plans out for voting, you get together and file a joint plan in place of the original one.

## How to Fight Off a Liquidation

If the competing plan suggests that a greater return will be from a sale of your assets, put your pen to paper and work hard to prove them wrong. Use your accountant to show how the return may not be what your creditors claim and how the costs of this action will increase the administrative costs; then, make sure this information is disclosed to anyone having to vote on the plan. Few liquidating plans return any payment to the unsecureds although their attorney may be paid. If your creditors are using unrealistic numbers, make sure the numbers are scrutinized.

If the liquidation is being proposed by a creditor who would benefit from the fact that you are no longer in business, that information should be brought to the attention of the court. File a motion explaining what the problem is and why these creditors should be denied the right to file their own plan. This is not an unusual circumstance, many of us do business with competitors from time to time and could find one of them as a creditor of our bankruptcy. Even if the judge does not decide to foreclose the possibility of this second plan, you will have brought the reasons behind the "other" plan to the attention of creditors who may be voting on both plans.

## GET CREDITORS TO VOTE ON YOUR REORGANIZATION PLAN

Your disclosure statement and plan will be sent to all creditors eligible to vote along with a ballot to return to the counsel for your company. Exhibit 12–2 shows a sample ballot (see page 208). The date for return will be entered on the ballot, and that is approximately 60 days, the time is set by the court. For the purpose of tabulation, only votes tendered are counted, not numbers of possible voters. Votes totaling one-half of the voting claims and two-thirds of the dollar amount of the voting claims are required for approval in each class.

You cannot campaign for a favorable vote, but you can ask your creditors to vote. It is important that those votes you know will be for

**Exhibit 12–2    Sample Ballot for Accepting or Rejecting a Reorganization Plan**

---

### IN THE UNITED STATES BANKRUPTCY COURT
### FOR THE WESTERN DISTRICT OF PENNSYLVANIA

---

IN RE: Pittsburgh Glove      Chapter 11
       Manufacturing Company      Case No. _____

       Debtor

#### Ballot for Accepting or Rejecting Plan

The plan referred to in this ballot can be confirmed by the Court and thereby made binding on you if it is accepted by the holders of two-thirds in amount and more than one-half in number of claims in each class and the holders of two-thirds in amount of equity security interests in each class voting on the Plan. In the event the requisite acceptances are not obtained, the Court may nevertheless confirm the Plan if the Court finds that the Plan accords fair and equitable treatment to the class rejecting it. To have your vote count, you must complete and return this ballot.

If equity security holder: The undersigned, the holder of (number) _____ shares of (describe type) _____ stock of the above-named Debtor, represented by Certificate No. (s) _____, registered in the name of _____.

If holder of a secured claim: The undersigned, a secured creditor of the above-named Debtor in the unpaid principal amount of $_____, and having a security interest in the following property of the estate, _____.

If holder of a general, priority, or administrative claim: The undersigned, a creditor of the above-named Debtor in the unpaid principal amount of $_____.

#### Check One Box

( ) Accepts
( ) Rejects
the Plan for the reorganization of the above-named Debtors.

Dated: _____, 19____

     Print or Type Name: _____
       Signature:
       (If Appropriate) _____
       By:             _____
       As:             _____
       Address:      _____
     RETURN THIS BALLOT ON OR BEFORE _____, 19____ to: _____

approval are returned so call and remind these creditors to return their ballots. Check with your attorney periodically and make follow-up calls if necessary. It's your own "get-out-the-vote" strategy.

## Understand the Confirmation Process

After the votes have been tabulated by your lawyer, they will be read into the record at the confirmation hearing. If you have achieved the level of votes needed for approval, the judge will confirm the vote and issue orders to that effect. Exhibit 12–3 shows a sample confirming order (see page 215).

If the vote goes against approval, however, several possibilities exist for what happens next. If the judge thinks that your plan has not met the criteria required by the Bankruptcy Code, he will deny approval, and then you will be required to go back to the drawing board to recreate a new plan, and the process will begin again.

If one class of creditor has voted in favor of the plan, however, it can be approved over the objections of those who have voted against it. This is known as a "cram down" and it can be forced on either the secured or unsecured creditors.

If you have offered payments in the full value of a secured creditor's interest in your collateral and the creditor is unhappy with the terms of the payback, the court can "cram down" on that class of creditor.

In the case of the unsecured creditors, if their class is receiving more by the terms of the plan than they would receive in a liquidation, the court can force this class to accept the plan that is being offered. In the case of a "cram down" on the unsecureds, no distribution would be available to the shareholders.

It is not as easy as it sounds to force a "cram down" on your creditors, and it will require some work on the part of your lawyer that will be costly to you in legal fees as well as time. If the case comes down to a real power struggle with one class of creditors, this becomes a negotiating play, and if the one class becomes absolutely unmanageable, it's another strategy in your arsenal.

## What Happens after Confirmation

Once the court has confirmed your plan, you are emerging from bankruptcy. You still have a 60-day period until the effective date when the case is no longer appealable to the court. During this period, you will also have the right to challenge any claims. You file a motion to "disallow" a claim and submit the documentation you have to substantiate your case. If the creditor doesn't respond, their claim will be voided. If they submit evidence to the validity of their claim, the judge will decide the matter.

Other than the settlement of claims, you will no longer have any court involvement in the day-to-day operation of our business. You will run your business much as you did before you filed for protection employing professionals, making contracts and making loans without any prior approval.

The court's only function where your business is concerned is to enforce the terms of the plan; if you fail to live up to those terms, it can be brought to the attention of the court for its action. This can result in a conversion to a Chapter 7 liquidation.

Your plan is a contract with your creditors specifying the debt you owe to each one and how you have agreed to make payments. After a confirmation, your creditors cannot demand a greater payback nor can they accelerate the terms of payback that were specified in the plan. The plan is binding on both sides.

You will no longer have the protection of the court from any debt you incur after your company has emerged from bankruptcy. Any creditors with claims arising after confirmation can proceed with all legal collection action through foreclosure. It is also forbidden for you to use your former status as a bankrupt company to dissuade any collection action, and the court could take action against your company for attempting this tactic. This could result in money damages being awarded to the creditor.

But the real joy is the accomplishment of sailing up these shark-infested waters and getting safely to port. It isn't easy but it is possible.

## SUMMING UP

Your plan of reorganization is your formal offer to repay outstanding debt over an extended period of time. Write your plan carefully, understanding its implications and be prepared to have it approved and consummated.

Exhibit 12–1   Sample Reorganization Plan   **211**

**Exhibit 12–1   Sample Reorganization Plan**

## IN THE UNITED STATES BANKRUPTCY COURT
## FOR THE NORTHERN DISTRICT OF MICHIGAN

RE: XYZ INDUSTRIAL SUPPLY                    Chapter 11
                                          Case XX-XXXX

### Plan of Reorganization

   XYZ Industrial Supply, the Debtor, hereby proposes the following Plan.

### ARTICLE I

### General Conditions and Terms

   A. All terms employed herein shall have the meanings set forth in the United States Bankruptcy Code, (11 USC § 101 *et seq.*) unless specifically defined to the contrary herein.

   B. When used herein, the words set forth below shall have the following meanings, except to the extent the context otherwise unambiguously requires:

1. "Administrative Expense Claim" shall mean claims pursuant to 11 U.S.C., Section 503, accruing from and after the date on which this Chapter 11 case commenced, including fees and expenses of professional persons retained or to be compensated pursuant to the Code.

2. "Allowed Claim" shall mean a claim which has been scheduled pursuant to 11 U.S.C., Section 521(1), other than a claim scheduled as disputed, contingent or unliquidated, or which has been timely filed pursuant to 11 U.S.C., Section 501(a), and, in either instance, with respect to which no objection to the allowance thereof has been made within the period of limitation set forth in this Plan, or which has been approved and fixed in amount and nature by Order of the Court pursuant to 11 U.S.C. §§ 502, 503 and/or 507.

3. "Claim" shall mean each duly listed and timely filed claim.

4. "Claimant" shall mean the holder of an Unsecured Claim, an Administrative Expense Claim and/or a Priority Claim in this proceeding.

5. "Confirmation Date" shall mean both the event and the date of entry by this Court of an Order confirming this Plan in accordance with Section 1129 of the Code.

6. "Court" means the Bankruptcy Court for the Northern District of Michigan.

**Exhibit 12–1** *(continued)*

7. "Disputed Claim" shall mean any claim as to which an objection to the allowance thereof has been interposed and not determined by an Order.

8. "Effective Date" shall be the date sixty (60) days following Confirmation.

9. "Interests" shall mean the Allowed Interests of all (a) holders of Stock in the Debtor, (b) holders of bonds of the Debtor, and all holders of options, warrants and similar instruments for the acquisition of the Debtor's Stock, and (c) persons who constitute "Equity Security Holders" within the meaning of Code § 101(16) arising from the equity securities of the Debtor as defined in § 101(15) which have been scheduled by the Debtor or have timely filed a proof of interest herein.

10. "Order" shall mean an order or judgment which has not been reversed or stayed and as to which the time to appeal or to seek review or rehearing has expired and as to which no appeal or petition for review or rehearing is pending and which is not the subject to an application for certiorari.

11. "Priority Claim" shall mean the portion of an Allowed Claim entitled to priority under 11 U.S.C. § 507(a)(1) through and including 507(a)(7).

12. "Pro Rata" shall mean the same proportion that an Allowed Claim in a particular Class bears to the aggregate amount of all claims in that Class.

13. "Rules" or "Rule" shall mean the Bankruptcy Rules promulgated by the Supreme Court of the United States, as the same may be amended.

14. "Secured Claimant" shall mean the holder of a Secured Claim.

15. "Secured Claim" shall mean any Allowed Claim, which is secured by a valid, perfected and enforceable lien on property of the Debtor, to the extent of the value of the interest of the holder of such Allowed Claim in such property of the Debtor as determined by the Court pursuant to 11 U.S.C., § 506(a), the amount of which Secured Claim and the value of which collateral have been fixed either by Order of the Court or settlement approved by Court order. To the extent of any deficiency in the value of the interest of the holder of the Secured Claim in such property, such deficiency shall be treated as an Unsecured Claim.

Exhibit 12–1    Sample Reorganization Plan    **213**

**Exhibit 12–1**    *(continued)*

16. "Unsecured Claim" shall mean an Allowed Claim which is not entitled to priority under 11 U.S.C., Section 507(a), or where the claimant does not hold a valid, perfected an enforceable lien or security interest, as defined in 11 U.S.C., Section 101(31) and (41); provided, however, that interest and other charges accruing, arising or imposed after the Filing Date, if any, shall not be part of an Unsecured Claim.

## ARTICLE II

### Classification of All Claims and Interests

Pursuant to Code Section 1123(a)(1), the Plan shall treat the following classes of Claims and interest in the following manner:

A. All Allowable Administrative Claims: All claims entitled to priority pursuant to Section 503(B) of the United States Bankruptcy Code consisting of the costs and expenses of and compensation for the services rendered by attorneys and accountants employed by the Debtor in such amounts as may be allowed by the Bankruptcy Court. This classification also includes those claims that arose in the normal course of business during the Debtor's post-petition operation.

### Class 1 Priority Unsecured Claims

These are the claims of the Internal Revenue Service and the State of Michigan Bureau of Employment which are pursuant to Section 507(a)(3)(4)(5)(6) or (7).

### Class 2 Secured Claims of Michigan Savings Bank

### Class 3 Small Unsecured Claims

These are claims of less than $1,000.

### Class 4 Large Unsecured Claims

These are all remaining unsecured claims of value greater than $1,000.

## ARTICLE III

### Treatment of Unimpaired Claims

Administrative Claims—This class which includes $6,800 of legal and accounting fees will be paid in full on the Plan's effective date or will be paid in accordance with agreements with the particular claimants. Trade claims in this class will be paid in accordance with ordinary business terms.

### Class 1 Priority Unsecured Claims

These claims include $21,600 due to the Internal Revenue Service and $14,050 due to the State of Michigan Bureau of Employment. The Internal Revenue Service shall receive

**Exhibit 12–1** *(continued)*

$5,400 on the effective date and the balance over 48 months at an interest rate of 8%. The State of Michigan Bureau of Employment shall receive $3,512.50 on the effective date and the balance over 48 months at an interest rate of 8%.

### Class 2 Secured Claims

The secured claims of the Michigan Savings Bank in the total amount of $56,000 shall receive 20% of their claim ($11,200) on the effective date and the balance shall be paid over 48 months at 9% interest.

### ARTICLE IV

### Treatment of Impaired Claims

### Class 3 Small Unsecured Claims

The Small unsecured claims are those less than $1,000 and they will receive 25% of their total allowable claims. Fifty percent of this amount will be paid on the effective date and the balance will be paid one year from that date. There are eight claims in this class.

### Class 4 Large Unsecured Claims

Unsecured claims in excess of $1,000 are included in this class and they will receive 25% of their total claim. This class will receive 10% on the effective date and the balance over 48 months at 9% interest rate.

### ARTICLE V

### Means for Execution

This Plan will be funded from the Debtor's fund of $42,000 acquired from the liquidation of certain inventory with permission of the court. The balance will be provided from the ongoing operation of the Debtor.

The Debtor shall be revested with all assets which will remain encumbered only as to Class 2 claimants as stated above. The Debtor is discharged from all debts upon consummation of this Plan. Debtor's assets may be subsequently sold, transferred, encumbered, liened or dealt with as may be appropriate in Debtor's judgment subject, of course, to valid liens, if any. Upon confirmation, Debtor's affairs will be managed without further supervision of the court.

### ARTICLE VI

### Special Terms

1. The Debtor's president, Jim Johnson, shall convert his note due from the Debtor into working capital agreeing to no further claim on this loan.

Exhibit 12–1   Sample Reorganization Plan   **215**

**Exhibit 12–1**  *(continued)*

2. The Debtor reaffirms all contracts pursuant to the purchase of all vehicles currently in effect with the Michigan Savings Bank.

3. The Debtor, through its attorney, shall continue to pursue legal action for collection of unpaid invoices due prior to the filing of this bankruptcy.

### ARTICLE VII

### Jurisdiction

The Court shall retain jurisdiction of this case pursuant to the United States Bankruptcy Code until such time as a discharge is issued by the Court. The venue shall remain in the Northern District of Michigan. The jurisdiction so retained shall include, but not be limited to, the authority to:

A. Hear, find, determine, fix, allow and disallow all claims against the Debtor, its assets and its estate.

B. To resolve any disputes arising out of the bankruptcy proceedings.

C. Hear, find, fix determine, allow and disallow all claims arising from the rejection of any executory contract and any objections which may be made thereto.

D. To make such orders as are necessary to carry out the provisions of the Plan.

E. To recover all assets and properties of the Debtor, wherever located. Nothing shall prevent the reorganized Debtor from pursuing action to recover assets of estate whether or not action was prosecuted prior to the filing in this case.

F. Permit the correction of any defect herein, the curing of any omission and/or the reconciliation of any inconsistency herein or in the order of confirmation.

G. Hear and adjudicate any alleged default under and enforce this Plan.

H. To enter a final order concluding the case.

Respectfully submitted,
XYZ Industrial Supply

Dated _____          by _____
Joe Johnson, President

Michael L. Martin, Esquire
Martin & Martin
204 Craig Street
Dearborn, MI 33104
Attorney for Debtor-in-Possession

**Exhibit 12–3    Sample Court Order Confirming a Reorganization Plan**

---

## IN THE UNITED STATES BANKRUPTCY COURT
### FOR THE WESTERN DISTRICT OF PENNSYLVANIA

---

IN RE: PITTSBURGH GLOVE                    NO. _____
      MANUFACTURING COMPANY            CHAPTER 11

### Order Confirming Plan

The plan under chapter 11 of the Bankruptcy Code filed by Pittsburgh Glove Manufacturing Company, on May 7, 1990, as modified by a modification filed on October 5, 1990, a summary thereof having been transmitted to creditors and equity security holders; and

It having been determined after hearing on notice that:

1. The plan has been accepted in writing by the creditors and equity security holders whose acceptance is required by law; and

2. The provisions of chapter 11 of the Code have been complied with; that the plan has been proposed in good faith and not by any means forbidden by law; and

3. Each holder of a claim or interest has accepted the plan or will receive or retain under the plan property of a value, as of the effective date of the plan, that is not less than the amount that such holder would receive or retain if the debtor were liquidated under chapter 7 of the Code on such date; and

4. All payments made or promised by the debtor or by a person issuing securities or acquiring property under the plan or by any other person for services or for costs and expenses in, or in connection with, the plan and incident to the case, have been fully disclosed to the court and are reasonable or, if to be fixed after confirmation of the plan, will be subject to the approval of the court; and

5. The identity, qualifications, and affiliations of the persons who are to be directors or officers, or voting trustees, if any, of the debtor after confirmation of the plan, have been fully disclosed, and the appointment of such persons to such offices, or their continuance therein, is equitable, and consistent with the interest of the creditors and equity security holders and with public policy; and

6. The identity of any insider that will be employed or retained by the debtor and his compensation have been fully disclosed; and

7. Confirmation of the plan is not likely to be followed by the liquidation.

Exhibit 12–3    Sample Court Order Confirming a Reorganization Plan    217

**Exhibit 12–3**  *(continued)*

It is ordered that:

The plan filed by Pittsburgh Glove Manufacturing Company, on October 5, 1990, a copy of which plan is attached hereto, is confirmed.

Date: _____, 1990

BY THE COURT,

_____

For 60 days after a plan has been confirmed, it is appealable by either the debtor or the creditors as to any claims or specific provisions. You may be likely to appeal the amounts of some specific claims. Your creditors may make a final appeal about how their claim was classified. If a creditor did not object at the disclosure process or at the confirmation, however, the chances are that they have lost most of their grounds.

Another issue that can be raised by creditors (and that extends this limbo period for up to 180 days) is that some fraud was involved in the plan or in securing the vote of creditors. The fraud that is most frequently charged is that an incentive was offered to some creditors to secure their approval. That is why it is forbidden that you discuss their vote with any of your creditors once the balloting has begun.

From the perspective of your right to file against any claim, that may be a subjective call. You should, as early in the case as possible, review all proofs of claim that have been submitted. I was quite surprised that some of my vendors submitted claims for more

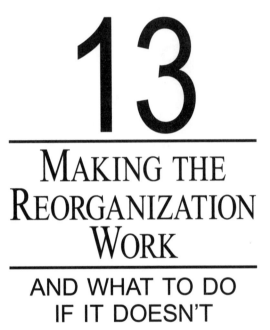

# 13

# MAKING THE REORGANIZATION WORK

## AND WHAT TO DO IF IT DOESN'T

than was actually owed to them. Their motivation may have been that because they expected to collect only a percentage of their bill, they raised the amount and would get a bigger percentage return. Or it may have been an inadvertent error. You may want to dispute these claims if their total cost is worth your time and effort. Remember, you may be arguing over the face value of a claim that you will be paying at 10% or 20%. And it may be a payment over time.

If a disputed claim is with one of your current vendors, it may be more beneficial in the long run to let it go. You have an ongoing business relationship to cultivate that is more important than this dispute. Remember that they will be writing off a portion of your debt, and it has taken some time to get paid at all. Don't make any offer to a creditor not to dispute a claim to get their vote—just make a prudent decision.

## KEEP TRACK OF ALL PAYMENTS MADE UNDER THE TERMS OF THE PLAN

On the effective date, you will make the first disbursements under the plan. These will be paid from the funds you have identified in your plan as being available for this purpose. If your plan specified the sale of some asset to create funds for this purpose, you can consummate the sale.

Regardless of when you pay and from what source, you will want to keep good records regarding your compliance with the plan. Send a cover letter to creditors stating whether this is an initial disbursement or a single payment. Record the case number on the check as your receipt of the payment. Keep a set of separate records so that you can document the completion of your plan when you go to court for the final discharge.

The payments you make under the plan must be sacrosanct to you. In the earlier months of payments, it wouldn't hurt to send remittance in advance as a way of reassuring your creditors of your intention of living up to your obligations. If you start out with a cavalier attitude, you won't be taken seriously and you won't take this second chance seriously. If you need some indulgence down the road from these creditors, you will be more likely to get it if you've been diligent when you began the reorganization.

## LEARN HOW TO REESTABLISH CREDIT

Going through the experience of bankruptcy gives one some real insight into the world of credit. What you learn is that you can't make someone pay a bill that they are equally intent on not paying. It is possible to sue them in court, to get a judgment, and to execute that judgment to take property including cash in a bank account. But each step is time-consuming and adds legal fees. And in the end, it is possible that the company that owes the money will file bankruptcy and pay little or none of their bill. And the creditor could get stuck with a legal fee!

Then how should credit decisions be made? The fact is that the best predictors of a small business are the ethics and intentions of the principals of the company. If you have gone through a financial reorganization, you have proved that your company stands by its commitments to the best of their ability and works through difficulties when they arise. That should be worth something, and you may want to point this out to vendors as you begin to reestablish some open lines of credit. It is difficult to make your business begin to grow again without the capital to fuel that growth. Vendor credit is one form of capital, and it could make an important contribution to the resurgence of your business.

The only way to find out if a vendor would be willing to ship you on open terms is to ask. Perhaps you can work a deal of limited credit to start with and the promise of an increase if all bills are retired in their terms. You might be surprised that your vendor will agree, and then it is up to you to win back the terms that will allow your business to prosper. One word of warning: If any vendor ties new credit to a recovery of the debt not paid under the plan, don't agree to these terms. It may jeopardize your standing with all creditors.

## Get Credit from Your Bank

Being able to find new lines of credit from the bank may be more difficult. The assets you have used as collateral for secured loans remain liened until the loans are repaid. There is very little chance of funding any unsecured loans to a company coming out of bankruptcy. What you may be able to do after you have repaid a portion of your original loan is to renegotiate a larger loan to take full value of the assets you have as collateral and provide working capital. Or you could develop a different banking relationship and negotiate a new loan that will retire your old bank debt and provide capital.

## Get Credit from Investors

Finally, there is the possibility of venture capital or equity capital that you might be able to attract if your business has the potential for a healthy rebound. If your reorganization has been an effective one, your debt service may be low enough that you have a favorable overall cost. If your company has become "lean and mean" through the experience, you may be positioned to be a competitive force in the market, that's part of what the process is about. This could attract the interest of outside investors and really allow you to find capital in return for either a stake in the enterprise or a stake in future profits. You are free to negotiate with any and all interested parties once your company has emerged, although, depending on the type of deal, you'll need to inform creditors, and you may want to complete the plan and seek a final discharge if you have the funds available.

The bottom line is that you really do have an opportunity to re-create your business as a new and profitable and growing entity. If the core business has remained intact, then the future has unlimited possibilities.

## COMMUNICATE WITH YOUR CREDITORS WHILE COMPLETING YOUR REORGANIZATION PLAN

There are several reasons to be in regular communication with your creditors. First, it is easier than it had been during your stay in bankruptcy. You are now sending regular payments, and it can be a reminder to include some updates on your progress. It doesn't have to be a complete statement, but one or two lines could have a good effect.

The second reason to reestablish a cordial ongoing relationship is so that if you need the indulgence of your creditor to delay a payment over a short period, this will not be the only contact they have had with you. Cooperation is more readily given to companies that know you.

And, finally, this approach is generally a good public relations strategy that could add a marketing push to let others in the business community know that you are doing well. That was evident as I looked for successful reorganizations to investigate in preparation for this book. The bankers and lawyers I spoke to in order to get names, first mentioned those companies who had made it known how they had successfully reorganized. It isn't an easy task, and, frankly, it does impress people who know what a challenge it can be. Why not turn that admiration into free publicity for your company?

## HOW TO HANDLE TEMPORARY CASH-FLOW SHORTAGES

The court will retain jurisdiction over your case as it pertains to the successful completion of the terms of your plan of reorganization. They will not oversee your case with any monitoring system; rather, they will respond to any formal notice from creditors that you are not living up to the plan. Therefore, if you find yourself with a temporary cash-flow shortage or the need to use your cash resources for a major purchase or repair, you can work out a deferred payment arrangement with your individual creditors. As long as they are satisfied with what you are offering, they won't take any outside action such as going back to the court. If you run into some temporary difficulties, go directly to your creditors first.

Depending on how you have redeveloped your relationships with creditors and how long you have been complying to the letter of the plan, you may find them very willing to work with you over a short-term difficulty. After all, it will take both time and legal fees for them to force you back into compliance and by that time, your difficulties will be over. And if you are forced to make payments that exceed your ability, your business may be jeopardizing its very survival and, with it, the hopes of your creditors to be paid back at least some return. At this point, their level of awareness of this risk is certainly heightened.

## WHAT TO DO IF YOUR PLAN WAS TOO AMBITIOUS FOR CURRENT BUSINESS LEVELS

Perhaps you weren't as diligent as you should have been when offering a plan to your creditors. Or in the heat of conflict or negotiating, you offered more to one class of creditor without considering how high the monthly payments were getting. Perhaps your plan was reasonable, but after it was confirmed, your company ran into a single troublesome event such as the need to move (which happened to my company) or the bankruptcy of one of your customers. Down the road, business conditions can deteriorate, shrinking your revenues, profit, or both. It doesn't mean that the company will fail. It does mean that steps will have to be taken to deal with your creditors early and effectively. Letting this situation get out of hand, even if the reason is a particularly compelling one, will be a disaster.

The logical first step is to go to a few creditors if an arrangement with them will make the difference. If relief will require an adjustment on your payment to the pool of unsecureds, it wouldn't be prudent to try to accomplish this casually.

You can go back to the court with a request to amend your plan. Have your attorney file a motion for "leave" to change the original document. Exhibit 13–1 shows a sample motion for leave to modify the plan (see page 224). If the court gives approval, you can try to work out a new plan.

Prompt action is a key factor in the success of any changes. The experiences of the past should teach you that avoiding problems does not make them go away. Once you've achieved the confirmation of a plan, it would be a tragedy not to complete it—particularly when it is possible to get further cooperation from creditors and the court to make it a success. Just don't let notice of any problems get to anyone's desk unless it is sent there by you.

This is the beginning of a new chance for your business, make the best of it!

## SUMMING UP

It is critical to be diligent about making all payments that are covered by the confirmed plan. If any indulgence of your creditors is needed, first got directly to the creditor in advance of due date. If your circumstances change drastically, you may file motions with the court to amend the original plan.

**Exhibit 13–1     Sample Motion for Extension of Time or for Leave to Modify the Reorganization Plan**

---

IN THE UNITED STATES BANKRUPTCY COURT
FOR THE WESTERN DISTRICT OF PENNSYLVANIA

---

IN RE: PITTSBURGH GLOVE          Case No. _____-_____
       MANUFACTURING COMPANY,

       Debtor

## Motion for Extension of Time and/or for Leave to Modify Plan

AND NOW, comes the debtor in possession, Pittsburgh Glove Manufacturing Company, and sets forth the following in support of its motion:

1. On or about December 13, 1990, this court confirmed the debtor's amended plan of reorganization, and on January 2, 1991, a post-confirmation order was entered.

2. Since the date of the entry of the order of confirmation and the post-confirmation order, debtor has made disbursement of all initial payments required under the plan to secured creditors, to its priority creditors, and to its administrative creditors.

3. To date, the only class of creditors to whom the debtor has not yet made disbursement is the class of unsecured creditors; however, the debtor in possession has filed objections to a number of the unsecured claims in preparation for disbursement.

4. On or about January 3, 1991, the debtor's landlord, _____, informed the debtor that _____ intended to terminate its business and vacate the building which it has been sharing with the debtor in possession.

5. On or about January 28, 1991, the debtor in possession's landlord advised the debtor in possession that the building where the debtor in possession's business is located would be closed within the next ten days.

6. The cost of heating the aforesaid building is so excessive that the debtor is unable to bear the cost on its own.

7. The debtor has had continuing problems over the last year with the landlord due to plumbing failures, broken windows which remain unrepaired, and lack of heat.

8. The debtor is hoping that it will be able to negotiate some type of lease with a prospective buyer which the landlord has; however, if the building is not sold, the debtor believes and therefore avers that it will be compelled to relocate its business to other premises.

Exhibit 13–1    Sample Motion for Extension or Modification of Plan    225

**Exhibit 13–1** *(continued)*

9. If the debtor is forced to relocate, the debtor believes and therefore avers that the cost of relocating its business, exclusive of income lost due to business interruption, would be between approximately $_____$ to $_____$, due to the cost of moving of the 35,000 lbs of machinery, inventory and equipment, the cost of rewiring premises to accommodate the aforesaid machinery (estimated to be $_____$ to $_____$); and other costs incidental to moving.

10. The debtor had planned to disburse the sum of $_____$ among its unsecured creditors upon resolution of the objections to claims proceedings.

11. If the debtor is compelled to relocated the debtor believes and therefore avers that it will be necessary for the debtor to invade the fund for unsecured creditors in order to accomplish the move.

12. The debtor is able to continue to make payments to its secured creditors pursuant to the terms of the confirmed plan, and believes that it would be able to make partial payments to unsecured creditors on an installment basis if it is granted leave to modify the confirmed plan.

WHEREFORE, debtor respectfully requests this Honorable Court to grant the debtor leave to file a modified plan permitting the debtor to make the payments which it intended to make pro rata to its unsecured creditor at the same rate but on an installment basis rather than making a lump sum distribution, in order to preserve the debtor's funds in case of a necessary move.

Respectfully submitted,

_____

Mary E. Bower

**Exhibit 13–1**   *(continued)*

## IN THE UNITED STATES BANKRUPTCY COURT
### FOR THE WESTERN DISTRICT OF PENNSYLVANIA

IN RE: PITTSBURGH GLOVE        Case No. _____-_____
      MANUFACTURING COMPANY,

      Debtor

### Order of Court

AND NOW, to wit, this _____ day of _____, 1991, upon consideration of the debtor's motion for extension of time and/or leave to modify its confirmed plan, it is ORDERED, ADJUDGED and DECREED that the debtor in possession is hereby granted leave to amend the confirmed plan by modifying the treatment of unsecured creditors pursuant to the confirmed plan. The debtor is directed to file its modified plan of reorganization with _____ days from the date of this order.

                    BY THE COURT,

                    _____ J.

It is possible at any time during the course of a Chapter 11 reorganization for a creditor to go to court to request a conversion to a Chapter 7 liquidation. The most frequent reason is that your company is continuing to lose money and the value of the "estate" is diminishing and will ultimately return less to each creditor.

It may be the action of the secured creditor to foreclose on their collateral which is pivotal to your operation. He may want to liquidate his loan quickly for a specific reason (such as the fact you are no longer making any payments) or simply because it is current policy of the bank which may have as much to do with the health of their organization as yours.

The office of the U.S. Trustee may move for a Chapter 7 conversion because no plan has been put forward, and it is noticed after a certain length of time. Again, this can sometimes be a relatively arbitrary situation having as much to do with the staff resources in the local office as anything else. In

# 14

# WHAT'S THE WORST THAT COULD HAPPEN?

## CONVERSION TO CHAPTER 7 LIQUIDATION

a small understaffed office, your case could "fall through the cracks" for a year or more. Then one day a new trustee will be assigned to the office and action will be taken. In my own case, a new trustee came and filed for a conversion against us. At the time, however, we did have a plan circulating but our disclosure hearing had been postponed by the action of the SBA. A case of one government agency not paying attention to another government agency.

One other reason that a conversion may be requested is your voluntary action. You may no longer want to go through the aggravation of the reorganization process, or it may become evident to you that it won't really work in the long run.

You should not be reticent about making this decision. It may be in the best interest of everyone concerned including you. Whether or not it is your decision, it is in your personal best interest to have a say in when the conversion begins and how an orderly liquidation takes place.

## WHAT HAPPENS IN A CHAPTER 7 LIQUIDATION

Once the court has granted a motion for a Chapter 7 conversion, all actions that had been a part of the Chapter 11 case are stopped such as any sale of assets. A trustee will now be appointed to oversee the orderly liquidation of your assets. Normally at this point, your business will cease operating. If it is in the best interest of the creditors that the business continues for the purpose of selling inventory or maybe even finding a buyer for all or part of the going concern, however, it may continue, and you may be paid to operate it. At this time, the control of the assets are out of your hands.

The clerk of the bankruptcy court will notify all of your creditors that a Chapter 7 proceeding has been ordered. A new meeting of creditors will now be scheduled and this could be far more difficult than the first. If you have been operating under Chapter 11 for any length of time, you may find yourself under great scrutiny of your creditors as to how resources were used during your operating period. They will want to know exactly what assets are still existing and what their value is currently.

## HANDLE PERSONAL BANKRUPTCY UNDER CHAPTER 7

If your company is not incorporated, this will also be a personal bankruptcy. To discharge the debts of an unincorporated company, the conversion will also include your personal assets. This could really add to the stress and difficulty of the entire situation and you will have to consider its implications before you voluntarily take this action.

In this circumstance, the questioning becomes very personal because all of your possessions are now possible assets for the trustee to liquidate and pay off your business creditors. There are several items that may be exempt (including jointly owned property of a certain value or the total value of a single main residence) under federal laws as well as under state laws, and you may elect one form over the other.

At this point, you should rely on the advice of your counsel, and you may want to check with a second attorney in addition to the one who handled the business reorganization. Your personal interests and those of your business may not always be the same. Although it will add to your cost, it may be prudent to employ your own attorney, particularly when you have a claim to assert against the liquidation of an incorporated business.

## WORK WITH A TRUSTEE TO LIQUIDATE YOUR COMPANY

Each district has a list of individuals (usually lawyers) who are qualified to serve as trustees in liquidation cases. As a case comes up, they are chosen to serve at random so you never know who may be the trustee on your particular case. The trustee, once a case has been assigned, will make sure there aren't any conflicts with his firm (they may have previously been representing a creditor), and then he will review the docket (in a Chapter 11 case it may be quite extensive) to see if this is an "asset" case. This means, are there any assets left in your company to sell or liquidate to pay creditors. The trustee is paid a fee of 3% based on the value of the estate and other fees for service that his firm performs. If all there is left is property on which there are secured loans, the trustee may try to give the asset back to the lienholder as satisfaction of the lien. Side deals are sometimes negotiated to authorize the trustee to actually conduct a sale of property as an agent of the lienholder. A "nonasset" case will get very little attention from anyone although a small fee will still be paid to the trustee to file all of the appropriate paperwork.

A case with assets will get work and effort from a trustee. He may begin by collecting all receivables and arranging to sell all tangible property. As mentioned earlier in this chapter, the business may be kept opened to sell inventory particularly in the case of a retail operation. You may be hired to run this final sale and paid by the trustee. You do not have to accept this role, and the trustee does not have to hire you. He may hire a professional liquidator.

There are reasons that you may want to participate in the sale as well as other aspects of the trustee's job that are discussed later in this chapter. If you have personal liability on secured debts or unpaid taxes, it is in your best interest to make sure that the greatest return is achieved from any sale of the company's assets. Your knowledge and experience can really make the difference in any sale. A liquidator may bring in other merchandise to include in "your sale," and prices will be cut to follow a formula not necessarily best in your market.

There is little doubt that this could be a very painful experience that you don't want to go through, and, again, you don't have to do it. Your decision will probably be one part logical and one part emotional.

Another role of the trustee will be to review all proofs of claim that are filed in the "new" Chapter 7 case. Because money will be disbursed to those who file new "proofs," it is in the best interest of the estate that these be reviewed by someone with inside information, namely, you. This task can be less difficult than the "going out of business" sale so you may want to consider participating in this aspect of the case. You will not be paid for this work.

The trustee has the ability to investigate the conduct of your company during its stay in Chapter 11 as well as before the initial filing. If your books and records are in fairly good condition and you are cooperative with the trustee, there's a good chance that he won't scrutinize every transaction but remember that he does have the authority to do so.

The trustee must convert all assets of your company to cash, and he has great latitude to accomplish this task. He can sell in bulk, and he can hold an auction. He will incur costs of either maintaining your current location or using storage or warehouse facilities before conducting the sale, which, under certain circumstances, will require approval of the court. You have the right to be one of the purchasers of any assets you desire either by making any offer to the trustee or coming to a public sale. There is nothing to stop you from starting up again in the same type of business, even using the merchandise of your old company. You can also buy the rights to the company name. It's been done before and occasionally with great success.

## HOW FUNDS ARE DISBURSED IN A LIQUIDATION

The secured creditors are permitted to foreclose on their property or to take the proceeds of any sale of their collateral less any fees that had been negotiated with the trustee. All other claims are retired in relatively the same order as a Chapter 11.

The first payments go to the administrative claims that by this time could have become very substantial. They will include any approved attorney and accounting fees left over from the stay in Chapter 11. Then there are the fees from the trustee, his attorney, and any other professionals they may have hired. All costs the trustee has incurred to warehouse, move, advertise, or sell goods to generate the cash will be paid as administrative debts.

Next on the list will be the priority unsecured debts, which are normally monies due to taxing bodies. In some instances, a trustee can reduce these debts to their principal alone, and have certain penalties and interest waived. If you are personally liable for these unpaid taxes, you will want to see that the money goes this far.

Last on the list are the general unsecured debts that would have received a percentage return under a plan of reorganization but seldom receive any distribution under a liquidation. This group may have formed into a creditors' committee on your initial filing, and they are given a second chance to form if there is a conversion to a Chapter 7. At this point, however, their attorney is far more likely to receive his fee than they are to receive any settlement.

## HOW A CHAPTER 7 LIQUIDATION COMES TO A CONCLUSION

If your company was unincorporated and your Chapter 7 was a personal bankruptcy that also covered your business, you will receive a discharge at the conclusion of the case. This will include any shortages on your secured loans because the discharge cancels any debts. The one area that may continue to be a problem is that of taxes. Except under certain very special circumstances (which will take some fancy legal work), the IRS, for example, can continue to pursue you for these taxes and most likely will do so. At some point when you are back on your feet financially, you will want to make an offer to settle these.

A corporation does not receive a discharge at the conclusion of a Chapter 7. Instead, the company ceases to exist, and for the most part the company's debts go with them. But some of your company's debt may become your personal debt. If you have personally guaranteed a bank loan, the bank can now look to you to make good on any shortage. Depending on the balances due and your obvious financial situation, they may pursue this debt vigorously or they may write it off. A settlement offer may be warmly received by your bank to close the books on the loan. Taxing bodies, including the IRS, will pursue you personally until they are paid, or you are deemed totally uncollectible, something that rarely happens. This is good reason to maximize the return from your company's liquidation, to pay off debts that could come back to haunt you.

## TAKE AN OBJECTIVE LOOK AT WHETHER A CHAPTER 7 LIQUIDATION MAY BE ADVISABLE

Once you have begun the process of a reorganization, all of your attention and energy is focused on the idea of keeping the business open and operating. You may have considered a liquidation, but giving up is not in the makeup of most entrepreneurs. But for some companies the time does come to make a graceful exit.

It may be the initial action of a creditor, but you can give it serious consideration and decide not to object to the conversion. Or you may take this action voluntarily. If the chance of a meaningful turnaround is slim, why continue to burn up assets that could be used to satisfy debts? Why not find a way to get out from under the crushing mound of debt and begin a new phase in your business life? Remember, you will take with you your single greatest asset, the talent and knowledge that you have developed over the years. You could put it to work where it will be better used and better paid. It is something to consider.

You can always go back into business again. It may even be in the same industry. You may need partners to find funding and get new credit. But several currently successful business owners have had a failure in their past. You certainly have learned from it. It is a tough call, but one you should have the courage to make.

## SUMMING UP

If the time comes to go into a Chapter 7 conversion, you should consider how to protect yourself from personal liability for any company debts. Cooperate with the trustee, and help him collect all that is due and pay only the fair debts.

If anyone believes that here isn't an enormous amount of stress involved in a bankruptcy, it's because they haven't lived through the experience. Even if your company is only considering the possibility of a filing, I'm sure you are feeling the stress of the financial pressure. It doesn't come on overnight, and at its peak you can feel immobilized.

Now that the worst of my run-in with bankruptcy is behind me, I can look back at the difficult period with a better perspective. There was a time when the ring of the phone could put my nerve endings on alert. My attorney would make a reasonable request, and I would feel incapable of handling the task. There were situations that now evoke a smile, although they didn't at the time. While I was moving the company bank accounts to a new bank, I went through a drive-in window to cash a check. There was some delay until the teller came back with the money, and I was expecting the Federal Bureau of Investigation to surround my car and demand an explanation

# 15
# AND LIFE GOES ON

of my withdrawal. I felt sheepish about this until someone else who had been through bankruptcy told me that he was at an out-of-town hotel attending a conference when he was paged. The first thought that streaked through his mind was, "My creditors have found me!"

I can assure you with absolute certainty that this does not last forever even if it feels as if it might. As the unknown becomes known, your feeling of loss of control will diminish. And the skills and talent that led you to the high-risk world of business will resume on autopilot, and the rebuilding process will begin. It may be in the context of your own business or it may be in another direction, but it will be.

# BUSINESSES DO GO ON
## AFTER CHAPTER 11 BANKRUPTCY

About the same time I filed for protection under Chapter 11 in 1986, the steel industry in our area was making it into a trend. The initial filing made by Wheeling-Pittsburgh Steel started the parade in April 1985 followed by LTV Steel in July 1986. They were later joined by Sharon Steel in 1988.

For Wheeling-Pittsburgh, it was the culmination of a period of losses and substantial capital investment that burdened the corporation with a substantial debt load but also efficient physical plants. A fragile refinancing agreement broke down, and the company went into Chapter 11. The early days added more difficulty with a strike that lasted 2 months. Against all the odds, the company did survive and manage to confirm a reorganization plan successfully, although it took more than 5 years. Sharon Steel also has completed a plan, and at the time of this writing, LTV Steel is into the final stages. Here are three companies in an industry in distress and during times that have been less than booming, making their way through the tough process of Chapter 11 and surviving with a chance to prosper again. All have cut costs and are positioned to face the future.

The next industry epidemic to break out was in retail, and it ran the gamut from Ames at the low end to the very chic stores of Allied-Federated such as Bergdorf Goodman. They have continued to operate and are beginning to file plans of reorganization. There will be fewer individual stores and fewer employees, but most likely the name stores that went into the process will survive.

Sometimes a company continues on with new ownership and a new name. Allegheny International filed under the weight of large losses and the accusations of mismanagement. Bought by Japonica Partners, the company has reemerged as Sunbeam-Oster, and it continues to manufacture and sell it consumer products. This is quite a feat if you consider the enormous legal fees the company ran up during the course of their case, with their lead attorneys billing as high as $300 per hour for the time of senior partners.

Midsize companies have triumphed over the difficult process including the Koss Corporation, a Milwaukee manufacturer of stereo headsets that were a standard in the industry. After an overambitious period of expansion, John Koss's company was 14 million in debt and operating at a loss. His bank would not cooperate with a restructuring, so Chapter 11 was his only alternative. After the trauma, Koss dug in and began a 7-day-a-week task of rebuilding the company, a job done well that ended with an emergence from bankruptcy and a return to profitability.

Reading Tube, Inc., another manufacturer, found itself in Chapter 11 proceedings in 1987. The Philadelphia-based maker of copper tubing used a highly communicative style to keep its creditors cooperating while it modernized its plant to keep it competitive. When the company emerged, the market prices of its product and the favorable cost savings it had achieved allowed the company to recover and pay its creditors.

Small companies such as my own make it through the strain of a filing by facing the situation, working hard for solutions, and having more than a little luck. Our group needed it because our stay in court was 4½ years, much longer than the average case, and this represented quite a risk that creditors would lose patience. We had other legal problems to solve and then a complicated confidentiality agreement to work out in light of the required disclosures, and it all took time. Our creditors could have filed for a conversion at any time because we were not diligent about keeping our exclusivity options renewed by the court. But we did make it through, and we are still producing and shipping a product.

And there are companies few of us know that have successfully accomplished a reorganization. While in the hall outside the bankruptcy court, I saw the owners of one of my favorite Chinese restaurants in Pittsburgh. I mentioned it to my lawyer and learned that the business had been reorganizing under court protection for a couple of years; I never knew—there was no reason I would. I did wonder, however, why they did not accept any credit cards at a time when virtually every other restaurant did. At their filing, these privileges were withdrawn but later reinstated. They made it through and are still serving great sweet and sour shrimp!

There is no magic involved, no slight of hand. Hard work, good strategy, and open communication can increase the chance that your company will continue and survive the challenge.

## EVEN IF THE COMPANY FAILS, THE PEOPLE DO NOT

I have not spoken with anyone who is going through a bankruptcy who hasn't suffered personally with symptoms ranging from sleepless nights to serious medical problems. Sol Stein makes a case in his book, *A Feast for Lawyers,* that the loss of control and self-esteem suffered by the CEOs and top managers brings on serious stress-induced illness. Because I too suffered the most critical medical crisis of my adult life only 8 months after I filed, I have no reason to doubt this conclusion.

Conversely, I have not spoken with anyone who hasn't made a recovery after the case had progressed relatively far or gone the distance, whether successfully or not. Most of us admit that we have changed, but most would probably describe it as a change for the better. We have learned to operate under adversity, to take an inventory of our value system, and even to have mellowed. And the recovery is also financial thanks to renewed resourcefulness.

The pain in Sol Stein's book is evident. His was a relatively vicious bankruptcy case with an active creditors' committee that forced his publishing firm into liquidation. His losses were devastating, and included his home and savings. In the end, however, his talent has even overcome these trials and he has created computer software to teach people how to write. The product is selling well, others are anticipated, and his income has been restored. This is a real tribute to the human spirit because in 2 years of studying cases, I never read an account that was tougher than the circumstances Stein & Day Publishing went through.

Another survivor of the bankruptcy process is Dan Whelan, a mechanical contractor who filed for bankruptcy several years ago. I first met Dan several years after his company had emerged from Chapter 11 proceedings. He has a head of white hair that stands out, but it's his wisdom and charm that takes over when he begins to talk. I had sent him a portion of my book to review because I wanted his opinion, and we began by talking about general business philosophy. The conversation soon drifted to talk of the trauma of making the decision to file, however, and the various struggles that went on while the case was open including the reactions of vendors who had been friends and then became unsecured creditors. We went back and forth for a while swapping war stories, and both agreed that this was not an easy experience. But Dan's company came back, and it was evident that he came with it. He has a realistic and objective view of how a small business should work and how it should be kept in perspective in one's life. It is good to see how complete a recovery can be, and we talked about working with others who are in the process.

My own "comeback" is still a work in progress, but I have come a long way. In some interesting way, it was the bankruptcy that has allowed me to accomplish a lifelong dream: to write a book. The first rejection letter I received from a publisher came in 1978, and it took 13 years and a financial disaster to become an author! Moreover, while waiting for my plan to be submitted and voted on, I started a new business with a few partners. It's just growing out of the start-up phase, but we are pleased with the progress and believe it holds great promise. My business continues, although it is smaller than it was 10 years ago. I'm excited about the future and feel prepared to meet the challenges of the 1990s.

## SUMMING UP

While in the heat of the battle, it may seem as if the difficulties you and your business face will never end. Yours may very well be one of the companies that surmount the odds, however, and go on to prosperity. Plan your strategy carefully and set your goals high.

# EPILOGUE

When the bankruptcy laws were changed in 1978, it was intended that the new code would give business a chance to rehabilitate themselves. The Chapter 11 process is a very complicated and costly one for any small business to survive without enormous effort of its principals and extra cooperation of its creditors. Much could be done to make the process easier and cheaper for debtors, and return more to the creditors.

Congress has responded to requests from many constituencies and in 1991 Senate Bill 1785 was introduced to establish a National Bankruptcy Review Commission to study Chapter 11, and submit a report and recommendations. They won't report for 2 years, but I hope they will streamline the process particularly as it pertains to the number of interest groups that can form and file adversary positions. The amount of legal cost incurred by the creditors' committee should also be reviewed.

This act also contains provisions for a small business bankruptcy chapter that will be in effect on a 3-year trial basis in 8 judicial districts. It is hoped that a fast-track process will make it easier for a company to reorganize successfully. I join that hope.

SUZANNE CAPLAN

# Glossary of Terms

**Adequate protection**  The protection that a debtor grants a creditor with court approval to prevent foreclosure on property. This can include a resumption of monthly payments.

**Administrative creditor**  All creditors holding claims for debts that were incurred after the bankruptcy was filed. This includes fees for legal and accounting professionals used by the debtor in possession.

**Adversary proceeding**  Matter of dispute brought before the court for determination. Many regard amount of debt, security interest, or use of cash as examples of issues to be settled by court action.

**Automatic stay**  Becomes effective on filing of a bankruptcy petition and prevents any creditors from taking further collection action against the debtor without court permission.

**Bar date**  The last date set by the court that a proof of claim can be filed to collect a debt owed by the bankrupt company.

**Cash collateral**  All proceeds paid or due to a company that have been pledged as collateral for a loan. Associated with the cash liquidation of inventory and accounts receivables.

**Collateral**  Assets that are used as security for a debt.

**Confirmation**  The action of the bankruptcy court approving the plan of reorganization and releasing at least a portion of the court's jurisdiction over the debtor.

**Conversion**  The voluntary or involuntary act of taking an operating Chapter 11 case into Chapter 7 liquidation. Also, an involuntary Chapter 7 can be converted into a Chapter 11 for the purpose of reorganization.

**Cram down**  Forcing one class to accept a plan of reorganization over the objections of that class. The plan would still be confirmed by the court.

**Creditors committee**  A group of 5 to 10 creditors that form to monitor the progress of a bankruptcy. May investigate questionable transfers, hire an attorney to advise them, and file a plan of reorganization of their own.

**Debtor in possession**    A new legal entity that is formed by the bankruptcy filing and operates until the case is discharged by the court.

**Disclosure statement**    A document that accompanies the plan of reorganization. This statement must include pertinent information needed by the creditors to vote on the plan.

**Foreclosure**    When property is sold by a court-authorized procedure for the purpose of satisfying a debt.

**Impaired claim**    A debt claim that will be paid at less than full value.

**Judgment**    A court decision against a debtor that creates a lien on property to satisfy an unpaid debt.

**Lien**    A document filed with the court that establishes a legal interest in property of the debtor by a creditor.

**Motion**    Legal documents filed in court asking for some action of the court.

**Plan of reorganization**    The document that a debtor files (in some instances creditors may also file), which states how and when debts are to be repaired.

**Preferential transfer**    Transfers of money or property made to one creditor in preference over another in violation of rules for such transfers. Certain transfers to insiders are also violations for 1 year before a filing.

**Priority creditor**    Certain unsecured creditors such as taxing bodies who hold claims that have a priority above other unsecured claims.

**Proof of claim**    The document filed with the court by a creditor to verify position as a holder of debt.

**Secured creditor**    A creditor who holds a lien on collateral as security for a loan on a debt. A secured creditor may also have some portion of debt as unsecured.

**Trustee**    An individual appointed by the court and authorized to oversee or take complete control of the assets of a bankruptcy case.

**Unsecured creditor**    Those creditors in a business bankruptcy who hold no property as collateral for their debt.

# INDEX